When English Language Learners Write

Connecting Research to Practice, K–8

KATHARINE DAVIES SAMWAY

HEINEMANN
Portsmouth, NH

Heinemann

361 Hanover Street
Portsmouth, NH 03801–3912
www.heinemann.com

Offices and agents throughout the world

The author and publisher wish to thank those who have generously given permission to reprint borrowed material:

Figures 1.1 and 1.2: from Hayes, John R. (2000). "A New Framework for Understanding Cognition and Affect in Writing." In *Perspectives on Writing: Research, Theory, and Practice*, Roselmina Indrisano & James R. Squire, Editors. Newark, DE: International Reading Association. Chapter 1, 6–44. Reprinted with permission.

Figures 2.2 and 2.3: from *Language Stories & Literacy Lessons* by J. Harste, V. Woodward, and C. Burke. Copyright © 1984. Published by Heinemann, a division of Reed Elsevier, Inc. Reprinted by permission of the publisher.

Figures 2.5, 2.6, 2.7, and 2.8: from Hoyt, L. (1993). "How Do They Learn to Read and Write? Literacy Instruction in a Refugee Camp." In K. Davies Samway & D. McKeon (Eds.), *Common Threads of Practice: Teaching English to Children Around the World*. Alexandria, VA: Teachers of English to Speakers of Other Languages, pp. 72–76. Reprinted by permission of the publisher.

Figures 2.11 and 2.12: from Taylor, D. M. "Writing and Reading Literature in a Second Language." In *Workshop 2: Beyond the Basal*, edited by Nancie Atwell. Copyright © 1990 by Heinemann. Published by Heinemann, a division of Reed Elsevier, Inc. Reprinted by permission of the publisher.

Figure 2.13: from Heald-Taylor, G. (1986). "Writing Development of One ESL Student." In *Whole Language Strategies for ESL Students*, ed. G. Heald-Taylor. Toronto, Canada: Ontario Institute for Studies in Education, pp. 50–55. Reprinted by permission of the publisher.

Figures 3.1 and 3.2: From Serna, I., and Hudelson, S. "Emergent Spanish Literacy in a Whole Language Bilingual Classroom." In *At-Risk Students: Portraits, Policies, Programs and Practices*, ed. by R. Donmoyer and R. Kos. Copyright © 1993. Published by State University of New York Press. Reprinted by permission of the publisher.

Figures 4.1 and 4.2: from *Turn up the Volume and Sing Along with Pedro* by Mary Jane Nations. Copyright © 1990 by Mary Jane Nations. Reprinted by permission of the author.

Figure 7.1: from McCarthey, S. J., García, G. E., López-Velásquez, A. M., Lin, S., and Guo, Y.-H. (2004). "Understanding Writing Contexts for English Language Learners." In *Research in the Teaching of English*, 38 (4), 351–394. Copyright 2004 by the National Council of Teachers of English. Reprinted with permission.

Figure 7.6: from Smith, K., Espinosa, C., Aragon, E., Osorio, R., and Ulloa, N. (2004). *Reconceptualizing Writing Workshop in a Dual Language Program*. Reprinted by permission.

Library of Congress Cataloging-in-Publication Data
Samway, Katharine Davies.
   When English language learners write : connecting research to practice, K–8 / Katharine Davies Samway.
      p. cm.
   Includes bibliographical references and index.
   ISBN 0–325–00633–4 (alk. paper)
   1. English language—Study and teaching (Elementary)—Foreign speakers. 2. English language—Study and teaching (Middle school)—Foreign speakers. 3. English language—Study and teaching—Research. 4. English language—Composition and exercises—Research. 5. Children—Language—Research. I. Title.

PE1128.A2S26 2006
808'.04280712—dc22   2005030150

Editor: Lois Bridges
Production coordinator: Elizabeth Valway
Production service: Denise A. Botelho
Cover design: Lisa Fowler
About the cover: Cover photograph of John David V., a fourth grader at Runn Elementary School in Donna, Texas
Cover photograph: Julie Farias
Composition: Argosy Publishing
Manufacturing: Louise Richardson

Printed in the United States of America on acid-free paper
10 09   RRD   3 4 5

Contents

Acknowledgments   v
Introduction   vii

Chapter 1: A Brief History of Writing Research   **1**
Writing Research: A Focus on the Product   1
Beginning to Focus on the Cognitive Processes Involved When Writing   3
Writing Research: Focus on the Writer/Writing Processes   4
A Social-Behavioral View of the Writing Process   14
A Sociocognitive Model of Writing   15
The Intersection of Writing, Sociocultural Factors, and Politics   17
Writing Research: What Now?   18
Implications of the Research for Teachers of Writing   20

Chapter 2: Core Research About the Writing of Children Who Are ELLs   **21**
What Does the Term *Writing* Refer To?   22
Young Children's Awareness of Functions of Print   22
Oral Language/Writing Connections   26
English Language Learners Can Write Before
    Orally Mastering the English Language   28
ELL Children Can Express Complex Thoughts and
    Emotions in Less Than Fluent English   30
ELL Children's Writing Is Developmental and Isn't Necessarily Linear   38
Knowledge of Writing Conventions May Be
    Transferred from the L1 to English   46
Being Taught to Write in the Native Language Is an Asset   47
ELLs Can Write in Both the Native and Nonnative
    Languages Without Being Confused   48
Similarities and Differences in Children's Writing
    in English and Other Languages   50
ELL Children Evaluating Writing   52
Prior Literacy Experiences May Affect How ELLs
    Respond to New Literacy Experiences   54
Implications of the Research for Teachers of Writing   58

Chapter 3: Sketches of English Language Learners Becoming Writers   **61**
Cecilia and Diana: Writing Development of Bilingual
    Kindergarten and First Graders   61
Alexis: A Struggling Second Grade Writer   66
Roberto and Janice: Different Responses to
    Invitations to Write Authentically   74
What Do These Sketches Tell Us About ELL Writers?   77
Implications of the Research for Teachers of Writing   77

Chapter 4: Gender, Race, Ethnicity, Social Class, and Writing   **79**
The Influence of Gender on Children's Writing   81
The Influence of Ethnicity and Race on Writing   84
Social Class, Socioeconomic Status, and Writing   94
Implications of the Research for Teachers of Writing   100

Chapter 5: Reading/Writing Connections   **101**
Focusing on the Craft of Writing Needn't Destroy the Reading Experience   102
Ways in Which Reading and Writing Are Connected   103
The Influence of Reading on Writing   109
Implications of the Research for Teachers of Writing   122

Chapter 6: Reflective Writing   **125**
Incorporating Reflective Writing in the Classroom   125
The Role of Reflective Writing in Language and Literacy Development   138
Journals as a Record of Experiences   138
Reflective Writing Supporting ELLs   139
Implications of the Research for Teachers of Writing   148

Chapter 7: The Influence of the Environment on Children's Writing   **150**
One ESOL Teacher Who Established a Workshop
    Approach to Literacy Learning   151
Influence of School and Community Writing Experiences on Children   152
Influence of School Experiences on the Writing of ELLs:
    An International Perspective   155
Influence of School Experiences on the Writing of ELLs in the United States   157
Influence of the Environment on Children Writing Bilingually   163
What Do ELLs Need to Become Successful Writers?   167
What Type of Writing Program Is Best for ELLs?   169
Implications of the Research for Teachers of Writing   177
Revisiting the Survey   178

References   180
Children's and Young Adult Literature   191
Index   192

Acknowledgments

I have had the extreme good fortune over the past two decades to have had stimulating conversations about teaching writing with many classroom and ESOL (English to Speakers of Other Language) teachers throughout the country. I value the many visits I have made to their classrooms, often for extended periods of time. Especially big *thank you's* go to Laura Alvarez, Susan Atencio, Angie Barra, Laurel Cress, Yolanda Dandridge, Audrey Fong, Joan Hagan, Michael Hagan, Jen Klem, Denise Leograndis, Kathy Maloney, Jennifer Jones-Martinez, Kathy Morgan, Mary Pippitt, Sonny Kim, Rachel Rothman, Barbara Schmidt, Choji Schroeder, Lydia Stack, Dorothy Taylor, Pam Webber, Gail Whang, Bernadette Whitman, Beverly Wilkin, and Siu-Mui Woo. They welcomed me into their classrooms, where I learned a great deal from observing them at work, from working with their students, and from the many rich conversations we have had. Other teachers have been very generous in bringing samples of their students' writing (and, sometimes, their own writing) for us to talk about, including Teresa Brandes, Sonia Davis, Leila Karzian-Banos, Maya Goetz, Heather Juhl, and Mingming Zhang. I value those occasions, also.

My interest in the writing processes of English language learners was fostered many years ago by two fine researchers and friends, Sarah Hudelson and Carole Urzúa. With their example to guide me and their long-distance support to sustain me, I first embarked on research into the writing processes of English language learners (ELLs). Theirs has been a long-standing gift that I continue to treasure.

I knew that writing a book like this would involve an incredible amount of library and Internet searching. I couldn't have completed the book without the very able assistance of Melinda Nettles, who located and tracked down references with good humor, patience, and ingenuity. I have also appreciated her emails inquiring about the book long after she had ended her stint as a research assistant. Those notes of encouragement did just that, and were a true gift. I am also very grateful to Lorene Sisson and Sue Kendall, librarians at my university, who were very helpful in navigating various research search tools and in locating research articles.

An editor can make a huge difference to a writer, and I feel very lucky to have been working with Lois Bridges all these months. She has a gift for coming into the foreground at just the right time and with just the right advice. I am also indebted to

Karen York for her invaluable assistance in getting permissions to reproduce some of the figures in the book. In addition, I am grateful for the considerable expertise that Denise Botelho, Amy Rowe, and Elizabeth Valway brought to turning my manuscript into this book.

Lucinda (Cindy) Pease-Alvarez is a wonderful friend and colleague, whom I met when I moved from western New York State to Oakland, California. We have worked together now for almost twenty years, years that I value beyond description. With regard to this book, I am particularly grateful for her careful, thoughtful and informed reading of draft chapters, and for steering me to some invaluable research and resources. Her friendship and the many stimulating conversations we have had over the years about literacy, language, English language learners, mandates, policies, and teaching continue to sustain me.

Tom Samway has been a constant support. He, more than anyone, knows how important this book is to me and how long I have been planning and working on it, and he has supported me from long before I ever wrote a word. If I hadn't heeded his queries about my progress, I may never have completed the book—as many people know, it can be easier to locate and read articles and books than it is to write, even when one finds writing satisfying.

Introduction

When educators refer to English language learners (ELLs) and writing, it is not uncommon to hear deficit views and myths, including the following:

- They can't write.
- They have writing problems.
- They are reluctant writers.
- They need to be taught the skills of writing before being asked to write independently.

It is true that the writing of anyone who is new to a language is likely to be different from that of native speakers. Also, the nonnative writer may find it more daunting to write in the nonnative language than the native language. However, with time and stimulating, purposeful writing experiences, ELLs can become effective writers, as much of the research reported on later in the book illustrates.

We are fortunate to have many excellent professional books that address the teaching of writing to K–8 children (e.g., Anderson 2000; Atwell 1998; Avery 1993, 2002; Calkins 1986, 1994; Fletcher 1996a, 1996b; Harvey 1998; Heard 1989; Portalupi and Fletcher 2001; Ray 1999, 2001) and, although they focus on English-speaking children, many of us who teach ELLs have found them to be very useful and inspiring. In contrast with these books, my book is an attempt to fill a gap, to explore writing research on ELLs, and to make connections from this body of research to the practice of teaching writing to ELLs.

I hope that this book supports the many educators (preservice and practicing teachers, administrators, teacher educators, and others) who would like ELL students to have a positive experience with writing, while becoming more skilled, effective writers. I hope my book will contribute to helping ensure that all learners, particularly ELL students, have positive, stimulating, and satisfying school-based experiences with writing.

An Overview of the Rest of the Book

We have at our disposal considerable research by university-based researchers as well as classroom teachers that has yielded tremendous knowledge about writing and writing processes. In the remaining chapters, the following topics will be explored:

- A historical overview of writing research, including a move from looking at only the product (the writing itself), to investigating learners' writing processes and the intersection of sociocultural factors and writing (Chapter 1).
- Core research about the writing of ELLs, including young children's awareness of print, oral language/writing connections, what ELLs can do as writers before they become fluent in English, and the role of the native language in their writing development (Chapter 2).
- An in-depth look at the writing development of five ELLs that illustrates key understandings about the writing and writing processes of ELLs (Chapter 3).
- Ways in which gender, race, ethnicity, and social class intersect with writing, including how literacy practices in nonmainstream cultures may be overlooked and misunderstood by teachers from the dominant culture (Chapter 4).
- How reading and writing are interconnected processes, how what children read influences their writing, and ways of fostering reading/writing connections (Chapter 5).
- Reflective writing (e.g., logs and dialogue journals), including how reflective writing supports ELLs and ways of incorporating it into the classroom (Chapter 6).
- How the environment in which ELLs are placed affects their writing, including the impact of adult expectations, the influence of school-based writing experiences, the role of a bilingual environment, and current developments in writing pedagogy (Chapter 7).

1

A Brief History of Writing Research

"No book writes itself."
GAIL TSUKIYAMA, AUTHOR

"I am not think(ing) well today so it's not a great letter."
BRIAN-MARTIN, SIXTH GRADE WRITER

Writing Research: A Focus on the Product

Prior to the 1970s, very little attention was paid to writing research, in part because America's structural linguists thought of written language as a poor relative of oral language. In fact, Bloomfield (1933) referred to writing as "not language, but merely a way of recording language by means of visible marks" (21). Most of the research devoted to writing focused on the product (e.g., descriptions of writing across age levels) and best methods for teaching writing (e.g., tests of which treatment was most effective). That is, researchers' concerns were grounded in what should be taught, how to assess writing, and the success of particular writing activities.

That this happened should not be interpreted necessarily as a lack of concern for knowledge about writing processes. In fact, in a monograph published by the University of Chicago Press in 1929, *Summary of Investigations Relating to Grammar, Language, and Composition*, R. L. Lyman, a professor of the teaching of English, commented on the limitations of research that did not investigate learners' writing processes. He wrote, "They measure pupil products and assume that by so doing they are evaluating the manifold tangible processes of mind by which those products were attained." In this monograph, Lyman provides brief reviews of "the most important studies" in the field of language-composition. The articles that Lyman included for review focused on the written product (e.g., rhetorical devices and usage/mechanical issues), and writing curriculum and methods. Interestingly, studies in spelling were not included in this analysis. (I say *interestingly* because I have by far the largest number of articles devoted to spelling research than any other aspect of writing; is this because it is less time-consuming for researchers to gather spelling samples than, for example, to observe children in the act of writing?) Lyman acknowledged the enormous difficulty of measuring writing, which he attributed to lack of sophisticated measuring devices, the complex nature of writing, and difficulties associated with objectively assessing attainment of mastery of any aspect of composition. Lyman concluded that composition "involves skills, habits, and attitudes which are difficult to isolate and measure" (3).

Early Research: A Lack of Emphasis on Writing Processes

Early research into children's writing tended to focus on the product, the actual pieces of writing and stages of writing, rather than on children's writing processes. For example, Britton, Burgess, Martin, McLeod, and Rosen (1975) looked at the writing across the curriculum of British school children aged eleven to eighteen, and described the following developmental stages in writing, with *expressive* being encountered first:

- Expressive—relatively unplanned, spontaneous writing that does not consider audience, such as a journal
- Transactional—information writing that is designed to clearly convey a message to others, such as essays and reports
- Poetic—literary or poetic writing, such as a story or poem

It should be pointed out that these *developmental stages* are closely tied to genres and they do not take into account writing processes, or how each of these broad categories of writing may draw on very similar processes. A decade later, Newkirk (1987) challenged the notion that young children first write expressively, as described by Britton and colleagues (1975).

Other early writing research focused on frequency counts, such as the incidence of different types of writing at different ages or the number of words per communication unit (T-units).[1] For example, Applebee (1978) reported on his investigations into children's conceptions of story and their revealing of this understanding orally and through writing. His findings reveal T-unit differences in oral and written responses. For example, he found that at nine years of age written responses were more linguistically complex than oral responses.

---

[1] T-units refer to the grammatical complexity of language and Kellogg Hunt conducted much of the related early research in the mid 1960s. He found that children used increasingly longer T-units (more grammatically complex sentences) as they got older. A single T-unit is made up of an independent clause and any dependent clauses or elements that are attached or embedded. Hence, *I walked to school* is one T-unit, but *I walked to school and I picked up my friend* is two T-units. See Constance Weaver's *Teaching grammar in context* (1996) for an interesting discussion of grammar, including T-units.

Writing as Subordinate to Oral Language?

Researchers such as Loban (1976), who conducted a twelve-year longitudinal study into the oral and written language development of students in grades K–12, focused on the primacy of speech and regarded writing as a manifestation of oral language development, rather than being a distinct subsystem of language (and worthy of study in its own right). Loban found that usage of dependent clauses in oral language increased steadily over the years and distinguished higher-ability from lower-ability students. However, a similar developmental pattern was not found in the students' writing. For example, he found that dependent clause usage leveled off for high- and average-ability students after grade eight, whereas low-ability students continued to use dependent clauses in their writing to the point where they exceeded higher-ability students' usage in this domain. Loban interpreted these findings to mean that the higher-ability writers had access to other ways of embedding when writing.

Other researchers have challenged the theory that writing is simply using written symbols to give permanence to oral language (e.g., Dyson 1983a, 1983b; Edelsky and Jilbert 1985; Goody 1977; Newkirk 1987). Edelsky and Jilbert (1985) found that Spanish/English bilingual children used formal language in their writing that they would not use in oral discourse (e.g., *gracias maestra*/thank you, teacher; *el fin*/the end). They also used repetitive refrains that they would not use in their oral speech (e.g., *me gusta* X, *me gusta* Y, *me gusta* Z/I like X, I like Y, I like Z), and although none of the children used telegraphic language in their speech (in fact, they were far beyond this oral language stage), sometimes telegraphic language appeared in their writing. In addition, whereas code switching frequently appeared in the children's oral speech, it rarely appeared in their writing.

Also in the 1980s, Newkirk (1987) investigated the nonnarrative writing of young children and observed, for example, that they wrote lists and labels and when they did so, they were not writing down speech; instead, he argues that they were appropriating and extending dominant and familiar forms of writing. Dyson (1983a) also argues that early writing does not grow out of speech; instead, she observed that early writing is typically labeling of pictures and is closely connected to drawing. Newkirk (1987) argues that the early years aren't a difficult time for children to write exposition, but a time of exploration and a time to make tremendous headway, if given opportunities (and here he argues against the deficit view that pervades the literature on children's writing development, when it is compared with the writing of adults).

Beginning to Focus on the Cognitive Processes Involved When Writing

Beginning in the 1970s, a focus on the cognitive processes involved in writing began to replace a focus on product and methodology. This was influenced by the recognition that good writing (like good reading) is hard to define, and the realization that the writing process merited its own investigation. Around this time there was also a shift in terminology, particularly in the research on adult writers. For example, the prevailing term *writing* was replaced by *composing*, in order to reflect a move from looking only at the words on a page to searching deep within the writer's mind, and exploring the cognitive processes involved when writing. Smith (1982) made the further distinction between *transcribing* (the act of putting words on the page) and *composing* (the thinking involved when writing).

According to Graves (1978, 1980), about 70 percent of writing research studies conducted until the 1970s were reports of experimental interventions that focused on the product. However, the 1970s saw the development of writing research that was influenced by anthropological, sociolinguistic, and psycholinguistic research that focused on the functional and communicative uses of language. This research explored the role of context in writing (e.g., ways in which purpose and audience affect the product, and how texts are created and judged by others), and ways in which homes, communities, and classrooms create social contexts for the development of writing and writers. Many of these studies used qualitative research approaches.

Writing Research: Focus on the Writer/Writing Processes

Between the 1960s and the 1980s, when writing process research took hold, two categories of writing process theories were in vogue, *cognitive* and *social*, with cognitive process theory dominating, in part because it built a model of the composing process. Bishop (1999) points out how, until that time, writing process research had relied on self-reports by literary writers (e.g., published authors of novels and poetry, such as Edith Sitwell and George Sand) that were not necessarily accurate and certainly didn't represent the writing circumstances of less-skilled writers. In addition, these self-reports, which were often self-edited to present a more interesting persona, sometimes generated misconceptions or misrepresentations (e.g., that writers must wait to be inspired).

Although self-reports often make for very interesting reading and may inspire others to write, Bishop argues that they can't be relied on too rigorously when teaching students to write. However, while it is clear that self-reports from published authors may not reflect the writing processes of younger learners or English language learners, I do think that it is interesting to and can be helpful for our students to know about the writing processes of accomplished writers for a variety of reasons. This type of experience can introduce learners to new strategies and confirm processes and experiences that less-experienced writers may have encountered. For example, one of my favorite writers is Gail Tsukiyama, author of *Women of the Silk* (1991), and not long ago, I heard her speak. She commented that it takes thought and a lot of research to write, whether a short story or an essay, which resonated powerfully with me. She added that she doesn't use an outline, just writes, but also warned, "No book writes itself" (2003). In this way, Tsukiyama challenged two common myths about writing, one that teachers often perpetuate (that writers [always] begin with an outline), and one that is rarely encountered in schools and that implies that the writer is simply a conduit for the writing of a piece, and doesn't really need to work hard at the act of writing. Although I don't usually begin with an outline when I am writing, I do find that it helps me to periodically create a schema of what I have produced in order to make sense of what I am writing and what I mean to write; sometimes I do this internally, but sometimes when I get bogged down I actually sketch it out. So, the latter comment of Tsukiyama's is particularly stimulating to me as a writer as it causes me to think hard about the role of outlines or their equivalents in my life as a writer . . . and in my life as a teacher of writing.

Cognitive Model of Writing

The *cognitive model* was grounded in research that provided insights into what had been previously invisible: what takes place inside a writer's head when composing. Writing process research methodology has been varied, but two distinct research methodologies have tended to prevail: a *social-behavioral model* and a *cognitive/developmental model.* Both approaches are concerned with the interaction between external performance and internal processes.

In a social-behavioral model, writers are usually observed while writing in naturally occurring settings, such as classrooms or the home (e.g., Graves 1982; Hudelson 1989; Samway 1987a, 1987b; Urzúa 1987), which allows for context to be taken into consideration. Researchers are interested in noting changes over time, and use ethnographic techniques (e.g., observational field notes, interviews, case studies).

In a cognitive/developmental model, specific and limited aspects of the composing process are investigated, writers may be observed in less naturally occurring settings, and attempts are made to develop a cognitively based theory of the writing process (e.g., Flower and Hayes 1981a, 1981b; Bereiter 1980; Scardamelia and Paris 1985). For example, one branch of *cognitive developmental* research investigates relationships between age and cognitive competence, whereas another branch looks at differences between expert and novice writers. This research is often experimental in nature, designed to discover what writers can/cannot do, and may use think-aloud protocols for data collection purposes.

Writing as a Meaning-Making, Thinking Process

Despite a common belief that writers know what they are going to write before they write it, this is not, in fact, the case. For example, in a conversation with students at the University of California at Berkeley, novelist Tom Wolfe remarked that he had decided that his next book would be about education. He wasn't sure what it would be about or where it would be set, and said, "All I know is it's dynamite and nothing has been written about it. I just sense it at this point. I can't wait to get in there, turn on the radar and find out about it . . . You don't have to know about a subject when you start. But then immerse yourself in it" (Hill 1998).

Tom Wolfe is an experienced and skillful adult writer, but what of less-skilled and experienced writers? Cognitive process research has generated detailed investigations of the writing processes of adults, young adults, and children and this research underscores how writing and thinking are interconnected. Janet Emig's seminal case study research (1971) into the composing processes of twelfth graders revealed the degree to which this is the case. For example, whereas up to that point a linear view of the composing process dominated (e.g., prewriting, writing, and rewriting), Emig found that the composing process was much more complicated than had been previously assumed, and was not linear. Instead, she found that it was recursive.

The Recursive Nature of Writing

Despite research findings and autobiographical accounts to the contrary, many teachers continue to refer to writing as a five-step process of prewriting (planning and goal setting), writing, revising, editing, and publishing, and the implication is that writers address their task in a rather static, simple, linear way. In fact, Emig (1971) found that writing is a complex, recursive process, one that involves going back and forth in the text while composing. For example, she found that students planned throughout the writing of a piece, not just in the early stages of composing, and constantly went back in order to move on, revealing an ever-changing interaction between words and thoughts. In the process, new ideas were generated and plans and goals were altered. This recursive phenomenon has been described in the following way:

> Composing does not occur in a straightforward, linear fashion. The process is one of accumulating discrete words or phrases down on the paper and then working from these bits to reflect upon, structure, and then further develop what one means to say. It can be thought of as a kind of "retrospective structuring"; movement forward occurs only after one has reached back, which in turn occurs only after one has some sense of where one wants to go. Both aspects, the reaching back and the sensing forward, have a clarifying effect. (Perl 1979b, 17)

Recursive writing has been documented for many groups of writers, including skilled native and nonnative English-speaking adult writers (e.g., Perl 1980b; Pianko 1979; Zamel 1982, 1983), less-skilled native and nonnative adult writers (e.g., Lay 1982; Perl 1979a, 1979b, 1980a; Pianko 1979; Raimes 1985), native English-speaking children (e.g., Calkins 1983; Graves 1982, 1983; Langer 1986), and nonnative English-speaking children (e.g., Samway 1987b; Urzúa 1986, 1987). For example, advanced adult English language learners interviewed by Zamel (1982) indicated that they used writing and revising to explore, rethink, and expand upon ideas. Although some students outlined (a procedure that is frequently recommended in a linear approach to writing), in most cases these outlines were discarded. One student explained it in this way: "How can I write an outline when my ideas are flying back and forth?" (Zamel 1982, 200).

In a study of younger writers, Langer (1986) found that 80 percent of the students in her study engaged in ongoing planning; that is, while they were actually writing, their plans changed. One fourteen-year-old student, Peter, commented, "As you're writing, the ideas come. It's like waking up in the morning. Things start waking up and the ideas keep coming" (113). Similar evidence documenting the connection between writing and thought is available for writers in the elementary grades. For example, researchers found that young children often did not know what they would write about, but in the process of writing, their thinking was stimulated and their stories emerged (e.g., Graves and Giacobbe 1982; Sowers 1979). In addition, even when their writing was not progressing smoothly, children were able to make insightful comments about the writing (Graves and Giacobbe 1982), an indication of thought being activated by writing.

Noted writer, Maxine Hong Kingston, captures the way in which writing is a thinking process in her book, *The Fifth Book of Peace* (2003). In one section of the book, she writes about the loss of a manuscript she had been working on when a fire in the Oakland/Berkeley hills destroyed her home and the manuscript. She recounts the reaction of another writer who lost a manuscript to a fire, Ralph Ellison. He had spent twenty years on a book before an electrical fire devoured it, and when asked how much time he had lost, Kingston reports that Ellison said, "You know, I'm not sure . . . Maybe four or five years. It wasn't as if I weren't working. I was trying to reimagine the situation. The characters are the same and the mixture of language is the same. But nuances are different. After all, *when I write I am discovering things*" (Kingston 2003, 61) (emphasis mine).

Writing Is Not Simply a Process of Transcribing Thoughts

Although writers may think about a topic for a long time before ever recording anything on paper or a computer screen, it is a mistake to assume that writing is simply a mechanism for expressing already-conceived, developed thoughts. In fact, through writing, we are enabled to explore and articulate our thoughts. Smith (1982) argues that through writing we discover what we think and know. As Flower and Hayes (1977) have argued, "a writer's normal task is a thinking task" (457). That is, writing is a complex, cognitive function. It is also a social act. This view of writing contrasts dramatically with what often passes for writing in school assignments (e.g., filling in the blanks).

It has been argued by Smith (1982) that knowing how to write involves being able to delicately integrate global and local conventions with one's own global and local intentions. He claims that when we write, we try out our theory of the world and in the process we discover what we know and think. As a consequence, our own thinking develops through writing. Thus, writing is an active, personal, theory-building, theory-testing process that facilitates the making of meaning. This is a process that both experienced, highly acclaimed writers and writing novices remark on. For example, upon finishing his memoirs that constitute the novel, *The Mimic Men*, the narrator in V. S. Naipaul's book comments, "So writing, for all its initial distortion, clarifies, and eventually becomes a process of life" (Naipaul 1967, 251). Similarly, twelve-year-old Brian-Martin captured this thinking/writing connection when he wrote to me, "I am not think(ing) well today so it's not a great letter." Writing does not require a specialized form of thinking; instead it is a means by which this theory-building and theory-testing may be put to work and is no different from any other kinds of learning (Smith 1982). It is therefore accessible to all writers, regardless of their relative proficiency in English.

When we write, we embark on a process that allows us to discover and understand what we want to write about; that is, texts unfold gradually as we engage in writing. This is true for children writing in their native language (e.g., Calkins 1982, 1986; Edelsky 1986; Graves 1979, 1982, 1983) and children writing in English as a nonnative language (e.g., Hudelson, 1989; Samway 1987a, 1987b; Urzúa 1987).

The Cognitive Processes of Skilled versus Less-Skilled Writers

Much of the early cognitive process research was conducted with older students, most particularly native English-speaking college students (e.g., Bridwell 1980; Perl, 1979a, 1979b, 1980a, 1980b; Pianko 1979; Shaughnessey 1977; Sommers 1980), and nonnative English-speaking college students (e.g., Raimes 1985; Zamel 1982, 1983). It provided compelling insights into, for example, differences in the writing processes of native English-speaking skilled and less-skilled writers and the writing processes of nonnative English speakers when writing in their native language and English.

Many studies found that skilled and less-experienced (often referred to as *basic*) writers relied on different processes when composing. For example, basic writers often relied heavily on rule-governed systems, and many of the limitations in their writing were related to applying ineffective rules and/or overapplying a rule (e.g., writing an outline, and then not allowing themselves to move away from the outline; or continually correcting their writing at the word or sentence level, thereby seriously interrupting the development of the piece of writing). In contrast, skilled writers tended not to rely on such systems, although they might attach an outline after completing a piece in order to comply with teacher expectations. In addition, skilled writers used a full range of revision strategies (e.g., addition, deletion, substitution, and reordering), whereas basic writers used fewer strategies and tended to rely on just adding and deleting. Skilled writers took into consideration the needs of their readers and checked the text written frequently to help guide its future development; basic or less-skilled writers did this rarely. Skilled writers had access to more flexible composing strategies than did less-skilled writers, and were more aware of the needs of readers and the demands of the rhetorical situation. Although most of this comparative research focused on adult learners, some researchers compared the writing of children at different ages (e.g., Langer 1986).

Hayes-Flower Cognitive Model of the Writing Process (and Modifications to It)

John Hayes and Linda Flower (1980) published a cognitive model of the composing process that was grounded in think-aloud protocol research. In think-aloud writing protocols (composing-aloud protocol research), writers are asked to describe their thinking processes orally, while in the act of composing. Although this clearly alters the composing process to some extent, it does provide access to a person's writing processes. The transcript of what the writer says is the protocol. The Hayes-Flower model, which has gone through several modifications over the years, identified the following three key components that work together recursively as a person composes (see Figure 1–1): the Task Environment, Cognitive Writing Processes, and The Writer's Long-Term Memory.

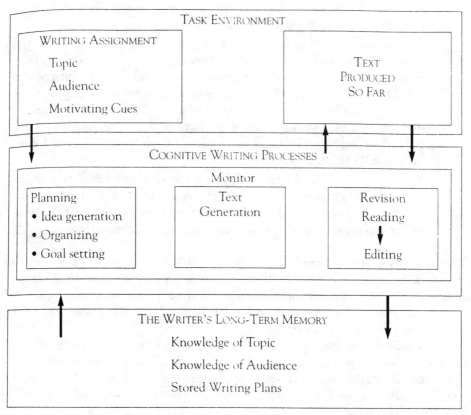

Figure 1–1. *The Hayes-Flower Cognitive Model of the Writing Process (1980)*

Task environment There are two elements, writing assignment and text produced so far:

- *The writing assignment* (i.e., social factors related to the writing assignment, such as genre, topic, audience, motivation to write, and the writer's goals)
- *Text produced so far* (i.e., physical factors, such as the text produced up to that point)

Cognitive writing processes There are three subprocesses (planning, text generation, and revision), which are all mediated by the writer's *monitor*, which determines how long a writer stays in a particular subprocess and what a writer will do next:

- *Planning* (i.e., generating ideas; deciding what to write and how to write the text; organizing or structuring the text; and goal setting, which writers engage in as they make decisions about what they need to do to effectively convey their messages) In this context, *planning* refers to an internal representation of knowledge (e.g., images, words, emotions) that is tapped into when composing, rather than the writing or drawing of a physical writing plan. Planning occurs throughout the writing of a piece.
- *Text generation* (i.e., turning plans into a written text, and translating often-complex ideas, images, emotions, and meanings into written language) This includes actually forming letters, selecting words, and deciding on syntax. This component has also been referred to as *translation*. For young children and ELLs whose native language uses a very different orthography from English, the forming of letters can have an impact on the process of generating text. Also, for ELLs, knowledge of English vocabulary and syntax can influence text generation.
- *Revision* (i.e., making changes to improve a text) This subprocess includes rereading and evaluating one's text, moving text around, adding and deleting text, and making editing changes. It often leads to additional planning and text generation, and can occur at any time in the writing process.

The writer's long-term memory Is a subprocess that is grounded in both the mind and other resources, such as books. It includes what the writer knows about a topic, about his or her audience, about the genre, and about how to solve writing-related problems that arise. The key for writers is to find the cue that allows them to retrieve useful information and knowledge.

More recently, this model has been revised to reflect increased knowledge about the writing process, particularly sociocultural aspects and influences (Hayes 2000). The revised model has two key components, instead of three: The Task Environment and The Individual (see Figure 1–2). The *Task Environment* is separated into the following two subcategories.

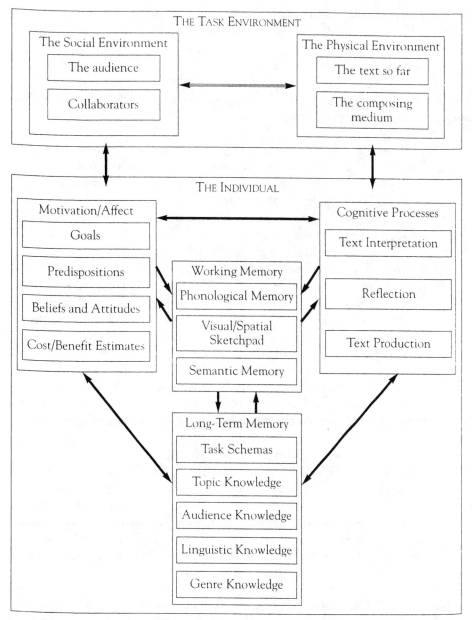

Figure 1–2. *New Hayes-Flower Model of the Writing Process (2000)*

- *The social environment* (i.e., the audience, people with whom we collaborate while writing, and other texts we read while writing)
- *The physical environment* (i.e., the text so far and the medium used to write, such as a pen, pencil, or word processor)

The Individual is divided into four subcategories: Motivation/Affect, Cognitive Processes, Working Memory, and Long-Term Memory

- *Working memory* (i.e., phonological, visual-spatial, and semantic memory) For example, the ability to quickly or automatically encode words and visuals, know where to put words or visuals on a page, and retrieve just the right word or visual for a given context.
- *Motivation/affect* (i.e., how writers' goals for, attitudes to, beliefs about, and engagement with writing affect writing performance) For example, writers who believe that writing is a gift are more likely to experience anxiety and lowered self-esteem than other writers.
- *Cognitive processes* (i.e., text interpretation, reflection, text production) Text interpretation involves reading and listening to texts, and interpreting graphics. Reflection includes inferring, problem solving, and making decisions. Text production refers to the physical production of both written texts and graphics, and includes the way in which all but the most emergent writers produce written language in sentence chunks, such as clauses (that is, not pausing after each word). Oracy is a factor in this category as writers often use oral language while writing (e.g., when conferring, when taking dictation from a co-writer, and when subvocalizing to figure out what we want to say or how we want to say it).
- *Long-term memory* (i.e., task schemas, topic knowledge, audience knowledge, linguistic knowledge, genre knowledge) Task schemas refers to internalized knowledge of how to go about a particular writing task, such as putting together a table of contents, encoding a word using sound/symbol correspondence, or how to lay out a cinquain. For example, once students know how to revise a piece through using carets and arrows, or cutting and pasting, they have acquired schema for the task of revision. Practice as a writer helps develop long-term memory.

In response to Hillocks' report, *Research on Written Composition: New Directions for Teaching* (1986), Hayes (1988) points to how, after years of study in the laboratory, he and his colleagues realized they needed to observe writers working in natural settings (e.g., in the classroom). The 2000 revised model reflects several developments in the field's knowledge of the writing process, including a greater understanding of the influence of the social environment in which writing occurs, and the influence of reading on writing.

A Misunderstanding About the Cognitive Theory of Writing

An unfortunate and unintended by-product of the cognitive theory of composing continues to plague writing instruction today as teachers often approach writing in a linear way, forgetting that the labeled processes identified by researchers (e.g., planning, writing, and revision) interact in a recursive, messy way. Consequently, they designate a day for planning/brainstorming, a day for drafting, a day for revision, and so on, with all students doing the same thing at the same time, without any real understanding of what writing involves. Clearly, writers work under deadlines (as I am while writing this book), but it is the responsibility (and right) of writers, no matter how old, or fluent in English, or experienced as writers, to figure out what step(s) in the process they need to be engaged in at any given moment (with help, if needed). While writing this book, I have often found that I spend a lot of time thinking about what to do next, that is, planning. However, there have been times when I realized that planning (or procrastinating in the name of planning) was interfering with writing, and it was at those times that I knew I needed to sit down at the computer to try out the ideas racing around in my brain; it was only in the act of hitting the keys that I could actually move on. Planning is critical, but it can all too easily interfere with the process of moving forward, a phenomenon that I have personally experienced and have observed in adults and children, both native and nonnative English speakers.

A Psychological Dimension

There is an additional perspective on writing that has received little attention, and that is a psychological dimension that transcends a straightforward intellectual (cognitive) experience. This was revealed to me by Lineah, a teaching credential program student, who captured in an end-of-semester commentary a dimension to writing that isn't often talked about, its *cathartic* power. Many of us have had the experience of discovering in the act of writing what it is we think or mean to say (a cognitive dimension). Many of us have also benefited from conferring with our peers and teachers on our writing (a social dimension). Writing is also a way of sorting through emotions and experiences, and for most of us, this may occur in journals. For other people, letters help. In the case of Lineah, it was through the act of composing a memoir that she finally made sense of an event that had occurred when she was fifteen. She wrote:

> One day in class, someone said something that sparked a memory for me. I began thinking about my uncle and my grandmother, who had both died within a couple of years of each other. I sat down at the computer and began writing. I finished my first draft in about an hour. The memories flooded my mind. It was an incredible experience. It is clear that writing is cathartic and should be encouraged in everyone. I had a new understanding of what had occurred

in my home when I was about 15 years old. I had put some missing pieces together that weren't there before because I was too young to understand.

A Social-Behavioral View of the Writing Process

Scholars who emphasize social aspects of writing argue that the composing process is much more complex than involving just the head (the cognitive model); instead, they argue that writing occurs in social contexts, and this affects how writers compose. A research methodological shift began to occur in writing research in the mid-1970s, when researchers began to focus on the social dimensions of writing. That is, they looked at how a range of socially constructed influences intersected with writing, including the classroom environment, the learner's community, student-student and student-teacher encounters and relationships around writing, social class, gender, and race.

Particularly when investigating children's writing processes, researchers began to embark on more long-term research projects that, instead of relying on data collected in experimental or quasi-experimental, controlled clinical settings, involved observing children over time as they engaged as writers.[2] Instead of trying to see if a particular strategy or program worked, or testing children's knowledge of writing in artificially occurring contexts, researchers observed them closely, in the home (e.g., Bissex 1980; Heath 1983; Schickedanz 1990; Skilton-Sylvester 2002; Taylor 1983), in classrooms (e.g., Blair 1998; Dyson 1989; Edelsky 1986; Franklin and Thompson 1994; Graves 1982; Han and Ernst-Slavit 1999; Harste, Woodward, and Burke 1983; Hudelson 1984; MacGillivray and Martinez 1998; Many, Fyfe, Lewis, and Mitchell 1996; Newkirk 1987; Samway 1993; Serna and Hudelson 1993; Smith, Espinosa, Aragon, Osorio, and Ulloa 2004; Urzúa 1987; Wollman-Bonilla 2000), and in the community (e.g., Huss-Keeler 1997; Moll, Amanti, Neff, and González 1992; Orellana, Reynolds, Dorner, and Meza 2003; Paratore et al. 1995; Skilton-Sylvester 2002). These researchers have documented the social nature of writing, and how writing occurs and is negotiated in a variety of settings, including school and the home. This research has relied on qualitative research methods; has used multiple forms of data collection (e.g., observations, audiotapes and/or videotapes of classroom interactions, and interviews of children, teachers, and caregivers); has focused on context; has been conducted over time (longitudinal research); and has sometimes included a participant-observer element.

---

[2]Some researchers argue that we should be doing research *with* students rather than doing research *on* students to find out about them. For example, Quandahl (1994) argues that because composition research involves a teacher-student interaction, the teacher's goal should be to explore *with* the students rather than aiming to know *about* the students. Others argue that research must ensure that participants are studied in their familiar, normal contexts rather than isolating them so that they are simply objects of study.

Ann Haas Dyson has spent many years carefully investigating the writing development and processes of young writers in urban classrooms, many of them African Americans, and her influential research is firmly grounded in the social nature of writing. For example, she has documented how children's writing is influenced by the kinds of classroom-based learning activities they encounter (1989, 1991); how they construct rules for writing while engaging in meaning making (1993, 1995); how cultural knowledge such as movies, cartoons, and neighborhood conversations influence their writing, as in topic choice (1992, 1994); the impact of social relationships on children's writing, such as writing on topics that amuse and entertain their peers (1992, 1994); and how children's ideas about writing and writers is influenced by how they and their peers work together (1989).

Several researchers have commented on the way in which children's metalinguistic conversations with peers and adults about their writing enhances their thinking (and subsequently their writing). This is true for both native speakers of English (e.g., Boutwell 1982; Calkins 1982, 1983; Graves 1983; Hubbard 1985) and nonnative speakers of English (e.g., Samway 1987a, 1987b; Urzúa 1987). For example, Boutwell (1982) reports on how this type of metacognitive engagement can be very helpful to children. As part of a classroom-based research project, a child was asked to record her own reading and writing processes. When the research project was completed, Boutwell took home the tape recorder. However, the young girl came back to school with her own machine and continued to consciously analyze her writing processes with her teacher.

The social context of writing is encountered in sometimes unexpected places. For example, not long ago, I was visiting a small town in Iowa surrounded by farmland, where I stayed in a motel. I was washing my hands at the sink and noticed a small basket on the washstand in which there were several pieces of stained toweling, each the size of a mini-washcloth. When I glanced over at the towels and washcloths on the towel rack, I saw that they weren't stained, so I wasn't concerned. I was curious, though, and wondered if they were for cleaning shoes. Then I glanced up from the sink and saw a sign that removed the mystery and illustrated the social context of writing (see Figure 1–3). I am an urban person and haven't ever gone hunting. I was visiting Iowa at the beginning of the hunting season, so the sign made perfect sense, and explained the presence of this small basket of fabric—use the scraps of toweling to clean your dirty hunting equipment, rather than the unstained towels.

A Sociocognitive Model of Writing

A combination of cognitive and social theories of writing has come to influence the work of many writing researchers, and has generated a sociocognitive view of the writing process that prevails today. For example, in my own early research into the writing processes of nonnative English-speaking children in the elementary grades (Samway 1987a, 1987b, 1993), I toyed with doing think-aloud protocols, but abandoned the

PLEASE NOTE

In an Effort to Keep Our Towel Supply Looking Its Best, We have Placed These Pieces of Stained, But Laundry Clean, Toweling Here for Your Use in Cleaning Guns, Fishing Equipment, Boats, Autos, Shoes or Any Other Use Needed.

YOUR COOPERATION IN THIS EFFORT WILL BE APPRECIATED.

Figure 1–3. *Sign in Iowa Motel*

idea, not because I did not think it was a valuable research tool, but because I wanted to observe the children's writing processes in their normal writing context, their ESOL (English to Speakers of Other Languages) class, and think-aloud would have altered that reality. In addition to exploring the social dimensions of, and influences on the children's writing processes, I did, however, explore their thinking when writing, such as asking them to rate pieces of writing, both their own and that of unknown children, and explain their ratings (Samway 1993).

Langer (1986) argues for integrating all research traditions (i.e., investigate the product, process, and context) and approach research from a sociocognitive perspective. She comments:

Rather than choose among the three emphases, it is time to integrate them into a sociocognitive view of reading and writing. Such a view will recognize that all learning is socially based, that language learning is ultimately an interactive process, that cognitive factors are influenced by context, and that they, in turn, affect the meanings that are produced. (7)

Currently, there is agreement (at least among researchers) that writing is a socially-constructed, meaning-making process. That is, writing is influenced and supported by writers' social and cultural experiences, which suggests that writing varies for people from culture to culture and within a culture. Many educators believe that the writing process is supported and developed by teaching that recognizes these sociocultural experiences. When there is no or minimal recognition of these experiences and differences, it is believed that children are not able to develop as writers to the extent that they would if their experiences and cultures were valued.

Despite the advantages of bridging home and school cultures, it isn't always a simple, uncomplicated process, as some researchers and teachers have reported. Both Stein (1993) and Hughes (2000) discuss experiences they had integrating home and school cultures and writing. In both cases, they invited children's family members to share their knowledge and expertise in school projects that involved family histories. Although these types of endeavors can offer extraordinarily effective ways of recognizing, respecting, and integrating the role of the family in the child's development and the collaborative nature of the home-school connection, there can be unexpected problems. For example, Stein (1993) comments on how some parents of her Soweto, South African students objected to being asked about family genealogy when preparing their family trees because of fears of revealing to the child (and others) events that the family would prefer not to have revealed or discussed. Hughes (2000) reports on how a series of ancestor-oriented projects designed to build community in his urban, multilingual, multiethnic class in California led to one family feeling uncomfortable at being asked to talk about what was essentially family disunity. Hughes had thoughtfully advised parents not to disclose anything that they would not like to have discussed publicly, but still he had to deal with unexpected problems that caused him to proceed more cautiously in the future. In important work that has integrated research and practice, Luis Moll and his colleagues have been instrumental in developing a form of inquiry study, *Funds of Knowledge*, that involves teachers becoming much more knowledgeable about, and respectful of community expertise, which they then weave into the curriculum (e.g., McIntyre, Rosebery, and González 2001; Moll, Amanti, Neff, and González, 1992).

The Intersection of Writing, Sociocultural Factors, and Politics

Sociocultural factors influence learning and writing development, and political issues are often embedded in sociocultural factors. For example, in an interesting reinterpretation of findings from a research project investigating the writing development of bilingual children that she conducted with Irene Serna (Serna and Hudelson 1993), Sarah Hudelson discusses how, in light of her greater understanding now of additional factors shaping learning, she would conduct the research differently (Hudelson 2005). For example, whereas she originally viewed children's spontaneous writing in English (referred to as *forays* into writing in English) from a constructivist perspective (i.e., the focus was on the children and their individual choices over when to use English) and as manifestations of their growing control of English, Hudelson now views them as manifestations of political realities. That is, her current interpretation of data from a decade ago is now informed by three additional influences:

1. Sociocultural perspectives, that is, the social construction of learning as a consequence of interactions with more knowledgeable others (e.g., Dyson 1989, 1993, 1997; Shannon 1995; Vygotsky 1962, 1978).

2. The lens of critical theory through which to understand that bilingual children are at the center of a struggle for linguistic hegemony, and that English is such a dominant language that it often leads to children abandoning their native languages (e.g., Shannon 1995; Tse 2001).

3. Ethnographic case study, which extends the detailed descriptions typical of case study research to include a sociocultural interpretation of the contexts in which the entity being studied is situated, such as neighborhoods, and views of community members and school officials when studying children's school-based learning (e.g., Merriam 1988).

Hudelson (2005) comments that she would conduct her research differently now in order to capture as complete a sociocultural picture as possible, including audiotaping and videotaping children in the act of writing, interviewing students and teachers, and observing the children both inside and outside the classroom. One of the major areas that Hudelson identifies as requiring more attention is the political nature of discussions about bilingual education in schools, communities, and at the state and federal levels. She comments that it is impossible for her now to discuss children's decisions to use English as simply an act of linguistic confidence; instead, she points out the influence of the dominance or hegemony of the English language, which undoubtedly encourages children to use it, devalues native languages, and almost certainly leads to the loss of the native language.

Writing Research: What Now?

The federal government funds national research centers, including the Center for Research on Education, Diversity and Excellence (CREDE), the Center for Research on the Education of Students Placed At Risk (CRESPAR), the Center for the Improvement of Early Reading Achievement (CIERA), and the National Research and Development Center on English Learning and Achievement (CELA). There used to be a Center for the Study of Writing located at the University of California, Berkeley and Carnegie Mellon, but that closed in the late 1990s. In an effort to ensure that I hadn't overlooked important research reports relating to K–8 ELLs and writing, I recently conducted a search on the U.S. Department of Education website, and located only one research report focusing on this population and topic. A similar lack of attention to writing and K–8 ELLs can be seen in the work of the now defunct Center for the Study of Writing. Of the forty-one Technical Reports and seventy-six Occasional Papers published by the Center (which are still available), only five of the Occasional Papers address this population to some degree; no Technical Report does. In fact, the vast majority of the Technical Reports are concerned with adult writers; Ann Haas Dyson's reports on her research investigating the writing of young, inner city, primarily African American children are a noticeable exception. These data suggest that the U.S. Department of Education doesn't view writing as important, and the research centers perhaps don't view the role of writing in the academic success of K–8 ELLs as relevant.

Despite the federal government's apparent lack of concern about and interest in writing, there are some who are strong advocates for placing more emphasis on writing in schools (which could be a mixed blessing, if ill-informed opinions about what counts in writing become politicized and polarizing and turn into rigid, poorly-conceived mandates, as has happened in reading). The 2002 National Assessment of Educational Progress (NAEP) report for writing (Persky, Daane, and Yin 2003) suggests that K–8 writing in the United States is improving, which may explain the lack of federal interest in writing. For example, the NAEP report, named *The Nation's Report Card: Writing 2002*, indicates that students' average scores on the writing assessment in grades four and eight[3] increased between the last assessment (in 1998) and 2002. Also, scores at the fourth grade for high-, middle- and low-performing students increased between 1998 and 2002; at the eighth grade level, scores for middle- and high-performing students increased from 1998 to 2002. Twelfth grade students didn't fare so well, suggesting that as students progress through school, writing tasks become more challenging, and students may not have sufficient experience writing to meet the demands for effective writing. Of great significance is the fact that Hispanic children and children from low-income homes (many of whom are ELLs) scored markedly lower than other populations at all three grade levels.

In reporting on the 1998 NAEP results, The National Commission on Writing in America's Schools and Colleges (2003), which is particularly concerned about how well students are prepared for college-level writing, commented that students can write, but they just can't write well. The commission comments that of the *Rs*, writing is shortchanged, and their report urges immediate attention, including the following:

- All states should establish comprehensive writing policies.
- The state policies should double the amount of time spent on writing in schools.

---

[3]The NAEP measures the writing skills of fourth, eighth, and twelfth graders.

- Writing should be taught in all grade levels and in all subjects.

Despite a lack of attention to writing at the level of policy makers, particularly with regard to ELLs, there is an important body of research that is a part of and builds on the research into writing and writing processes discussed in this chapter. Future chapters explore several of the areas that have been the focus of important research for those of us who work with and on behalf of ELLs. They include chapters on core research about K–8 ELL writers (Chapters 2 and 3); the intersection of gender, race, ethnicity and social class, and writing (Chapter 4); reading-writing connections (Chapter 5); reflective writing (Chapter 6); and the influence of the environment on children's writing (Chapter 7). Much of this research is classroom- and/or community-based, and sociocognitive in nature.

Implications of the Research for Teachers of Writing

The writing research discussed so far provides us with some very clear guidance about teaching writing. First, we must recognize the complex and idiosyncratic nature of writing and writing development and focus on the individual writer and his or her development and needs. Similarly, we must recognize how cognitive and sociocultural factors intersect with writing. Through carefully observing children in the act of writing, and talking with them (and family members) about their writing and writing processes, we can become knowledgeable about the writing strategies and skills that students have access to, and then teach them additional strategies and skills that enable them to become more effective writers. In this way, our assessments of students' development and needs will be richer and more accurate than if we rely exclusively on written products.

Finally, we must resist the allure of overly simplified and misconstrued views of the writing process that conceive of it in a linear rather than recursive fashion. For example, although most writing involves some preliminary planning, this also occurs throughout the writing of a piece, as does revision and editing. This suggests that we must strenuously resist efforts to impose writing approaches and programs that require that students proceed in a lockstep fashion, as if all learners' writing processes, development, and needs were identical.

2

Core Research About the Writing of Children Who Are ELLs

"This is hard, isn't it?"

AHMED, FOURTH GRADE WRITER

Before reading any further, take a few moments to complete the following survey about English language learners. If possible, then talk about your responses with a colleague or friend.

	True	False
1. English language learners should have lots of experience with writing exercises that allow them to practice the component parts of writing before being expected to write on their own.		
2. English language learners can write before they can read.		
3. Writing instruction should be delayed until an English language learner is orally fluent in English.		
4. The types of reading and writing experiences that English language learners have in school influence their writing.		
5. The native languages of English language learners affect their writing in English.		
6. In order to learn to write well in English, English language learners should be discouraged from writing in their native languages.		

What Does the Term *Writing* Refer To?

It is important to be very clear about what one means when referring to *writing*. For example, when commenting on the *goodness* of students' writing, some teachers refer almost exclusively to mechanical features that are often the easiest elements for us to notice, such as spelling, punctuation, handwriting, and grammar. For others, *writing* refers to any acts involving encoding words, whether on paper, a sidewalk, or a computer screen, whether artificial (e.g., copying a poem from a blackboard) or authentic (e.g., writing one's own poem). When I refer to *writing*, I am thinking of the creation of an original text, no matter how complex or simple the message. I am not referring to the copying of sentences, the making of sentences from a word list, or filling in blanks, which often comprise the school writing experiences of many students, particularly young children and English language learners.

When I think of good writing, I am thinking of the clear and evocative writing that captures my attention, whether my intellect and/or my emotions, and both children and adults can do this, as well as native and nonnative speakers of English. I am not thinking of the overly dense and convoluted language that sometimes characterizes academic writing. Although we all need the opportunity to rely on a form of shared language, almost like a shorthand, that is accessible to members of the same community, academic language (and legal and bureaucratic language intended for public consumption) sometimes seems more intended to confound and distance the writer from readers. I also use the term *writing* to include the early, scribble writing of young children, which is often accompanied by drawings; most often the drawings precede the writing, but some children write before drawing.

Although there is a solid body of research focused on children's writing, the majority of studies have focused on native English-speaking children. It has only been in the last twenty to twenty-five years that writing research has focused on nonnative English-speaking children. Contrary to curricular advice implied or stated in many instructional and methodological materials, it is now known that nonnative English-speaking children are capable of much more than is generally expected of them. What follows are some key insights into the writing of children for whom English is a nonnative language; in some cases, these findings are discussed within a context that refers to native English-speaking children's writing development in order to contextualize and more fully explore the issues.

Young Children's Awareness of Functions of Print

Research tells us that very young children are aware of functions of print, and this is reflected in differentiated scripts for drawing and writing. For example, as Figure 2–1 shows, a two-and-a-half-year-old child, Jamie, drew a picture made up of clusters of slash marks, and at the top of the paper, he drew single slashes, which he indicated read, "This is a kitty cat"; he very clearly understood that writing and drawing are distinct, even if he didn't use standardized drawing and writing symbols. Harste,

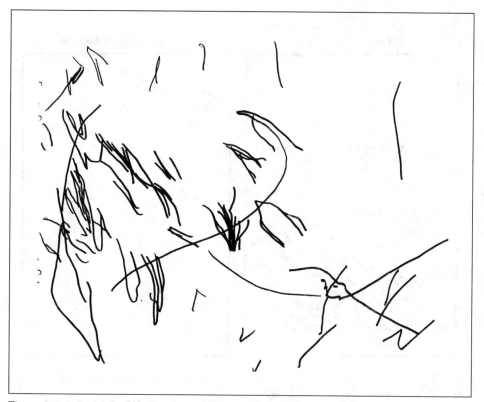

Figure 2–1. *Jamie's Scribble Drawing and Writing. The lines along the top make up Jason's writing. He said he had written, "This is a kitty cat." The rest of the lines make up his drawing.*

Woodward, and Burke (1984) illustrate how young children's early writing is organized and how they often use differentiated scripts for their writing and drawing (see Figure 2–2). Here, a three-year-old, DuJulian, uses an up and down, linear format for his uninterrupted writing (left frame) and circular marks for his drawing (the top part of the right frame). The top of this right frame was a picture of him, and the linear strokes on the bottom were his name. These examples point to how very young children are aware of the multiple functions of print.

Awareness of Features of Written Language (How It Looks)

Harste, Woodward, and Burke (1984) also found that young children across distinct languages and cultures reveal an awareness of the particular features of their native written languages. Figure 2–3 illustrates how three children from different language backgrounds, English, Arabic, and Hebrew, incorporated features of their written native languages. For example, the writing of Nageeba, a Saudi Arabian child from

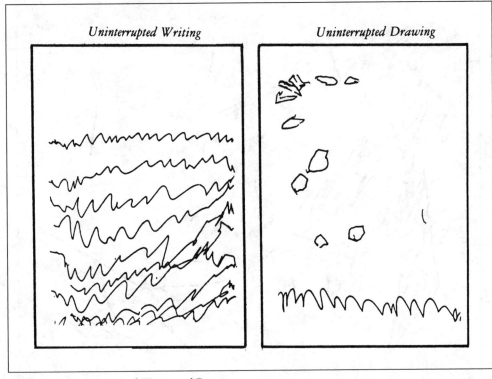

Uninterrupted Writing   *Uninterrupted Drawing*

Figure 2–2. *Uninterrupted Writing and Drawing*

Dawn
United States

Nageeba
Saudi Arabia

Ofer
Israel

Figure 2–3. *Early Writing Influenced by the Native Language* an Arabic speaking home, is reminiscent of Arabic in the curved lines and diacritical marks above the letter approximations. Ofer's writing is reminiscent of printed Hebrew, and includes some diacritical marks, which are used with young children and adults who are learning Hebrew to denote vowels. In contrast, the writing of Dawn, whose native language is English, is reflective of cursive English. This type of language- and culture-specific early writing points to the socially constructed nature of writing.

Understanding How Writing Works

Emilia Ferreiro has spent many years investigating the writing of young children and their understanding of how writing works. In a two-year study in Mexico City that focused on the hypothesis-making about written language of children who were not yet reading and writing, Ferreiro (1980) and her colleagues asked children from poor and middle-class backgrounds to decide if different forms of print were readable. The children were asked to respond to cards with various print configurations, including single letters and numbers; strings of two to six letters that displayed both real words and impossible letter combinations, such as XYZ; strings of the same letter; capital letters; and handwritten letters. The children were not asked to read the cards, just indicate if the text on the card could be read.

Results from this study indicate that the children relied first and foremost on the number of letters and letter variety (i.e., the same letter could not recur) when hypothesizing about the readability of a card. So, if a card had the same letter repeated, children classified it as unreadable because it was always the same letter. Also, a card that contained one or two letters was also rejected as unreadable as the children said there had to be several letters. Although the children were not explicit about how many letters were needed for readability, the data revealed that three was the magic number.

Other interesting findings from Ferreiro's research include the following:

- Variations on the minimum of three letters being required occurred when the size of the referent came into play (e.g., more letters could be used for a larger object, such as a house or an older person).
- Conceptual similarity was more important than sound similarity. Hence, children used the same letters to write *gallina* (hen) and *pollitos* (chicks).
- A syllabic hypothesis, whereby children attributed one letter to each syllable. At this stage, the minimum number of letters requirement coexisted with the syllabic hypothesis, which caused children some confusion when monosyllabic words came into play.
- Children eventually realized that an alphabetic principle is involved (i.e., sound/symbol relationships).

This important research underscores the creative construction principle at work as children emerge as writers. That is, children are actively (and usually internally) figuring out the way in which written language works and, in the process, are continually trying out their hypotheses. Sometimes they overgeneralize, which leads to the misapplication of a learned element (e.g., when children use the regular past term marker, *–ed*, with *go*, to make *goed*). However, with time, and as they gain more experience with and understanding of language, children revise their hypotheses. As Ferreiro comments, "Children have shown us that they need to reconstruct the written system in order to make it their own. Let us allow them the time and the opportunities for such a tremendous task" (56).

Oral Language/Writing Connections

Young children can write before being able to read, write before being orally fluent, and use drawing to explore their thoughts; this is true for both native- and nonnative-speaking children. Drawing, talking, and writing are interconnected mechanisms that allow young writers to symbolically represent their thoughts, and their writing is often a socially-constructed activity. This means that drawing and talking are key elements in early writing development.

The Role of Talk in Young Children's Writing

Ruth Hubbard (1985) explored the role of talk in the writing of first grade children who experienced a daily writing workshop. Over the course of several weeks, she tape recorded whole class sharing sessions that ended each writing workshop. Students volunteered to share their writing and looked forward to these sharing sessions, when they knew that their peers would ask lots of questions about their writing, which consisted sometimes of just a few words. Hubbard found that, although the children could anticipate the kinds of questions they might be asked, knowing this did not lead to them adding to their writing. Instead, they looked forward to the ensuing conversations, and the act of orally sharing and talking about their piece appeared to act as a form of validation of the stories they carried within them and an opportunity for them to refine their thinking. Hubbard comments, "The written text might be a kind of conversation starter, and the sheer event of speaking the most important thing" (627).

When analyzing the kinds of comments made and questions asked, Hubbard found that they fell into the following four categories: textual (about the text that was read), drawing (about accompanying illustrations), process (referring to the author's writing), and supplementary (not referring to the text itself). Hubbard found that the children asked questions most of the time, rather than making supportive comments, such as "I liked . . . " or "My favorite part was. . . ." Hubbard argues that this signals a profound engagement on the part of audience members/respondents and an interest in what peers had written about. She also points out how conversations would almost certainly have ended quickly if the "I like" kinds of comments prevailed, as the texts the children wrote were often very short (e.g., "The big field"); instead, the conversations were dynamic and allowed the children, through their questions, to express interest and support.

The majority of questions asked by the children were textual, indicating that the texts created by their peers were at the center of the conversations. In most sessions, the children also asked questions about illustrations, which were equally related to content (e.g., "What's coming out of his mouth in the word bubble? What's he saying?"). The next most frequently occurring questions related to process (e.g., "How long did it take you to write it?"), which illustrates how the children were interested in how others wrote.

The Role of Talk in Developing ELLs' Literacy

In a study in the mid-1990s, Ernst and Richard (1994/1995) investigated the interplay between reading, writing, and talk in a pullout ESOL classroom that served elementary-aged children. The students in the program spoke twenty languages and came from very different backgrounds (e.g., refugees, immigrants, and expatriates). In their ESOL class, they were surrounded with print, including some print in their native languages, and their ESOL teacher integrated all language modalities (listening, speaking, reading, and writing), including newcomers to English. Ernst and Richard found that talk was an important influence on the students' developing fluency in English, both oral and literacy. For example, through class discussions in response to literature read by the teachers, they were able to bridge familiar experiences and new experiences they were encountering.

In other cases, immersion in oral, traditional literary forms, such as nursery rhymes, acted as a conduit for students to experiment with the English language in meaningful ways. For example, after learning several nursery rhymes, which class members read, recited, drew, and wrote, Hyun-Tae, a fourth grader from Korea in his first year in English, wrote a birthday card to his teacher that was clearly influenced by the nursery rhymes that his class had been enjoying and studying. He wrote the following (325):

Dear Mrs. S
Happy Birthday
Mrs. S
I love this classroom.
I'm a sheep
You are
a little Bo Peep.
I'm a dog
You are   (continues)

a old mather Houber
Have a good day
January 1990, 18 Thursday

English Language Learners Can Write Before Orally Mastering the English Language

Several researchers have found that sophisticated oral language development is not necessary for English language learners to successfully communicate their thoughts and experiences in writing (e.g., Edelsky 1982a; Han and Ernst-Slavit 1999; Hudelson 1983, 1984, 1989; Urzúa 1986, 1987; Samway 1987a, 1987b, 1993; Samway and Taylor 1993a, 1993b; Taylor 1990, 2000). Even when the English system of syntax and semantics has not been mastered, children are able to express their thoughts effectively (Urzúa 1987). In fact, children can write very early in their exposure to English as a consequence of being surrounded by environmental print written in English, such as advertisements, product packaging, and television (Hudelson 1983); this writing growth reflects a growing development in oral fluency (Hudelson 1983).

ELLs Can Convey Important Messages in Writing

The ability to communicate effectively, even with limited control of the language, is well illustrated in the case of Maya, a sixth grader who was a newcomer to the United States, whose writing development was reported on by her ESOL teacher, Dorothy Taylor (1990). Maya was a native speaker of Russian who didn't speak a word of English when she came to the United States. She was in a pullout ESOL program, where she was introduced to reading and writing in English on her first day. Because Taylor had great difficulty finding appropriate reading materials for the recent newcomers, particularly students in the intermediate grades, she began to rely on student-authored books to introduce ESOL students to English reading. They read books written by each other and by students in previous years, and children in the lower grades read the books written by the older students, also. Maya's story, "Things That I Love," is an example of the kind of writing that newcomers produced in their first weeks in the United States (see Figure 2–4). In this short book, Maya relied on pictures, speech bubbles (*I love books, I love to walk in parks*), labels (e.g., *book, Boston Globe,* and *My chair*) and a repetitive refrain (*I love to*). Thus, although her oral language in English was at a beginning stage, she was able to successfully communicate an important message in writing, which others understood and appreciated.

Listing Leading to More Complex Writing

In another part of the world, Lauren Hoyt provided staff development to teachers working in a refugee camp for Southeast Asian students located in the Philippines,

Figure 2–4. *Things That I Love (Russian/English)*

and she reported on the English literacy development of the students (1993). The children were exposed to meaningful literacy experiences throughout their program, including independent reading, read-aloud, shared reading, dialogue journals, Language Experience Approach (LEA) and, about midway through the eighteen-week cycle, writing workshop. At the beginning of the program, one of the students, Somlith, wrote short entries that relied on language patterns and vocabulary that had been taught and that were displayed in the classroom, such as classroom objects and location words (see Figure 2–5). As can be seen, these read like top to bottom lists.

Listing continued in Somlith's writing, but by the sixth week of the program, he had begun to write about topics that captured his interest, such as monsters, and his listing was formatted as continuous prose and included the conjunction *and* to link sentences (see Figure 2–6). In the eleventh week of the program, Somlith wrote a letter to his teacher about his New Year's wish, to go to America. Although listing continued to characterize his writing, he also used the conjunction *because* to explain why he had included several objects in the first half of his letter (see Figure 2–7).

This type of listing and using of available vocabulary is frequently found in the early writing of newcomers to a language, and it often acts as a bridge to more independent writing. This development is reflected in a piece that Somlith wrote in the eighteenth and final week of the program, when he wrote a story about a dog going to a town called Balanga, a nearby town; in this piece, he developed ideas and included a story line, and also illustrated his writing (see Figure 2–8).

ELL Children Can Express Complex Thoughts and Emotions in Less Than Fluent English

English language learners are able to use writing to express complex thoughts, even if they do not have control of the English writing system. For example, Hudelson (1986) discusses the expository writing of intermediate grade ESOL students who had been in the United States for only two years and were not yet fluent writers in English. However, they were clearly able to convey their messages very effectively, albeit with nonstandardized grammatical forms and spellings that are often encountered in ESOL writing, as the following excerpt written by Khamla illustrates:

> One day it was hot and cool it was at summer time. My father sad we will to Disenearland. A day pas buy. We were of to Disenearland. 5 day later we were at Disenearland. We check in to hotles. it were night time. My father said get to bed you want to get up erlee. We got a big day tomorrelow. (Hudelson 1986, 43)

As this excerpt reveals, Khamla was, first and foremost, able to communicate the core and details of his piece about going to Disneyland with his family. On the level of grammar, he successfully used the past tense (e.g., *it <u>was</u> hot, My father <u>said</u> get to*

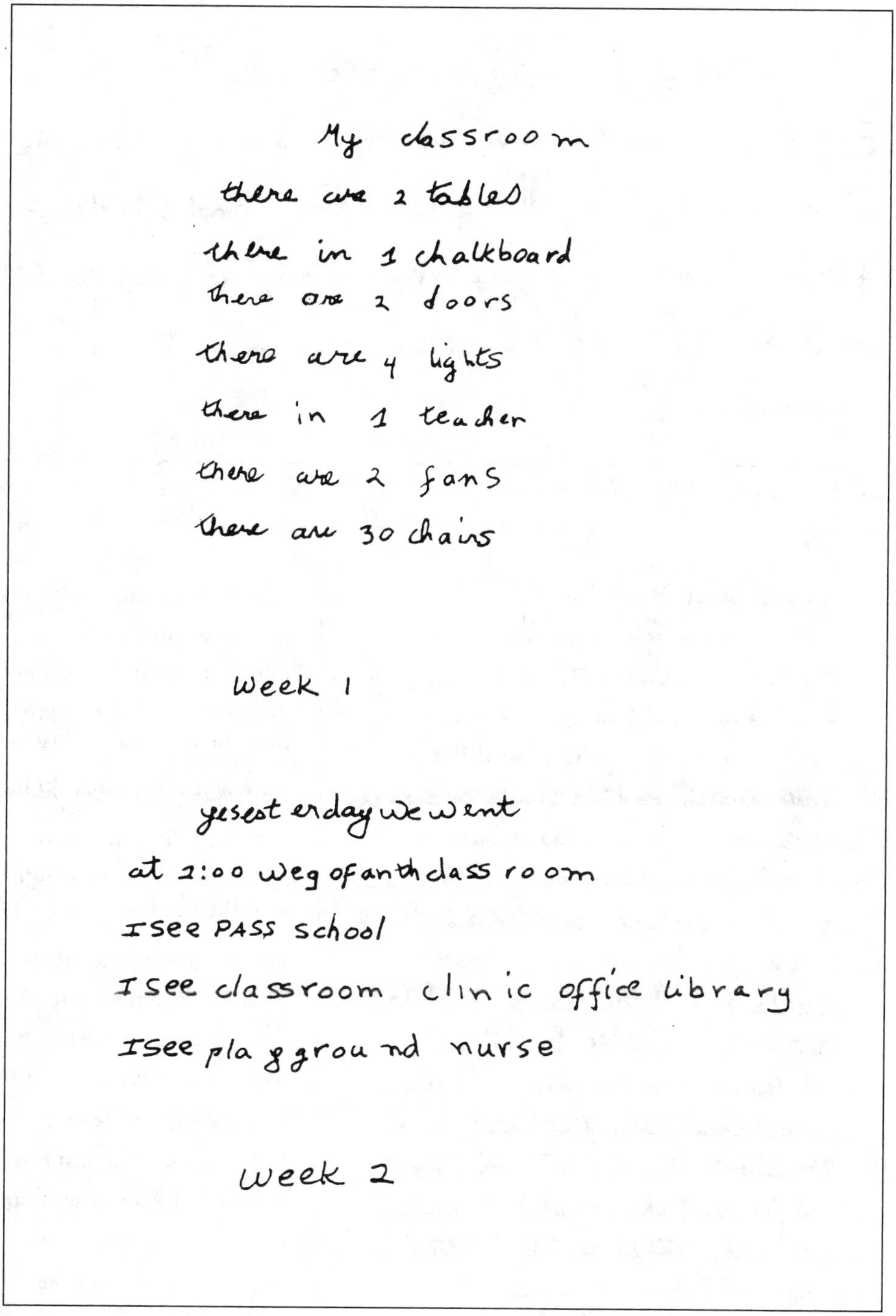

My classroom
there are 2 tables
there in 1 chalkboard
there are 2 doors
there are 4 lights
there in 1 teacher
there are 2 fans
there are 30 chairs

Week 1

yesesterday we went
at 2:00 weg ofanthclassroom
I see PASS school
I see classroom clinic office library
I see playground nurse

week 2

Figure 2–5. *Somlith's Writing, Weeks 1 and 2*

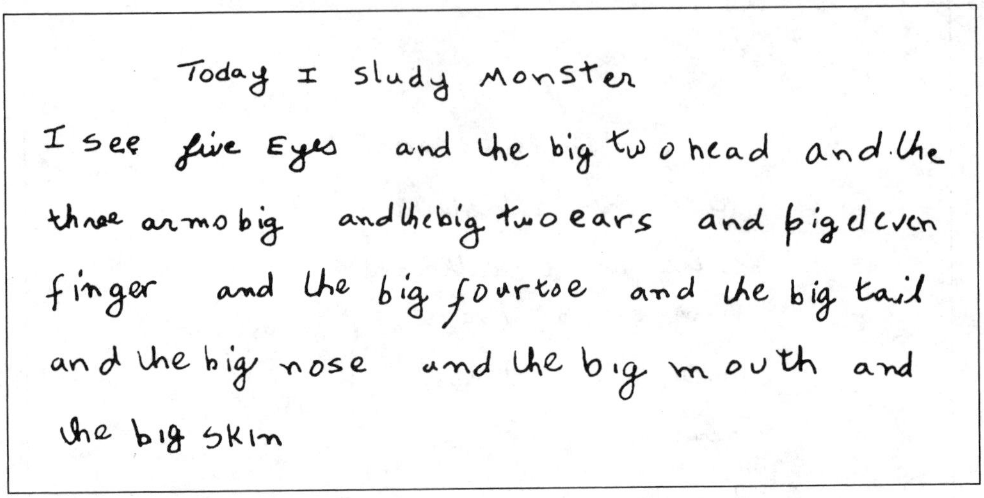

Today I sludy Monster
I see five Eyes and the big two head and the
three armo big and the big two ears and pigd even
finger and the big fourtoe and the big tail
and the big nose and the big mouth and
the big skin

Figure 2–6. *Somlith's Writing, Week 6*

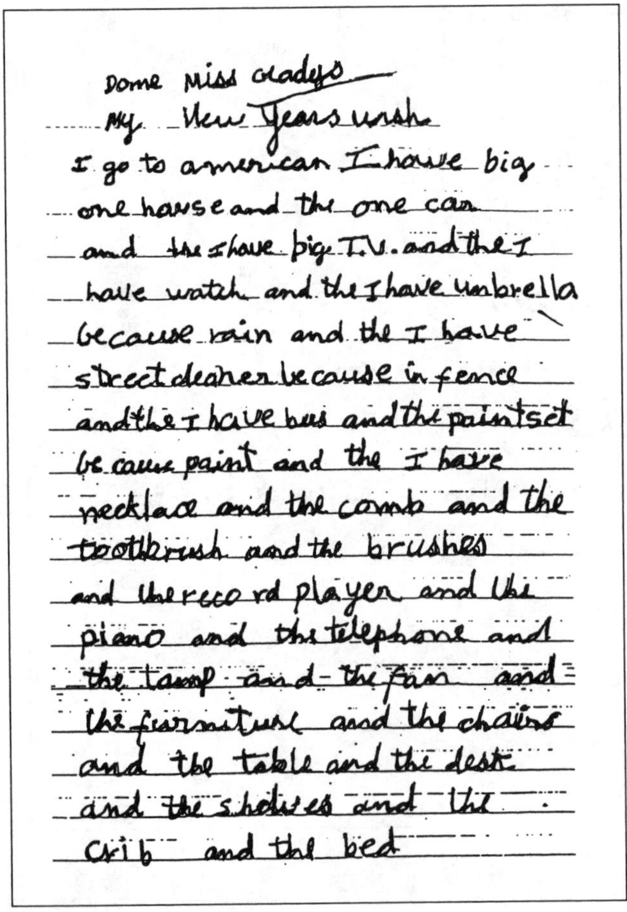

Dome Miss Gladys
My New Years wish
I go to american I have big
one house and the one car
and the I have big T.V. and the I
have watch and the I have umbrella
because rain and the I have
street cleaner because in fence
and the I have bus and the paintset
be cause paint and the I have
necklace and the comb and the
toothbrush and the brushes
and the record player and the
piano and the telephone and
the lamp and the fan and
the furniture and the chairs
and the table and the desk
and the shelves and the
crib and the bed

Dear Miss Gladys

My New Year's wish

I go to America. I have big

one house and the one car

and the(n) I have big TV and the(n) I

have watch and the(n) I have umbrella

because rain and the(n) I have

street cleaner because in fence

and the(n) I have bus and the paintset

because paint and the(n) I have

necklace and the comb and the

toothbrush and the brushes

and the record player and the

piano and the telephone and

the lamp and the fan and

the furniture and the chairs

and the table and the desk

and the shelves and the

crib and the bed

Figure 2–7. *Somlith's Writing, Week 11*

Figure 2–8. *Somlith's Writing, Week 18*

bed), pronouns (e.g., *we, My, it, you*), articles (e.g., *A day*), and English word order (*big day* [adjective followed by the noun]). However, his use of grammar reflects that he is a nonnative English speaker. For example, on one occasion, he omitted the verb (e.g., *we will* [go] *to Disenearland*), although he included the future tense marker (*will*). There were also some occasions when he used the present tense rather than the past tense (e.g., *We check(ed) in to hotles, A day pas(sed) buy,*" and used the third person plural form of the verb *to be*, instead of the third person singular form (*It were* instead of *It was*). These are very common written miscues among nonnative English speakers. When looking at Khamla's word usage, what is striking is that he accurately uses words and terms (e.g., *later, check in*), even if he uses nonstandardized spellings (e.g., *buy*/by, *sad*/said, *hotles*/hotels, *erlee*/early, *tomorrelow*/tomorrow). Also, he uses colloquial expressions successfully, such as *get to bed* and *We got a big day*.

ELLs Understanding More Than They Can Write

Typically, ELLs are able to understand more than they are able to express in writing. Although obviously hampered by a lack of fluency in English, newcomers to the language are nevertheless able to express complex thoughts and emotions. For example, intermediate grade students in Dorothy Taylor's ESOL class were studying the conditions that plants require for optimal growth, and they recorded observations about the progress of their plants' development in science journals. Pedro was a relative newcomer to English, but he still managed to convey humor very effectively in a short entry in which he remonstrated about his pea plant not growing (see Figure 2–9).

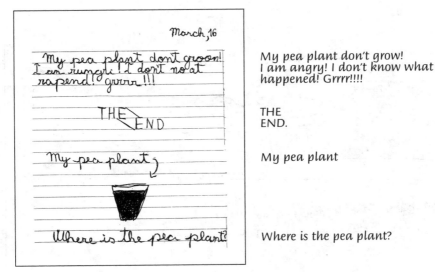

My pea plant don't grow!
I am angry! I don't know what happened! Grrrr!!!!

THE
END.

My pea plant

Where is the pea plant?

Figure 2–9. *Pedro's Writing, Science Log #1*

Pedro used exclamation points; a colloquialism to indicate anger (*Grrr*); a captioned drawing of a pot filled with dirt, but no sign of plant life, and the words, *My pea plant;* and an arrow pointing to the pot, accompanied by the words, *Where is the pea plant?* An entry he wrote five days later maintained this humor (see below, Figure 2–10).

Using Symbols to Express Complex Thoughts

In some cases, ELLs use invented or borrowed symbols to express ideas that their developing command of English does not enable them to communicate effectively, or to emphasize a point. For example, Taylor (1990) reports on the symbols her recent immigrant students used "because of the thrifty way they convey embedded meaning" (111). As Taylor points out, sometimes these symbols were simply "pictorial clichés," such as hearts and flowers, but at other times they allowed the writers to convey more complex thoughts than they were able to express in English. For example, the students did not have sufficient command of English to write complex beginnings and endings, but they followed the lead of Sasha, who substituted written leads and closures with pictures of books at the beginning and end of stories. Other students adapted this popular pictorial marker, such as using a waving hand at the end of a story.

Another example of students borrowing useful pictorial devices began with Maya in her book, "About My Family" (see Figure 2–11). As can be seen, she used a large X to express a negative, to indicate that her mother didn't like to wash dishes. Both newcomers and more fluent English speakers read this book widely, and it inspired seventeen additional versions of "My Family," which were devoured by the students. As Figure 2–12 illustrates, other students picked up on this use of an X, and began to

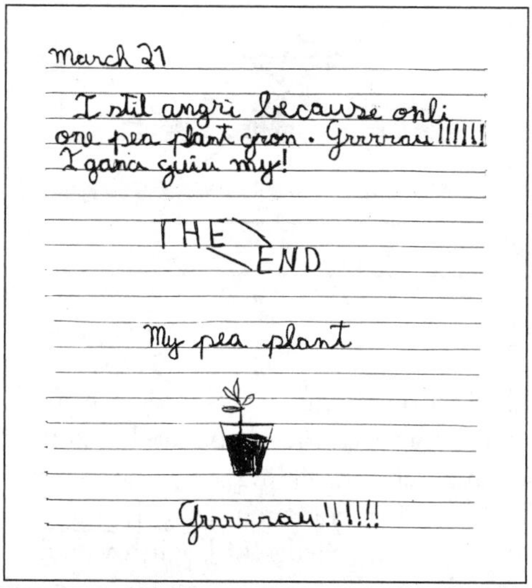

I'm still angry because only
one pea plant has grown. Grrrrow!
I'm gonna (indecipherable) my!

THE
END

My pea plant

Grrrrow!!!!!!

Figure 2–10. *Pedro's Writing, Science Log #2*

Figure 2–11. *Maya's Book: About My Family*

use it in their own writing, much as published writers borrow stylistic devices from other writers. As this figure shows, Maya's peers borrowed the symbol and used it in a variety of situations, such as to underscore an absence of siblings (A), the loss of a dog (B), and being fired from a job (C). Taylor (1990) points out that the pictures allowed the students to convey meanings that their knowledge of English wouldn't permit and, as Taylor comments, the illustrations were the "most joyous and creative part of their books" (112).

Figure 2–12. *Using X in Many Ways*

The texts in these student-authored books were very simple (e.g., *I am . . ., My name is . . .*) and were, in some ways, similar to commercially published texts written for emergent readers that often aren't interesting to the readers, particularly older students. However, these simple texts were devoured by the students, which Taylor attributes to the texts allowing the students to get to know each other. At the same time, these self-selected texts (the content and format were entirely the responsibility of the student writers) helped ELL students figure out how written English works, and allowed them to express themselves in writing in meaningful ways.

ELL Children's Writing Is Developmental and Isn't Necessarily Linear

It has been well documented that children's writing development is irregular, regardless of whether it is in the native language (e.g., Calkins 1982, 1983; Edelsky 1982a, 1982b; Graves 1982; Newkirk 1985) or in the nonnative language (e.g., Edelsky 1982a, 1982b; Hudelson 1984; Samway 1987b; Urzúa 1987). Writing development varies from student to student, even when they have had similar amounts of exposure to and instruction in English and share the same native language (e.g., Hudelson 1986, 1989; Samway 1987b). It should be remembered that this is true for native speakers of English, also (e.g., Graves 1975, 1982; Calkins 1983). Although Edelsky (1982a) found that patterns of development existed for individual nonnative English-speaking children, she did not find that there was a developmental pattern that was common across children. Writing development is irregular, such that there is often variation in quality and quantity across pieces and within drafts for the same writer (e.g., Hudelson 1984; Samway 1987b; Urzúa 1987). For example, I observed that Pedro took a month to write a piece and minimally revised it, David was a quick writer, but he also minimally revised, and Ahmed usually made major revisions from draft to draft (Samway 1987b).

Developmental Stages in Early Writing

Writing is a developmental process, and young children go through various nonrigid stages as they become more skilled writers. There are several developmental stages in early writing, and I will use the example of Linh's writing, reported by Gail Heald-Taylor (1986), to illustrate these stages, where appropriate. Linh was a native Chinese-speaking Vietnamese refugee living in Canada. She had lived in Canada for a few months before enrolling in first grade, and spoke just a few words and simple phrases in English. Over the course of about fifteen months, spanning first grade and part of second grade, her writing developed enormously (see Figure 2–13).

- *Scribble writing (and drawing) stage:*
  - Scribbles often reflect the orthography of the native language.
  - Letters are often approximations of standardized letters.
  - Scribbles for writing and drawing are often differentiated.

In mid-September, Linh used scribble to accompany her drawings, and the scribble resembles Chinese characters, which she would have probably seen in her home as her father had been a teacher in Vietnam (see Frame 1). By early October (see Frame 2), her scribble resembled early writing in English (the cursive text was written by an adult).

- *Strings of letters stage*:
  - There is no sound-letter correspondence.
  - Numbers and other symbols are often interspersed.
  - Spacing between letters is often absent.

Figure 2–13. *Linh's Writing Development (continues)*

Frame 3

Obc de fgh IJKLMno p q r
s t u v w x yz–ABC DE

My friend went out
trick or treating. She give
me candy. Her name is
Binh. I give her a candy.
Then I go home and give my
sister one candy or two. My
mom came home and said
I can't go out.

Linh Nov. 1, 1983. Age: 5.11

Frame 4

rain – day

I went outside with my
cousin. My cousin's name
Kiew. My and my friend
is coming and we go inside
and we had hot water.

Linh Nov. 15, 1983. Age: 5.11

Frame 5

my mom m
a c r r a
a c my mom
I am m f
m c

My mom make me a cookie.

Linh: Dec. 1983. Age: 6.0

Frame 6

It is fun to go to
skating. c
I like to go skating

It is fun to go to skating
because it's fun. I like
to go skating.

Linh: Jan. 5, 1984. Age: 6.1

Figure 2–13 (continued). Linh's Writing Development

Frame 7

I wecnd to the fr~~
hu~ and my fr~ gr~~
Me a big pr~~ and I Su~
to my fr~ fr~~~ fu~
a P~~~ and I wechd
h~~ and I eat su~~~ I h~
fu~ g~~ to my m~~

I went to the friend
house and my fried gave
me a big present. And I
said thank you
to my friend for
a plesent. and I went
home and I eat supper. I had
fun. Showed to my mom.

Linh: Jan. 23, 1984. Age: 6.2

Frame 8

I went to the party
yest erday and I had fun
and I eat Chinese food
and I dancing goob!

Linh Jan 20, 1984 Age: 6-2

Frame 9

I am a rain drop.
and I'm droping
down. And I'm.
geting cold.

The End.

Linh May 8, 1984 Age: 6-6

Frame 10

Next week me and my mom
and dad and my sister
is going to my grandmother
house to sleep over when
we have long of mondys
do you no when I'm go have
3 days When I'm there. my
grandmather is going
to give me a dess

Linh Sept. 20, 1984 Age: 6-10

Figure 2–13 (continued). *Linh's Writing Development*

Frame 11

Once a upon a time there were a farm. And they are eating lunch. And then the two children went outside to play. And one of the children open the door of the cow's door. And then they went inside. And then when the door was still open. And then the cow went out. And then the little children went out to play again. And then they saw the cow was gone. And then they run. And go find the cow. And then they went to the woods. And then they hear a sound like a cow. And then they went into the woods And then they found the cows. And they went out of the woods. And then they saw someone with a light. And it was the children's mother. And then they went home.

Linh Nov. 6, 1986. Age. 6.8

Figure 2–13 (continued).   *Linh's Writing Development*

By the beginning of November (see Frame 3), Linh was incorporating random letters, in addition to scribble, to accompany her drawings.

- *Letters represent whole words or thoughts stage*:
  - There is some sound/symbol correspondence.
  - There are some correctly spelled words, which are frequently sight words and high-frequency words that may be displayed in the classroom (e.g., *rain-day* in Frame 4, *my*, *mom*, and *am* in Frame 5, and *skating* in Frame 6).
  - Some spacing between words (and sometimes between letters) appears.
  - There is a simple message, which is often in the form of a label.
  - Pictures are often as important as the writing.
  - At first, writers of English tend to capture beginning consonants, then ending consonants, then medial consonants, and finally vowels (see Frame 5, written in December); this is similar to the spelling development of native English speakers.
  - At this stage, students may have difficulty reading their own texts.
- *Stylized sentence writing stage*:
  - Writing is often patterned in nature (e.g., This is . . . , This is . . .).
  - Writers may rely on familiar words, often those displayed in the classroom.
  - Texts become longer, and include more conventional spelling.
  - Students can usually read their own writing.
- *Emerging standardized writing stage*:
  - Messages are longer, often reflecting the writer's eagerness to focus on quantity, and *bed-to-bed/and then* writing is frequently found (see Frame 11).
  - Punctuation may not be used conventionally.
  - Spelling may become more unconventional as the writer takes more risks in incorporating less familiar or frequently occurring words.
- *Standardized writing stage*:
  - Writing is better organized and more focused.
  - Word choice is more varied and voice is more apparent.
  - Spelling is more standardized, except when writers are using vocabulary that is not familiar.
  - Punctuation is more conventional and varied.

Heald-Taylor reports that by late January (see Frame 7), Linh had begun to focus more on the content of her writing and by the end of that month was no longer using scribble to act as a place holder for unknown spellings of words or parts of words (see Frame 8). This increased focus on the content of her writing continued and by the end of the fifteen months of data collection, in November of the following academic year, her writing integrated attention to conventions, as well as content (see Frame 11).

These developmental stages were also reflected in the very early writing of Laurel Cress' Spanish/English bilingual kindergarten children, who signed in each morning, rather than the teacher taking roll call. Figure 2–14 below shows the emergent writing development of Johanna—the three signatures are from September (top), November (middle) and January (bottom). Her September signature is made up of random, letter-like marks. By November, she signed her name with all its letters, but the *a*'s and *n*'s are backwards. By January, all the letters in her name are standardized.

Irregular, Nonlinear Writing Development

Although there are developmental writing stages, it would be a mistake to expect that children will move through these stages smoothly, or even go through all the identified stages. In fact, they often do not, a reality that is often reflective of students' confidence and engagement as writers. Some children will write only words that they know are correctly spelled (e.g., words that are displayed on the word wall). As they gain more confidence, however, they become more willing to take risks and their once correctly spelled writing includes less familiar words that they do not know how to spell correctly, but attempt to approximate through knowledge of sound-symbol correspondence (a process that is often referred to as *invented* or *developmental spelling*). Some adults may interpret this phenomenon as a regression or lack of care, when actually it often reveals growth as a writer.

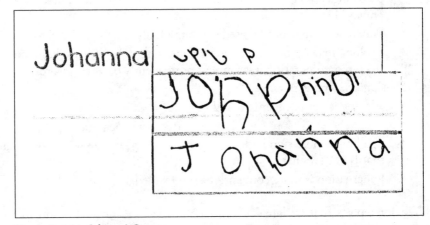

Figure 2–14. *Johanna's Signatures*

Contextual Influences on Writing Development

Other factors that can influence writing development include contextual issues, such as motivation and familiarity with a genre. For example, when children write on a topic that is of importance and interest to them, their writing is often better developed than writing in which they are less invested. This can be seen sometimes in the prompted writing of children who have had many opportunities to select their own topics—children who can write vibrantly when they select their own topics may write less well-developed pieces when given writing prompts that do not resonate with them. Similarly, students who try new genres may exhibit less skill over organization or word choice than they previously demonstrated. Additional environmental factors also influence writing, such as tiredness and even the kind of materials that writers have at their disposal. For example, some children write more fluently when they are using markers or when they are working on a computer.

Edelsky and Jilbert (1985) point out how writing development is not a linear process of accumulating discrete skills, but is more a process of reorganizing systems as children sometimes appear to regress (just as children do when learning their native language and as children and adults do when acquiring a nonnative language). For example, they found occasions when previously conventional spelling became unconventional when children tried a new genre or writing implement. Also, when working with more difficult content, children used more unconventional segmentation. Edelsky and Jilbert comment, "Examining the idea of textness reveals even stronger evidence against the idea that children accumulate separate and separable skills and in favor of the idea that they construct and successively reorganize total systems" (63).

Hudelson (1986) found that intermediate grade ESOL students' writing varied from piece to piece and from child to child. Variations encompassed both quality and quantity and appeared to be related to such elements as students' interest in and personal involvement with a topic or assignment, availability of resources (e.g., prior experience with a topic [schema] and availability of books and other materials on a topic), experience with a writing form, personality, and amount of time available for writing. An additional influence that Hudelson comments on is related to children's views of themselves and their sense of efficacy as writers. For example, whereas the majority of children expressed confidence as writers, wrote even when it was not assigned, and used writing to express themselves, one child, Vuong, wrote only when it was assigned. Also, his writing did not reveal the same kind of personal involvement that was reflected in the writing of the other students. Hudelson makes a very important point when she comments that to determine a student's writing based on one piece would not provide a complete or true picture of that writer: "No single piece of writing by itself provided as complete a picture of each child as a writer as did an examination of all the pieces, assigned and unassigned, produced by each child" (48).

Knowledge of Writing Conventions May Be Transferred from the L1 to English

The writing of ELLs often contains both standardized and nonstandardized spellings, and many of their developmental spellings reflect how their knowledge of the writing system of the native language (L1) is used as a resource when writing in English. For example, Pedro's science log entries about his pea plant not growing (Figures 2–9 and 2–10, shown earlier) reflect features of his native language, Spanish. He correctly spelled "My pea plant," which he may have seen on charts in his classroom, but wrote "I an rungri!" for "I am angry." These nonstandardized spellings probably reflect letter/sound correspondences that he heard when pronouncing the words or hearing them. He wrote two words ending in *i* instead of a *y* (*angri*/angry and *onli*/only), but it should be remembered that, although it is unusual to end a word with an *i* in English, it is very common in Spanish (e.g., *si*/yes, *aquí*/here, *comí*/ate). Similarly, it is not unusual for Spanish speakers to write the English *h* with a *g* as the Spanish *g* makes a similar sound to the English *h*. For example, Paul Ammon (1985) reports that Maria wrote *gr* for *her*.

What do you think is the native language of the ESOL student who wrote the science log entry that follows (see Figure 2–15)? Some of the clues include the use of diacritical marks over dirt (*dört*), give (*gif*) ending in the hard "f" sound, and the spelling of water (*watter*). In fact, the student is a native speaker of German, and these elements are reflective of German sounds and spelling patterns.

Influence of the Native Language, English(es), and Interlanguage on ELLs' Writing

Bruce Cronnell (1985) investigated the writing of third and sixth grade Mexican American children living in the metropolitan Los Angeles area; the writing was written in response to a district-wide end-of-year assessment. Cronnell found that the students' writing showed evidence of the influence of Spanish, Chicano English, and *interlanguage*, that is, a form that occurs in the process of learning a language, and that seems to be influenced by the creative construction process in which learners engage, sometimes

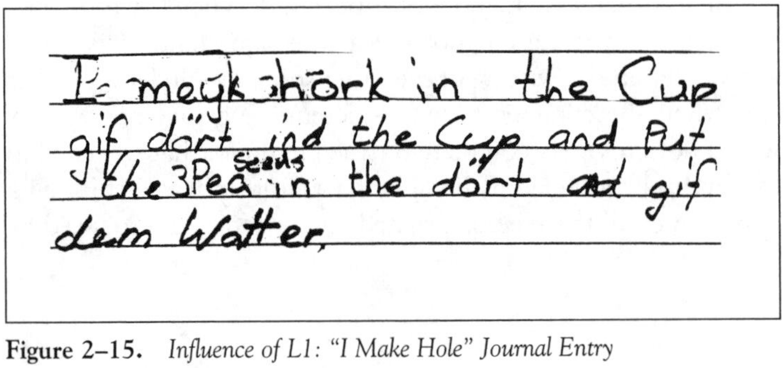

I make hole in the cup
give dirt in the cup and put
the 3 pea seeds in the dirt and give them water

Figure 2–15. *Influence of L1: "I Make Hole" Journal Entry*

overgeneralizing and *inventing* forms. Cronnell analyzed deviations from standard written English (except punctuation and capitalization), and found the following:

- Twenty-seven percent of third graders' and 36 percent of sixth graders' deviations from nonstandard English were identified as possibly being influenced by Spanish, interlanguage, or Chicano English.
- Third graders tended to make more spelling, pronunciation, and verb-based errors than sixth graders. Spanish spelling has regular vowel sounds, such that the Spanish /i/ is spelled *i* and the Spanish /a/ is spelled *a*. Therefore, when spelling English words, it is common for Spanish speakers to spell English words with these letter-sound correspondences in mind (e.g., Cronnell found *clean* spelled *clin* and *making* was spelled *mekin*). Spanish pronunciation also influences the spelling of words. For example, in Spanish, the /b/ and /v/ are not differentiated, so that it is common for Spanish-speaking students to spell *very* as *bery* or *convince* as *conbins*, as Cronnell found. Cronnell acknowledges that the writing prompts themselves may have contributed to grade-based differences in verb tense usage. That is, the third graders were asked to write a story based on a picture prompt of an elephant and a monkey on roller skates at the start of a race, whereas the sixth graders were asked to write a persuasive letter to a friend. He conjectures that it is likely that the story prompt elicited more use of the past tense than the letter prompt.
- Sixth graders tended to make more vocabulary and syntax errors than did third graders. Idiomatic language use was the genesis of many of the vocabulary-based deviations from written English that Cronnell found. For example, the preposition *in*, which is visually similar to the Spanish *en* (and means both *in* and *on*), was frequently overused, as in "in your mark," "in skates," "in television," and "in channel 2." The word *out* was similarly overused (e.g., "The program comes out at 7:00), and this may be explained by Spanish usage of *salir*, which means "to come/go out" (i.e., to leave), but is also used with regard to the appearance of a television program (meaning to "come on").

Many of the students' deviations from standard English, while common amongst nonnative speakers, sometimes appear in native speakers of a nonstandard version of English dialect (e.g., speakers of Chicano English), such as using the double negative (e.g., "don't have nothing"), misuse of reflexives (e.g., "their self"), and misuse of superlatives (e.g., "most funniest").

Being Taught to Write in the Native Language Is an Asset

As part of a study investigating language socialization in Mexican immigrant and Mexican American families living in the San Francisco Bay area of California and San Antonio, Texas, Sandra Schecter and Robert Bayley (2002) explored the English and Spanish narrative writing of children in fourth, fifth, and sixth grades. They collected thirty prompted essays written in Spanish and forty-one written in English, and found that those children who had acquired some proficiency in Spanish writing wrote equally as well as those children who wrote only in English. As Schecter and Bayley point out, these children had actually outpaced their monoliterate peers because they were literate in two languages. They also found that children who were not taught Spanish literacy, but were exposed to oral Spanish, did not acquire Spanish reading and writing. These findings, which suggest that children who were taught Spanish literacy were at an advantage due to their biliteracy, provide a compelling argument for maintenance bilingual/biliteracy education.

ELLs Can Write in Both the Native and Nonnative Languages Without Being Confused

There has been considerable debate about whether children can cope with being taught to read and write in two languages at the same time (simultaneous or sequential instruction, or indirectly through being exposed to print in two languages), and whether this can lead to confusion and possible language interference. Edelsky and Jilbert (1985) found that children could cope with both Spanish and English without confusion, were acquiring two systems simultaneously, and were able to differentiate between the two written systems. For example, children in this year-long study never used tildes (~) when writing English words and used the letter *k* only when writing in English (*k* is used in Spanish only for foreign words).

Errors as Hypothesis Testing

Edelsky and Jilbert (1985) found that children's writing errors were not random, but evidence of hypothesis-generating and testing; they found this with spelling, segmentation, and punctuation. For example, children invented unconventional spacing (segmentation) that was used systematically, such as no spaces within a sentence (e.g., Eslipdclorda/es libro de colorear/It's a coloring book). They also put periods at the end of every line. These findings underscore the way in which children incorporate into their writing features that they have not been directly taught (e.g., writing one sentence per line and then separating lines with stars and separating words with hyphens). I encountered a similar ability to differentiate in Laura Alvarez's fourth/fifth grade bilingual class, where certain subjects were taught in Spanish and others were taught in English.

Errors as Evidence of Language Resourcefulness

Children draw upon their knowledge of their native language until they have internalized the rule in English. This is not language interference. Instead, it is using the language resources that are at their disposal. For example, children are likely to use their knowledge of the orthography of their native language, such as Spanish, when writing in English. This can be seen in the following message written in English by a native Spanish-speaking child: ai joup llu gou agien/I hope you go again (Edelsky and Jilbert 1985, 68). This reflects knowledge of Spanish spelling (e.g., *ai* for the /i/ sound in *ai*/I, and the double *ll* for the /y/ sound in *llu*/you). Edelsky and Jilbert report that, as the children became increasingly more knowledgeable about English writing, English phonics generalizations were at the heart of their invented spellings in English.

Children Can Write in More Than One Language

Despite the much-heard refrain, "These children can't speak/write in Spanish *or* English," Edelsky and Jilbert (1985) found that the children's bilingualism enhanced their options for making meaning, rather than reducing or limiting it (as is often assumed). They were well able to maintain their writing in either Spanish or English, were not confused about which language they were using or needed to use, and used code switching for very specific reasons, such as to indicate direct quotations and for emphasis. For example, one child wrote ". . . *y le pegó al cocodrilo y el cocodrilo se murió y el Popeye dijo—yeay*/and he fought the crocodile and the crocodile died and Popeye said, 'Yeah'" (70). In this case, the child used Spanish for writing the narrative, but when writing what Popeye said, the child switched to English and wrote *yeay*/yeah. Children also code switched when emphasizing a point, such as reaching the end of a piece, as the following example illustrates (70).

What the child wrote	Standardized Spanish	English translation
y se fueron a juera	y se fueron afuera	and they went outside
y una biejita yego a	y una viejita llegó a	and a little old lady came to
la casa de los ositos	la casa de los ositos	the three bears' house
Fin The end	Fin The end	The end The end

As can be seen, the student wrote "The end" twice, first in Spanish (*fin*) and then in English, as if to emphasize the completion of the story.

Code Switching in Writing

It is interesting to note that, although the children in Edelsky and Jilbert's research (1985) frequently code switched when talking, they rarely code switched when writing, and when they did, it tended to be single words. Also, although they were more fluent in Spanish, they were much more likely to code switch when writing in Spanish than when writing in English (which challenges the myth that code switching is a reflection of limited language competence). In addition, the code switching that occurred in English writing seemed to be more like the slip of a pen, as when articles and conjunctions were written in Spanish, such as when a child wrote, "*y el dinasaur is gonna be*/and the dinosaur is gonna be" (70). As Edelsky and Jilbert comment, it appeared that the children realized that, although they were in a bilingual program, English was the more valued language of the school, with norms that were less like oral language and, therefore, less conducive to code switching.

Similarities and Differences in Children's Writing in English and Other Languages

Writing processes for children are very similar across languages. For example, Marilyn Chi (1988) investigated the early writing/spelling processes of Chinese-speaking children in Taiwan ages three to six. Her findings indicate that, like children whose language is alphabetic, such as English and Spanish, these children, whose native language is logographic rather than alphabetic, invented spelling/writing symbols. That is, they used cues from Chinese logography to write their own unique symbols. Chi found that there were developmental stages, such as the following:

- Scribbling; iconic picture writing, such as drawing a picture of a hand instead of writing a character to represent *hand*
- Using strokes to represent unrecognizable characters
- Using strokes to represent recognizable characters
- Writing using condensed, but distinguishable characters
- Writing by homonym character, in which words with the same pronunciation and some of the same strokes/part of the graph carry different meanings
- Conventional writing

Chi found that the younger children, such as three-year-olds, were more apt to use the lower levels of writing (e.g., scribbling, and iconic pictograph writing) than the older children. The data also revealed that there was some overlap in how the children progressed through stages, such that their writing might fit into more than one developmental stage, which is similar to what is known about the development of English writing. Chi points out, however, that there were differences in the writing strategies used by Chinese-speaking children when compared with English-speaking children. These include Chinese-speaking children using global visual features to guide their construction of characters, whereas English-speaking children rely on sound-symbol correspondences.

There are frequently many similarities found in children's writing when they write in their native and nonnative languages. In a study funded by the National Institute of Education (NIE) involving first, second, and third graders in a Spanish/English bilingual program who were taught literacy in Spanish before being formally taught literacy in English, Edelsky (1982a, 1982b) reports on the following similarities in the children's writing in their native and nonnative languages.

- *Personal style*—the same writer would tend to use the same type of stylistic devices in both languages, such as overusing *para*/for when writing in Spanish and overusing *then* and *and* when writing in English. Children also used the same strategies for ending a piece of writing. For example, the same student ended pieces with a pleasant, upbeat comment, such as "*y gracias maestra*/thank you, teacher" when writing in Spanish and "*y*/and it's fun. *Thank you*" when writing in English. In addition, children used the same strategy in both languages for making a piece longer, such as repeating phrases.
- *Spelling*—the students invented spellings in both languages, which is particularly interesting when one considers that Spanish is considered to be a very regular language grapho-phonically, unlike English. When writing in English, the children usually used their knowledge of Spanish orthography, such as when one child wrote *ba llana uwen* for "bionic woman."
- *Segmentation*—students segmented according to a variety of factors, including: (a) *syntactic*, such as putting spaces between, but not within, noun phrases (e.g., *los reyes*/the kings would be written as one word), (b) *morphological/phonological*, such as segmenting by syllable (e.g., *estaba*/ was written as two words, *es taba*).

Edelsky (1982b) also found differences in the children's native and nonnative writing, including the following:

- *Tildes and accents*—Students knew that accents and tildes (the diacritical mark placed over the *n* in Spanish, as in *mañana*/tomorrow) were used in Spanish, but not in English, and accents and tildes did not appear in the children's English writing.
- *Syntactic complexity*—Children's writing was often syntactically more complex in Spanish than in English. For example, a child's writing in Spanish would include some relative and adverbial clauses, but in English the writer tended to use subject-verb-object declarative sentences. These differences were related to the English language proficiency of the child.
- *Handwriting*—Third graders wrote more often in English than did the first and second graders. They also chose to write in manuscript. About midyear, there was a shift toward cursive. When writing in Spanish, they wrote in manuscript and cursive. When beginning to write in English, many students wrote only in manuscript.

Many educators working with Spanish-speaking students notice that young children's early writing in Spanish is filled with vowels, whereas early writing in English is dominated by consonants. Irene Serna and Sarah Hudelson (1993) encountered this reality, which they attribute to the morpho-phonological structure of the Spanish

51

language in which vowels occur in each syllable and receive equal or more stress than consonants. In contrast, in English, consonants receive more stress.

ELL Children Evaluating Writing

Many myths surround ELL students and what they are capable of doing, and one that I sometimes hear is that they can't be expected to do complex cognitive and linguistic tasks because they don't have enough English. In a small study that was part of a larger study investigating the writing processes of ELLs in a pullout ESOL program in a city school district, I explored the criteria that nine second to sixth graders used when evaluating writing (Samway 1993). I asked each child to rate a standard set of six pieces written anonymously by fifth grade students as part of a statewide writing test; when time allowed it, the children also rated their own writing (five students did this). The pieces represented a range of writing abilities and included well-written and not so well-written pieces, short and long pieces, and conventional and unconventional mechanics, such as spelling.

The evaluation process involved the following steps: (a) I met with each child individually, (b) I explained what the writers had been asked to do, reading from the test administration directions (occasionally students chose to read the directions, usually aloud), (c) the student read each piece (if unconventional spelling caused difficulties for a student, I read the piece to him or her), (d) the student put each piece in one of three piles: *very good*, *okay*, and *not so good*, and (e) I interviewed the student about his or her evaluations, asking questions, such as, "Why did you put this story in the *Okay* pile?" or "What would you do to make this story a *very good* story?" Later, I coded their responses using a modified version of Hilgers' (1984, 1986) classification scheme for evaluation statements. The coding categories included *retelling* (i.e., paraphrasing all or part of a text), *liking* (i.e., indicating personal liking of an element or an association with the text), *surface features* (i.e., about the form of the text, such as spelling, length, or handwriting), *understanding* (i.e., efforts to process or make sense of the text), *crafting* (i.e., about how well a text was developed), and *entertainment* (i.e., the degree to which a text prompted an emotional response).

Displaying Reflective Powers

The children were clearly unfamiliar with this type of writing-related activity, and it was often hard for them. For example, at one point Ahmed commented, "This is hard, isn't it?" However, the students responded with enthusiasm and displayed a capacity to thoughtfully evaluate writing. It was clear that these ELL students were capable of engaging in a demanding linguistic experience.

Although many of the anonymous texts that the children rated contained unconventional spellings, which sometimes made them hard to read, the students rarely made *surface features* comments (only 3% of all comments). In fact, the largest percentage of comments fell in the *crafting* category (47% of all comments), followed by *understanding* (14% of all comments), *retelling* (10% of all comments), and *liking* (9% of all comments). Approximately half of the children rated their own writing, as well as that of the anonymous pieces, but the task did not appear to affect their evaluative comments. In fact, there were similar percentages for each category, regardless of who had written the piece; the one exception was, not unsurprisingly, in the *understanding* category (9% of all comments for own pieces and 24% of all comments for anonymous pieces). However, age may have been a factor in the children's responses, as the second/third graders were more likely to make *understanding* comments than the fourth/sixth grade students.

Attention to Crafting Issues

The preponderance of *crafting* comments is particularly compelling as such a focus demands that the reader/writer must look at the entire text, rather than simply using the text as a cueing system to past experiences, as *liking* comments, for example, typically reflect. Even when the mechanics of the texts inhibited the children's understanding, still they focused on the overall impact of the piece and constantly revised their evaluations, as the following excerpt from Ahmed's interview illustrates:

> AHMED: (Reading) *The day I turned into a giraffe. I was waking up. I got out of bed and banged my head on the ceiling. "Ouch," I yelled, "Come quick," I yelled. She ran up the stairs. Who's, He said, I yelled. She ran up the stairs.* What does it mean, *She ran up the stairs?*
>
> SAMWAY: Maybe if you read on you might get the rest of it.
>
> AHMED: Okay. *I was waking up. I got out of bed and banged my head on the ceiling. "Ouch." "Come quick," I yelled. She ran up the stairs.* I don't know. She should put, "I ran up the stairs." (He continues reading.) Is it *lotion* or *potion?*

Ahmed came to the text with some understanding of wizards and, by the time he had finished reading the story, he understood it and gave it a *very good* rating.

This excerpt also illustrates how the students were critical evaluators (e.g., Ahmed made suggestions for the absent author). A younger student, Pablo, also made insightful comments when he rated this same story involving a giraffe. After I asked him why he had put it in the *very good* pile, he said, "It (pause). It like tells you about it. You know. It tells you and they don't have to tell you that you had a dream. You can figure it out easily." That is, Pablo recognized that good writers don't have to tell everything, but can leave it to readers to figure out or infer some of the meaning.

Partial Understanding of a Craft Element

Sometimes the children's *crafting* comments indicated an incomplete understanding of an element. For example, second grader, Hector, said that he thought that the author of a piece about a bird had done a good job because "He describe the other birds." In fact, the description of the other birds made the piece less focused and cohesive, but it is possible that the extra details made the piece more interesting to Hector. In other cases, the students used language that seemed routinized, such as when Pablo commented that a piece about a baloney sandwich was *very good* because "It's got a beginning, middle, and end," when in fact, the piece was a listing of ingredients. As Pablo was unable to point to which parts corresponded with "a beginning, middle, and end," it is possible that he was using terminology that he had periodically encountered in his ESOL class, and was using it to indicate that he understood the piece. Examples such as these suggest that the students sometimes had partial understanding of a criterion and were experimenting with it, thereby indicating a developing awareness of writing and evaluation criteria.

Influence of the Classroom Environment

The findings in my study were noticeably different from those of Hilgers (1984, 1986) in several respects, including the following:

- Whereas 47 percent of the ESOL students' comments in my study fell in the *crafting* category, only 8 percent of comments in Hilgers' study fell in this category.
- In Hilgers' study, the children were much more likely to make *liking* comments (47 percent of all comments), whereas only 9 percent of all comments in my study fell in the *liking* category.
- Whereas 3 percent of all comments made by children in my study fell in the *surface features* category, these comments accounted for 19 percent in Hilgers' study.

The predominance of *crafting* comments in my study, along with the relative absence of comments in other categories, such as *liking* and *surface features*, may be explained by events in the ESOL class. Ms. Olsen, the ESOL teacher, did not pay much attention to mechanical conformity and accuracy, instead stressing the importance of the content of one's writing. This may explain the absence of comments relating to spelling, punctuation, and handwriting, and the overwhelming reliance on *crafting* comments.

Prior Literacy Experiences May Affect How ELLs Respond to New Literacy Experiences

Many ELLs may encounter markedly different literacy learning experiences in their English-medium schools from those they had earlier in their lives or continue to have outside school. This is true of children who have already received some schooling in their native lands, as well as children who have not, but whose parents have different understandings from teachers about writing and how best to support its development.

Literacy for Social Cohesion versus for Individual Expression

In an overview of differences between the writing experiences and expectations of Japanese and Chinese students and what they often encounter in western, English-medium classrooms, Carson (1992) comments that Chinese writing instruction is grounded in memorization of writing styles and word choice, and encourages group rather than personal or individual sharing. That is, language and literacy are a means to express social cohesion, rather than to provide for individual expression. Consequently, students are encouraged to copy established writing styles, and writing may appear to lack the interesting range of word usage and writing styles that one typically finds in other languages. Creativity is viewed as emerging from internalizing others' styles; creativity comes from discipline and proficiency. Whereas hard work in Japanese and Chinese writing is manifested in memorization and learning the forms, in U.S. writing classrooms, hard work manifests in planning, writing, and revising. Carson points out that these are quite different concepts and potentially alien to non-native English-speaking students (and their parents) who come already literate in their native languages.

According to Carson (1992), most Japanese children enter school able to read, even though letters and characters are typically not taught in nursery schools or kindergartens. Carson attributes this to parents (particularly mothers) reading picture books written in the phonetic *hiragana* (phonetic symbols with sound-symbol correspondence) and *kana* blocks that children play with. Once in school, children are taught *kana* using a whole word method, and are taught *kana* writing using a kinesthetic method involving tracing the word in the air or on a table while pronouncing the syllable. Then they trace the syllable on dotted lines. Carson concludes that as Japanese and Chinese writing is product-oriented and English writing is often process-oriented, English-medium teachers need to be aware of any previous writing experiences that their immigrant students may have experienced prior to coming to their new, English-medium school.

Part-Whole versus Whole-to-Part Approaches

Despite a trend toward more process-oriented approaches to writing instruction, many students are taught to read and write using a part-to-whole, skills-based approach. In many Spanish/English bilingual programs, Spanish reading and writing are typically taught this way. That is, children are first taught vowels, then consonants, which are added to the vowels to form syllables (e.g., *ma, me, mi, mo, mu*). They are then taught how to form words (e.g., *casa, mira*), then sentences, followed by paragraphs and finally stories. In English-medium classrooms that adhere to a skills-based approach, the emphasis is usually first on consonants, followed by vowels.

Thereafter, the sequence is similar (words, sentences, paragraphs, and stories). In a part-to-whole, skills-based approach, students tend to spend quite a bit of time practicing the skills they have been taught (e.g., on worksheets, in workbooks, and with skill games); only when they are considered to have mastered the conventions of writing are they encouraged to write authentically (i.e., write original messages that they have composed).

In other classrooms, children are taught to read and write using a whole-to-part approach in which they are taught with complete texts, such as shared reading books (big books) and authentic story/personal narrative writing, and are taught skills and strategies in the context of these complete texts. Sometimes, ELLs experience these two different approaches (part-to-whole and whole-to-part) in the same year. This can occur either in the same classroom or in their Spanish- and English-medium classrooms, if different teachers are responsible for instruction in English and the native language, as sometimes happens in two-way immersion programs. It can also occur from year to year, either in the same school or in a different school, if the student moves. One might assume that this is very confusing for ELLs, but in fact they are often quite resilient and adapt well to different learning experiences and adult expectations.

Resilient Literacy Learners

An example of resiliency is reported on by Han and Ernst-Slavit (1999). They observed Tong-bing, a young boy from China who entered kindergarten in March, and documented how he responded to the writing experiences available in his classroom. When Tong-bing arrived in the United States, he spoke no English, and "appeared as a silent stranger" (146). Tong-bing's first grade classroom had several literacy experiences that were designed to build a "literacy community," including time to read in a well-stocked reading area, literacy centers, a Read-at-Home project, and a writing workshop. Children rotated through four literacy centers each day, and the teacher used a chart to explain where children were to go.

Although there were three other Chinese-speaking children in the class, the teacher placed them in different center groups, so Tong-bing didn't have access to anyone with whom to interact in his native language. When he was in the literacy centers, he was "like a mute instrument, not knowing which part to play" (149). However, he excelled in one of the centers, one that was skills-oriented and included copying words that an adult wrote on a whiteboard—his handwriting was very well developed, which may have been influenced by the fact that his parents asked him to practice his handwriting at home each day.

Another center activity was journal writing, which was very difficult for Tong-bing as he was unclear about its purpose—perhaps if he had been writing in a dialogue journal with an adult, he may have had a much clearer understanding of its purpose, as well as opportunities to learn from the adult as she talked through what she was doing while writing a response to his entries. In addition, Tong-bing did not know how to sound out letters. A further complication was presented by the notion of *inventing* spellings being at odds with the Chinese literacy practices that his parents exposed him to at home, including the expectation that he would spell words correctly. For example, each day at home, he memorized words from a Chinese-English dictionary and copied the words into a notebook, a practice that is consistent with Chinese educational practices, where calligraphy is integral to good writing and children in the primary grades practice Chinese logographs/characters, both in school and at home.

Despite the differences in expectations of him as a writer at school and home, Tong-bing's resilience as a second language learner is reflected in how he adapted to journal writing by writing words he had memorized, such as animal and color words, and using environmental print. For example, when writing about the colors of animals, such as "See my duck. He ce yellow," he found the color words on the crayons in front of him (151). As he became more fluent in English and more familiar with classroom routines, he began to write more and with less concern for whether words were spelled correctly; this seemed to coincide with his growing comfort in the classroom. If he had been paired with another Chinese speaker, it is possible that the literacy center experiences could have been more successful from the beginning of the year.

Collaborative Learning Styles

Often, the collaborative learning experiences that are available to children in North American classrooms, for example where writing workshops are in place, can be very beneficial to nonnative English-speaking children whose home cultures value working together on behalf of the group. Such was the situation that Mary Jane Nations (1990) observed when studying the literacy development of mainstreamed Spanish-speaking third graders. For example, she found that Pablo struggled with literacy events that involved solitary activities (e.g., seatwork assignments and independent reading) and whole class instruction, but thrived in a writing workshop environment, where he was able to work interactively with others. Pablo also had many collaborative literacy experiences at home, such as working on the computer with family members.

The Potential for Dissonance

If students come to English-medium instruction with already well-established expectations of what constitutes teaching and learning, they may encounter educational dissonance when placed in classrooms where typical learning experiences are very different from what they have experienced in the past. This was seen in the discussions of Tong-bing and Pablo.

Despite dissonances, however, L2 students often respond very favorably to unfamiliar pedagogies and learning experiences. For example, in Nepal, the most common teaching practice is recitation, which involves rote learning. A few years ago, I was walking through a town outside Kathmandu, from the bus terminal to a school I was going to visit. Along the way, I passed several schools, and I could hear children reciting their lessons in unison. The school I was visiting had been working with a Volunteer Service Overseas (VSO) volunteer, a teacher from England, who had spent almost two years working closely with teachers, instructing them in interactive English as a foreign language (EFL) teaching practices. In one classroom, I observed a Nepalese English language teacher, who actually spoke very little English, engaging her students very effectively in several variations of group learning, which I was told is not commonly found in Nepalese schools. In the early part of the lesson, she tested the children's knowledge of days of the week in English (via print) through a game in which boys competed against girls. In this activity, the children used both English and Nepali print (which does not use Latin letters).

Later in the class, the children went outside to work in mixed-gender small groups to place the days of the week in order; the teacher had printed the days on cards made from the backs of packaging for foodstuffs. In this activity, the children had access to print in only English, and I observed that the children were engaged in considerable conversation (in Nepali) and negotiation, such as trying to decide where a particular card should go (see Figures 2–16 and 2–17). So, although the most common form of learning and teaching that these Nepalese children had encountered was whole class and did not involve much collaborative work with peers, in this EFL class they experienced a new pedagogy, and responded successfully.

Implications of the Research for Teachers of Writing

Although newcomers may not be as fluent when writing in English as they are in their native languages, and their writing may not be as fluent or as standardized as that of their fluent English-speaking peers, they are clearly able to use writing to express their thoughts and emotions. When working with ELLs whose writing is filled with unconventional uses of English, it is important to keep in mind that writing is a developmental process, whether writing in the native or nonnative language.

It is common to find influences from the L1 in ELLs' writing, and instead of interpreting this phenomenon negatively, we need to view it as something to celebrate, as it indicates that students are active learners—they are using what they already know about print to construct and refine understandings about how written language works in another language. Given that children are able to distinguish between languages, we need not fear that their native language is hindering their development. Instead, knowledge of the native language's writing system is frequently a huge asset in an ELL's writing development.

In many classrooms, teachers aim for a very quiet environment, but particularly with young children and ELLs, opportunities to talk about their writing, both while writing and at the end of a writing occasion, are invaluable. This talk also needs to

Figure 2–16. *Nepal Group Work 1*

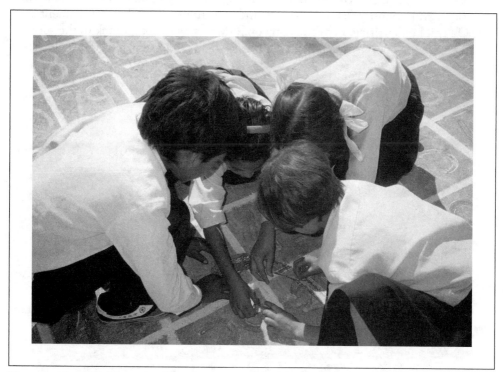

Figure 2–17. *Nepal Group Work 2*

focus on evaluating writing (their own and that of others), and identifying influences on their writing, including the texts they read and hear.

Another dimension to the interplay of oracy and writing relates to whether ELLs should be asked to write in English before their oral language in English is fluent. As the research discussed in this chapter indicates, ELLs need to be introduced to writing in English at the beginning of their English-medium schooling. Also, these early writing experiences should not be worksheets that focus on the component parts of English writing; instead, they should be real opportunities to express thoughts and emotions, and written for an authentic audience, such as peers, teachers, and others. Although ELLs' early texts may be relatively simple at first, in time and with authentic audiences and purposes for writing (and focused instruction tailored to their needs as writers), texts become more sophisticated and the writing becomes more fluent and native-like.

As this body of research illustrates, children are influenced by the literacy experiences they encounter in the world around them and in school. Unless they have grown up in a community that has no access to print (and there are very few communities in the world today for which this is true), ELLs come to school aware that writing is functional. However, children may have had markedly different prior literacy experiences in their native lands and communities, and we need to be aware of and sensitive to this, and explain the purpose and value of unfamiliar teaching strategies and learning experiences to both students and their parents.

Future chapters will explore in greater depth the following writing-related topics as they affect or intersect with ESOL writers: gender, race, and ethnicity; reading/writing connections; reflective writing; and the influence of the environment on ESOL children's writing. Before reading on, however, why not go back to the survey at the beginning of this chapter and see if you would modify any of your responses.

3

Sketches of English Language Learners Becoming Writers

*"I don't know what I'm going to write next.
I've got more things in my mind."*

Alexis, Second Grade Writer

It can be helpful to look more closely at the writing development of individual children in order to see similarities and differences in writing development. In this chapter, I will explore the writing, writing processes, and writing development of five English language learners living in different parts of the country. In each case, the sociocultural context in which these children wrote is a key element.

Cecilia and Diana were in Spanish/English bilingual classrooms and wrote in Spanish, whereas Alexis, Roberto, and Janice were placed in mainstream classes and attended pullout ESOL classes, where they wrote in English. These sketches are based on the research of Irene Serna and Sarah Hudelson (Serna and Hudelson 1993; Hudelson 1989), as well as my own research (Samway 1987b).

Cecilia and Diana: Writing Development of Bilingual Kindergarten and First Graders

Serna and Hudelson (1993) report on the writing development of two Spanish/English bilingual students, Cecilia and Diana, in their kindergarten and first grade classrooms in Arizona. The children were taught reading and writing through a learner-centered, whole-to-part approach, where they were read to often in both Spanish and English, engaged in whole class shared reading using predictable texts in enlarged format (big books), corresponded with the teacher in dialogue journals, and wrote self-selected stories and other genres. These two young writers were similar in that their writing became more skillful and their use of writing strategies increased over the two years. Also, their development wasn't linear in the sense that it didn't go cleanly from one stage to another. Although their writing development shared some characteristics, it was markedly different in many ways and reflected the idio-syncratic nature of writing development.

Cecilia in Kindergarten

Cecilia was born in Mexico and her family had lived in the United States for approx-imately one year when she entered kindergarten. She had been read to a lot at home in Spanish and had some early experiences with writing. At the beginning of the school year, she wrote journal entries in Spanish, which consisted of drawings and strings of random letters that did not represent specific words for her. Then, for a short time in November and December, she seemed to regress, and started to use lines and circles instead of letters. At this time, interestingly, her drawings contained more details and she included more letters to accompany her picture. She also began to incorporate words that she saw around her in the classroom (e.g., book titles). Her writing then progressed through various stages, including labeling pictures using devel-

Mi hermanito me topó

(My little brother hit me.)

Figure 3–1. *Cecilia's Writing: "My little brother hit me"* opmental spelling (which reflected her growing awareness of how Spanish spelling works), and writing sentences about the main action in her pictures (see Figure 3–1). In late February, she began to write stories, which she continued to do for the rest of the school year. Over the months, her spelling in Spanish became more standardized and in April, she began to use lines and periods to indicate spaces between words. By the end of the school year, she began to accurately use accent marks.

Cecilia's writing also developed in other ways. For example, whereas she wasn't always able to read her writing word for word at the beginning of the year (instead, reading for meaning), by April she was able to read her own writing word for word, both her handwritten copy and the final, typed copy. She also wrote in several genres, including an informational science report about turtle habitats, dialogue journal entries in which she asked questions of and answered questions from her teacher, science log entries about the development of a plant, and a group report on turtles for which she took dictation from group members. Both her peers and the adults working in the classroom viewed Cecilia as a competent writer, and her help was valued.

Cecilia in First Grade

In first grade, Cecilia continued to be viewed as a very competent writer, and children sought her out to help with various projects involving literacy. She was an independent writer from the beginning of the year, and wrote her personal narrative and expository texts phonetically while vocalizing each syllable. Her writing became increasingly more fluent, more complex grammatically, and more standardized in segmentation and spelling over the course of the year. Her writing experiences also included writing in a dialogue journal to her teacher and being a very active contributor to a classroom newspaper, including taking dictation from other students. By March, she had begun to revise her writing, which ranged from expanding on invented (developmental) spellings, to adding more information, and editing grammar.

Diana in Kindergarten

Diana was born in Guatemala and, in contrast with Cecilia, she entered kindergarten with little experience with school-related tasks, including reading and writing. At the end of September, she was introduced to journal writing, and her entries consisted of colorful pictures. Sometimes, when asked a question in writing, she would respond with letter forms that resembled the letters *P, T, O, I, E, S,* and *F;* these letter-like forms did not represent sounds or words, however. By October, her journal pages were filled with letter approximations. Interestingly, in November, she seemed to regress and reverted to drawing in her journal, almost always without any writing. Although strings of letters returned in January, she attached meaning to her pictures, rather than to her writing.

In February, Diana's teacher recognized her reluctance to write independently, and invited her to dictate stories to accompany her drawings; an adult wrote down what she said. Diana willingly dictated her stories and added on or changed her stories in response to questions she was asked. Although she couldn't read her dictated story, she could remember what she had dictated and would complete sentences that she had dictated that an adult was reading aloud. Some of Diana's peers had been writing books and in April, Diana began writing a story about an imaginary friend, Erica. It took her more than a month to complete this story, which included topics such as Erica's birthday and how she wanted to live with her father. In this story, Diana wrote some of the message herself. Although she didn't know most of the letters of the alphabet, she had seen other children sounding out words and locating letters to represent the sounds they made, and she began trying to do this. Often, the letter she wrote didn't correspond with the sound, which meant that only Diana and people who had been present when she wrote could read her writing.

In May, Diana wrote two words that she had memorized, *mama*, and *Erica*, on the penultimate page of her story (see Figure 3–2). This page was collaboratively written with an adult and includes the word *chocolate*, which she wrote with assistance, and words that she dictated to an adult (e.g., *Cuando la mama le dió un*). She was able to retell her story from the pictures and from remembering what she had written and dictated. In addition to personal narratives and this story, Diana also wrote entries in a science log that consisted of mostly random letters; she could retell what she had written, illustrating that she was attaching some meaning to the letters she wrote. Also, she provided pictures to accompany a piece of informational writing about the life cycle of a butterfly that she worked on collaboratively with another child.

Diana in First Grade

When Diana entered first grade, her writing once again consisted of pictures and strings of letters that had no letter-sound correspondence. However, she could retell what she had written. This continued until November, when her writing began to incorporate some spellings that could be read by others (e.g., *esabimis* for *estabamos/ were*). Serna and Hudelson point out that, unlike other children, Diana did not verbalize as she wrote, which might have helped her to sound out more words and make more letter-sound correspondences. Because the adults had noticed that Diana was able to write using letter-sound correspondence when given adult assistance, they decided to up the ante and no longer accepted her strings of random letters. Instead, they began to ask her to use environmental print in the classroom to help her write words. For example, she had used a string of random letters (*AebNA*) to write a science journal entry, which she read as "*El pescado se cayó del agua y se murió*/The fish fell out of the water and it died" (311). An adult asked her to look for the word *pez* or *pescado* (fish) in the classroom, and she found *peces* (fish) on a fish food container, which she copied into her journal. She also copied another word (*cayo/*fell), used the letter name *c* for *se* and was assisted in writing *agua/*water by peers. Diana also continued with shared writing, in which she wrote some of the words, while the adult wrote the rest. In March, she elected to write personal narratives about her family,

PAPA
ERICA
18/Mayo/00
MA MA

la mamá

Cuando ∧ le dió un

CHNOCOLATE

ERICA ya no estaba

enojada.

| *Cuando la mamá le dio un chocolate Erica ya no estaba enojada.* | (When her mother gave her a chocolate Erica was not mad anymore.) |

Figure 3–2. *Diana's Writing: "When her mother gave her a chocolate"*

which she wrote with assistance in hearing letter-sound correspondences. Although she was not yet writing independently, she had begun to write alphabetically, albeit with assistance, and could read her texts.

Two Children: Different Learning Styles and Writing Development

Serna and Hudelson point out that these very different children became increasingly more competent as writers through being immersed in meaningful, learner-centered reading and writing experiences. They also point to individual differences, both in terms of experiences prior to entering school, amount of time needed to acquire skills and processes, rates of progress, need for individualized adult support, and response to literacy experiences and instruction. That is, even in a learner-centered environment, children will inevitably respond differently to learning experiences according to their learning styles, prior experiences, and temperaments.

Alexis: A Struggling Second Grade Writer

The writing of second grader, Alexis, over the course of one semester also illustrates the developmental nature of children's writing (and influences on it), including its irregular development. I got to know Alexis when conducting research into the writing processes of nonnative English-speaking children in the elementary grades (Samway 1987b). Alexis turned eight at the end of January. He was a repeating second grader, a native speaker of Spanish who was orally fairly fluent in English, but struggled as a reader and writer. He was a shy child with an ironic smile lurking around his lips most of the time. A veneer of bluff, macho bravado was tempered by his shyness and off-hand sense of humor.

A Cautious, Vulnerable Writer

Alexis' vulnerability could be seen in how he responded on occasion to his peers. One day he was willingly and proudly reading his writing to me when Dilia approached. He stopped reading and challenged her: "Why you here?" Dilia's response, "I'm not looking at you," did little to calm Alexis and when he returned to his story, he was abashed that he had lost his place. Alexis' vulnerability and lack of self-confidence as a writer were evident on another occasion, when I was looking through his folder. After I had read a two-sentence piece, he quickly pointed out that he had written another, longer story.

On other occasions, Alexis would mask his paper with his hand, suggesting that he was a rather self-conscious writer who lacked confidence. The other children wrote in front of their peers with greater ease and had come to view writing as a social, if not collaborative act. It took Alexis much longer to approach that stage. He was proud that I wanted to hear his stories and did not mind when I copied his stories into my notebook using standardized orthography. With his peers, though, this ease was often missing. Sometimes, he spent two or more days arduously composing a piece, as if he weren't sure what he could or should write about.

Alexis' ESOL Class

Alexis attended a pullout ESOL class every day for approximately 40 minutes, which he enjoyed enormously, even if he was sometimes uncertain. In his regular classroom, Alexis had a reading textbook (an older version of Open Court) and rarely wrote, except to complete worksheets. In his ESOL class, the students read trade books, and wrote on topics of their own choosing. His teacher, Ms. Olsen, was beginning to implement a writing workshop, having just read and been impressed by Lucy Calkins' *The Art of Teaching Writing* (1986). She wanted to give her students freedom over what they wrote and because her own writing was often influenced by what she read (e.g., topics and style), she often encouraged her students to borrow from what they read; sometimes, the suggestions she made for writing topics were seemingly interpreted as mandates, despite the fact that she really wanted the children to write on topics about which they were passionate. Students met with Ms. Olsen for group writing conferences, and students could decide whether or not to join these conferences held at the round table designated for book discussions and writing conferences. Although Alexis rarely shared his writing in these groups, he sometimes joined the conference group.

Searching for a Topic

For most of the semester, Alexis was a constrained, self-conscious writer who lacked confidence. On the first day that I observed him, he was writing a response to Langston Hughes' short story, "Thank You, M'am," which the students had read and talked about with great energy and engagement. As a follow-up to this animated conversation, Ms. Olsen asked the students to write a response to the prompt, "Why did Roger steal the purse?" This clearly stumped Alexis, who wrote the question (see Figure 3–3). When I observed him a few days later, it was after the Challenger space shuttle had exploded with the teacher, Christa McAuliffe, on board, and the children and Ms. Olsen had a very intense, emotional discussion about the tragedy. After the conversation, she suggested that the children write about something important. Alexis was clearly struggling to find a topic and did not write that day, even after Ms. Olsen quietly conferred with him about what he'd like to write about. His third piece took him three days to write, and was about his love for Puerto Rico (see Figure 3–4).

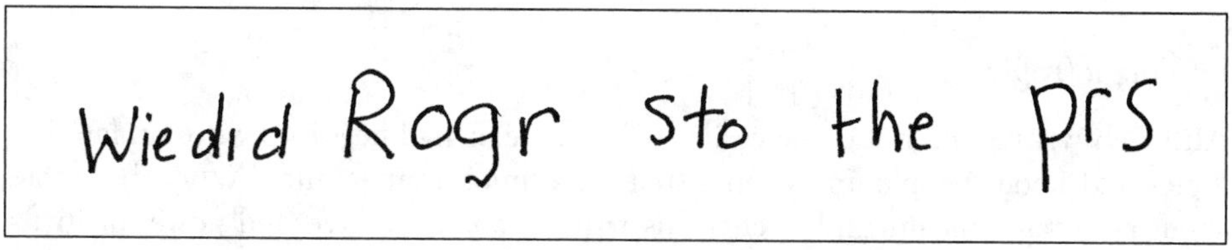

Wie did Rogr sto the prs

Figure 3–3. *Alexis' Writing: Roger*

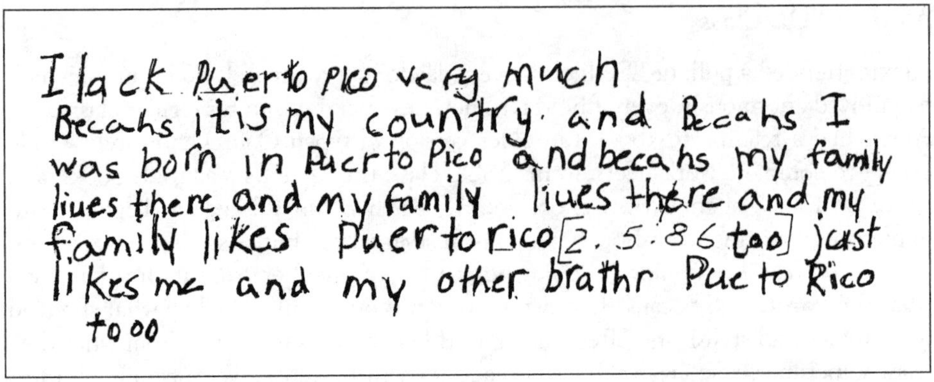
I lack Puerto Pico very much
Becahs it is my country. and Becahs I
was born in Pucrto Pico and becahs my family
liues there and my family liues there and my
family likes Puerto rico [2.5.86 too] just
likes me and my other brathr Pue to Rico
tooo

Figure 3–4. *Alexis' Writing: Puerto Rico*

He appeared to have taken his teacher's advice to write about something that was important to him, but he was clearly unsure where to go with it.

Alexis rarely conferred and did not usually seek out a conference, as other children did. Neither did he come to the conference table very often just to listen and participate as a reader. Some children begged to read, impatiently waiting for a reader to finish, and eager for the praise, recognition, and suggestions that invariably followed the reading of a piece. Other children would be willing readers even when they did not seek out a conference with any great urgency. Not so with Alexis, who tended to stay at his own table, struggling alone. Once, he said to me, "I don't know what I'm going to write next," in a voice tinged with desperation. Ms. Olsen was aware of his struggles, was empathetic, and made sure to touch base with him often, but still he struggled, seemingly influenced by his awareness of what he couldn't or didn't know how to do.

The following week, I observed Alexis making a few small editing changes to a piece he had written in January, and I asked him what he would do next. He opened his writing folder, turned to his friend, José, and asked, "Which one you think I should work on?" He eventually began recopying a piece he had written in January. Later in February, he began to write pieces that were grounded in his family life (see Figures 3–5 and 3–6). Alexis' writing in these two pieces is much more fluid than his earlier writing, where he struggled for a topic and content.

Finding a Topic

Although writing did not come easily to him, Alexis had begun to write on familiar topics and about people and events that were important to him. When he wrote about personally meaningful events, his writing was evocative and powerful in its intensity, as the following piece about how he almost got run over illustrates (see Figure 3–7).

My fathr awas go to wrk rly in
the mrny and cams bak in the
naet at 12:00 and my mother has to
mak my fathr soom food and my
fathr gifs my brathr a Cis are huet.

My father always go to work early in / the morning and comes back in the / night at 12:00 and my mother has to / make my father some food and my / father gives my brother a kiss at night.

Figure 3–5. *Alexis' Writing: Father*

Wén my mather das the dish
she sanme to soueD tha flor
So I dans with the brom than
I hap my mother clen up the
ho hauss so my sistr haop me
clen my rom so I hap hor
clen hor rom war we or finish
We cacoorsals smspagar thn we
go to se crtun.

When my mother does the dishes / she say me to sweep the floor / so I dance with the broom then / I help my mother clean up the / whole house so my sister help me / clean my room. So I help her / clean her room. When we are finish / we cook ourselves some spaghetti. Then we / go to see cartoon.

Figure 3–6. *Alexis' Writing: His Mother*

Almost every piece that Alexis wrote was on a different topic and when Ms. Olsen reminded him that he didn't need to begin a new story each time he wrote, he said, "I don't know what to write." It is possible that he did not see the need to revise his writing, but it is also possible that he didn't know how to revise, except to rewrite, which was a very tedious task for him (as it is for most writers). Three quarters of the

> Yastrday I omos gat ran
> ovr becas I was rag my balk
> in the mire, of the stret so I
> was tra p in the stret becas
> tow cars was won in frat and wan
> was in bak of me and wan
> my mathre same she cat
> so scir and I ran my baik
> in the siwako

Yesterday I almost got ran / over because I was riding my bike / in the
middle of the street so I / was trapped in the street because / two cars was
one in front and one / was in back of me and when / my mother saw me
she got / so scared and I ran my bike / in the sidewalk.

Figure 3–7. *Alexis' Writing: Almost Got Run Over*

way through the research project, Alexis wrote a noticeably longer story when
encouraged to write on a self-selected topic (see Figure 3–8). In this case, he retold
the story of the *Three Little Pigs*, a favorite story that he told me he had at home and
liked to read, particularly the part where the wolf blows down the house. This topic
happened to be the last of eight topics that he had written on a list and placed in his
writing folder earlier in the semester. He wrote this story with noticeably greater ease
and was clearly proud and relieved that he had written something that contained
more words than had been the case in the past. Although the story did not convey
the dynamism that his piece about almost being run over had, it served a very valuable purpose in freeing Alexis from some of the self-imposed constraints that he
appeared to be wrestling with. It is possible that this very cautious writer who lacked
self-confidence benefited from the security of rewriting a well-known and much-
loved story.[1]

---

[1]Emergent and less-confident young writers often retell favorite stories, movies, and TV shows,
which sometimes distresses teachers, who urge their students to write their own stories. As retelling
appears to act as a support to and bridge for emergent writers, and given that published adult authors frequently retell familiar stories, including fairytales, folktales, and legends, perhaps it would be wiser for
teachers to teach about retelling, as in a genre study.

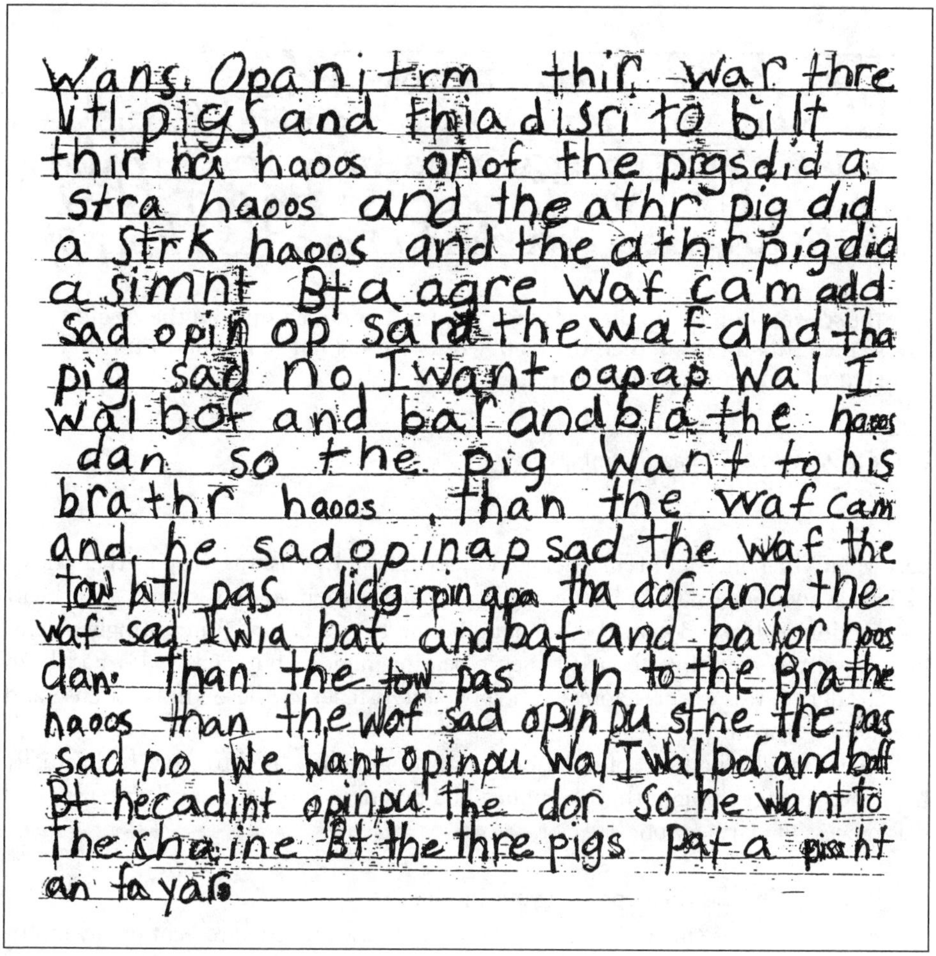
Wans Opanitrm thir war thre
litl pigs and thia disri to bilt
thir haoos onof the pigs did a
stra haoos and the athr pig did
a strk haoos and the athr pig did
a simnt Bt a agre waf cam add
sad opin op sa the waf and tha
pig sad no I want oapap wal I
wal bof and baf and bla the haoos
dan so the pig want to his
brathr haoos . than the waf cam
and he sad opinap sad the waf the
tow litl pas didg rpin apa tha dor and the
waf sad I wia bat and baf and ba lor hoos
dan. than the tow pas ran to the Brathe
haoos than the waf sad opin pu sthe the pas
sad no we want opinpu wal I wal bof and baf
Bt he cadint opinpu the dor so he want to
the chaine Bt the thre pigs pat a pisht
an fa yars

Figure 3–8. *Alexis' Writing: Three Little Pigs*

Taking Risks

Toward the end of the semester, Ms. Olsen asked the students in Alexis' ESOL class to write about the scariest day of their lives. Alexis wrote about a personal event, and was the only child *not* to write about goblins and monsters (see Figure 3–9). Alexis declined to read this piece in a conference on the day that he finished it, but did so two days later, when it generated a great deal of discussion and interest, much as his earlier story about almost getting run over had. His peers asked for more information and commented on what they had enjoyed about the story. Pablo was impressed by the sense of relief and happiness that the story conveyed and said, "I liked when, when it started when he said, 'I was happy that I celebrated.'" Bernardo liked best the

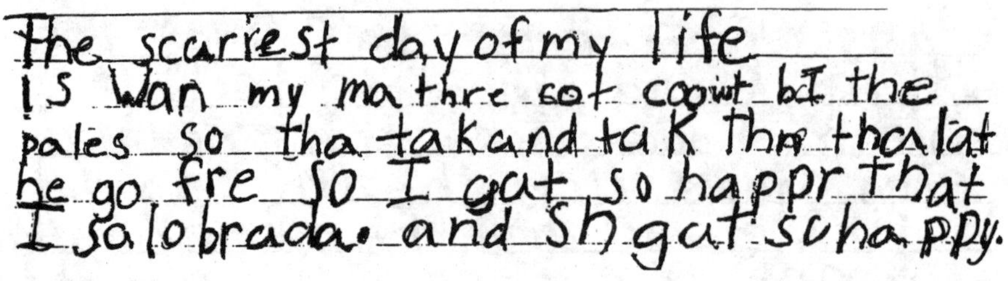

> The scariest day of my life
> is Wan my mathre sot coowt bI the
> pales so tha takand taK Thr thalat
> he go fre so I gat so happr That
> I salobrada. and Sh gat schappy.

The scariest day of my life / is when my mother got caught by the / police so they talk and talk then they let/her go free so I got so happy that / I celebrated. And she got so happy.

Figure 3–9. *Alexis' Writing: Scariest Day*

part where the police let his mother go. Understandably, this was the part that Alexis liked best too. Pepe said, "I likeded the part when, when you got scared, your heart was beating real fast. Boom, boom, boom, boom, boom, boom." Interestingly, Alexis hadn't written anything about his heart beating rapidly, but Pepe, who had been present during this event, expressed how we often react in these kinds of tense and frightening situations.

The class also had lots of questions, some of which related to what had actually happened as they thought that the police had taken his mother away. Pablo initiated this process of clarification:

PABLO: Why did the cops take your mother?

ALEXIS: Because my father. He came to my house and tried to beat up my mother. Then, then, then they call the police. He went to his house. He was gonna break the, uh, car's windows. The police came and took her in the car. Talked with, er, what happened. They told her next time he do that to call the police (inaudible) stay at home. He was gonna take him, but she I (inaudible) so they didn't took him.

Given Alexis' lack of confidence as a writer, one can assume that he had risked a lot in sharing this story. He exposed himself as a writer, as a human being, and as a member of a family. He had trusted his audience and that trust was not betrayed. This brief and stunning account was compelling to his audience. Tales of monsters, bats, witches, and ghosts may scare us, but we instinctively know that they are figments of our imagination. On the other hand, the possibility of one's mother being taken away is a real and deep-seated human fear that most people can identify with. Alexis was clearly proud of the impact that his story had on both his peers and Ms. Olsen.

The Impact of Teachers' Actions

Although written late in the semester, this piece of writing was shorter than most of Alexis' previous pieces, and remained a first-draft-only piece, like almost all his writing (bar a few minor editing changes). This occurred even though his piece had been received well by his peers and teacher, he had received constructive remarks in the group conference, and he said at the end of the conference, "I've got more things in my mind." The absence of further writing may be an indication that Alexis had chosen not to divulge any more personal information. He was, after all, an intensely shy and private person. However, the two stories about his scariest day and almost getting run over were stories that he had chosen to write about. It is possible that he did not revise this piece because he did not know how to revise, despite the fact that other children in his ESOL class did make quite marked changes to their writing and did take into account the remarks of both their peers and Ms. Olsen.

Some of Alexis' struggles may have been grounded in the use of terminology. During the conference, Ms. Olsen referred to this scariest day piece as a *story*. Alexis quickly pointed out, "Not a story! A *real life* story," which led me to wonder if Ms. Olsen's use of the term *story* to mean any piece of writing had contributed to his difficulties in finding a topic. After all, in his ESOL class, they read and discussed novels, which they referred to as *stories*, and they were encouraged to get inspiration for their writing from their reading. Did Alexis assume he had to write about fictional events? Could it be that the ambiguity of language had been holding him back all semester? Is it possible that the use of the term *story* conjured up for him images of imaginary events that he was not able to handle just then as a writer? Calkins (1983, 1986) and Graves (1983) have argued that children should write on topics they know a lot about in order to develop their voices as writers. It is possible that Alexis didn't have sufficient experience writing on familiar topics. It may be that he was hindered by his perception of what he thought was expected of him and what he felt he could do.

This reminds me of how reluctant I used to be to write short stories as this was a genre that I particularly enjoyed reading; however, I didn't think I had the imagination to be able to generate fictional topics. It wasn't until several years after this research project ended that I realized that authors don't necessarily invent everything from scratch. This happened after I had read a story whose plot was almost identical to a newspaper account I had read a couple of years earlier—it was like an epiphany to realize that writers are inspired by, not just their own life experiences, but what they read and hear about, and they/we borrow the cores of ideas liberally. The skill is in the telling of the story, and it was very freeing to realize that I might be able to write short stories, after all. I wonder if Alexis had felt a similar kind of constraint that I had experienced.

By the end of the semester, Alexis' writing continued to exhibit his idiosyncratic spelling and punctuation, but he was clearly getting the hang of the writing workshop and the expectation that he should write about what interested him; when he did, the rest of the class was captivated. Although Alexis had spelling tests in his mainstream classroom, his spelling did not improve noticeably over the course of several months. His ESOL teacher, Ms. Olsen, was very new to writing workshop, and was finding her way into it. For example, she did not spend time exploring possible topics with the students, or place much emphasis on teaching skills and strategies, even in context and as needed, which may have benefited Alexis enormously.

Roberto and Janice: Different Responses to Invitations to Write Authentically

Sarah Hudelson (1989) reports on striking individual differences in the writing development of two ESOL second graders who were both relative newcomers to English, Janice and Roberto. Whereas Janice had recently arrived from Puerto Rico, Roberto was in his second year in an American school, having come from Cuba in first grade—he was placed in a first grade special class for recently arrived Cubans that focused on acclimatizing the children to the language, customs, and routines of American schools. Both children had been assessed by an English proficiency test as beginners, and were in the same second grade classroom and ESOL class. The children did not have any authentic writing opportunities in either of these contexts; instead, they were asked to copy letters, syllables, words, and sentences.

About twice a month, Hudelson worked with the two children outside the classroom, where she invited them to write on self-selected topics. The process involved first drawing (as the children were reluctant to write before drawing), talking about their drawings, and then writing. Despite their shared writing experiences in their mainstream and ESOL classes (and with her), Hudelson reports on clear differences in their development as writers. Whereas at the beginning of the year both children were very much influenced by the quasi writing experiences in their other classes (e.g., copying sentences on worksheets), Janice was able to move beyond this kind of writing more easily than Roberto.

Roberto's Writing

Roberto was reluctant to express himself in written English unless he was copying or reproducing something he had memorized, such as language that he had practiced in a workbook accompanying a reading series, *The Miami Linguistics Readers* (Robinett, Rojas, and Bell 1970). For example, he wrote (left column) and read (right column) the following (88):

Roberto's writing	What Roberto read back
Nat the rat is drikig milk	Nat the rat is drinking milk
e dog is drikig e milk Yes	A dog is drinking milk Yes
e lede is etie cake	A lady is eating cake

74

When asked to write his own messages, Roberto wrote just a few words, asked for a lot of assistance, and his drawings carried most of the meaning of his messages. By the end of the year, his writing consisted of single sentences or lists of words. For example, he drew a picture of superheroes, some of which he labeled (e.g., *superman* and *uok*/Hulk); he also wrote about what the Hulk was doing (*is faring with Superman*/ is fighting with Superman).

Although he continued to draw and talk about another superhero, Spiderman, he refused to write anything else. Roberto was an enthusiastic drawer, which served as a means of self-expression, as well as rehearsal for writing, and throughout the year, his pictures were more detailed and complex than his writing, which is frequently found with emergent writers, both native and nonnative speakers. Roberto did not often ask for help in how to write something in English or even talk about his writing. Hudelson conjectures that Roberto's limited control of English, combined with a lack of confidence in his ability to express himself in English, an unwillingness to take risks, and an absence of opportunities to write authentically in his mainstream and ESOL classes, appeared to influence the degree to which writing in English was difficult for him.

Janice's Writing

Like Roberto, Janice's early writing reflected the kinds of inauthentic writing experiences that she encountered in her regular and ESOL classes (e.g., reproducing workbook sentences and being concerned that her writing was spelled correctly). However, she was more willing than Roberto to write her own messages. For example, in January, she drew a picture of a television showing a person and a house, which she labeled "*un television y una nina y una casa*/a television and a girl and a house." Like Roberto, Janice enjoyed drawing, which served as a rehearsal for writing. In February, she drew a colorful picture of a house with flowers, trees, and grass and then wrote the following (92):

Janice's writing	What Janice read back
My Haus is Red and	My house is red and
dlue and Iigot	blue and I got
faurr and trree	flowers and trees
and I gad aporl	and I got apples
dad is Haus my	that is house my
garnmo (crossed out)	
Grandmotho	grandmother

By the end of the year, Janice was writing extensive texts and was revising her writing. Janice also interacted a great deal with Hudelson about her writing (e.g., asking how to say something in English, and responding to questions about her writing), which often led to questions from Hudelson about the content. For example, in April, she drew a picture of two buildings connected by a road on which there was a vehicle. Next to the road was a person standing next to a bench. She then wrote the following (92):

What Janice wrote	What Janice read back
I gad a hotel	I got a hotel
and ono tree	and one tree
and ono bus	and one bus
and ono Street	and one street
and ono house	and one house
and ono gere	and one girl
ueeirin	waiting
the Bus	the bus
take to the hotel	take to the hotel
dezit him gamer	visit him grandmother

Janice had stopped after writing *and ono gere*/and one girl, but after Hudelson asked her what the girl was doing, she said in Spanish that she was waiting for a bus. Hudelson responded, "Oh, she's waiting for the bus," and Janice wrote the words, "*ueeirin the Bus*/waiting the bus." After a brief conversation in which Janice and Hudelson talked about why the girl was waiting for the bus and how to say it in English, Janice added the final two lines, "*take to the hotel dezit him gamer*/take to the hotel visit him grandmother." In this way, Janice began to revise her writing.

The Intersection of Personality, Learning Styles, and Writing Development

Hudelson suggests that some of the differences between Roberto's and Janice's writing and writing development may have been related to differences in personality and social and cognitive styles. For example, whereas Roberto was a rather quiet, serious student who did not often initiate interactions with peers and appeared reluctant to take risks as a language learner, Janice was more outgoing and very popular with her peers, and was willing to take lots of risks as a language learner, including making mistakes. She also used her native language, Spanish, to seek help with English.

Hudelson reports that she visited the school the following year and met with Janice and Roberto, who were then in third grade. Roberto volunteered to narrate and then write a summary of a wordless picture story. He drew a picture of the sun shining on a dragon that was breathing fire on a tree. He then wrote and read the following (97):

What Roberto wrote	What Roberto read back
Sun is hot. The fire is in	Sun is hot. The fire is in
The tree. The rock is in	the tree. The rock is in

fire too. The lonw is blue.	fire too. The lawn is blue.
The danasorn is down.	The dinosaur is brown.
The danasorn has fire in	The dinosaur has fire in
his mouth.	his mouth.

Although Roberto's classroom writing experiences continued to focus on spelling lists and workbook pages, Hudelson points out that his actions here suggest that he had gained sufficient confidence and knowledge of how English writing works in order to begin taking risks.

What Do These Sketches Tell Us About ELL Writers?

Several themes emerge from these five sketches of young ELL writers, including the following:

- The environment, including teacher expectations, teacher responses to the needs of learners, and the kinds of writing experiences offered to children, exerts a powerful influence on the writing development of ELLs.
- Writing development is highly idiosyncratic, and even when the types of writing experiences offered to children are identical, children differ from each other in how they approach writing, how they develop as writers, and the rate at which they make progress.
- Writing development isn't linear, with children passing through particular stages in a straightforward manner. Instead, it is often very recursive so that, after children appear to have made a lot of growth, they may suddenly seem to regress. This type of developmental pattern is often explained by attempts to incorporate new elements and/or a lack of engagement with the piece at hand.
- Personality, confidence, and differences in learning styles may play a role in ELLs' writing development. The more that children are able to take risks as writers, the greater the chance that they will develop as writers.

Implications of the Research for Teachers of Writing

Although educators often recognize that there are individual developmental patterns and needs among writers, in many schools children are treated alike and held to identical expectations. When children are viewed and treated as distinct learners and writers, it is possible to attend to the individual differences and rates of learning that the research illustrates, while also holding high standards for all ELLs. At times, this means being willing to up the ante, as happened when Diana's teacher asked her to use print in the classroom to help her write words, instead of relying on random letters. Of course, this type of challenge to students needs to be grounded in careful and sensitive observation of the learner.

Factors such as self-confidence and personality, as well as understanding of the writing task and writing expectations, all converge to influence how children respond differently to writing (e.g., whereas Roberto rarely used Hudelson as a linguistic resource, Janice was willing to ask questions, including the English words for words in Spanish). It is important to both recognize these differences in temperament and learning styles, while also teaching students additional strategies that may be helpful to them.

For many young children and newcomers to English, drawing provides a valuable rehearsal for writing, yet many older ELLs are urged to write without the benefit of this experience. ELLs often need time to draw as this is sometimes the most effective way for them to express meaning. We must recognize this, particularly with newcomers to English, while also providing a range of writing options (e.g., writing in the native language and another student or an adult writing the English translation; and positively receiving early efforts in English that may be much less complex than those that native English speakers are writing). We also need to pay attention to what ELLs are attempting to accomplish in their writing, and teach the words, expressions, and grammatical structures that they demonstrate a need for; of course, this means carefully selecting one or two items for instruction, rather than bombarding them with so many teaching points that they are unable to internalize them. That is, we must challenge them realistically.

How one's writing is received and responded to is of major importance as writing is a risky proposition, as the case of Alexis, in particular, illustrates. Although he was not one of the most accomplished writers in his ESOL class, the environment fostered trust among participants and gave him time to understand and absorb the structure of the class. Over time, Alexis began to develop as a writer, risked a lot, and was rewarded for his efforts through the positive way in which his writing was received. In similar ways, we need to establish classroom routines and learning experiences that build ELLs' confidence as writers, including developing a supportive classroom environment and teaching to the needs of learners.

4

Gender, Race, Ethnicity, Social Class, and Writing

"It was as though they had no voice."

HEATHER BLAIR, RESEARCHER

"By focusing on child behaviors compatible with those already valued in schools . . . it presents an anemic . . . view of literacy."

ANN HAAS DYSON, RESEARCHER

Some years ago, I was working in a third/fourth grade class, helping the teacher implement literature study circles (Samway and Whang 1996). The children selected their groups based on which books they wished to read and talk about in small groups, and groups almost always had both girls and boys present, regardless of whether the protagonist in the book was male or female. One day, I met with a group of three boys and three girls to talk about *Tuck Everlasting* (Babbitt 1977, 1989). As I could see from the girls' written notes that they had read the book and they said that they had finished it, I was surprised that they did not contribute to the conversation, despite my invitations to them to do so, their smiles and obvious interest in the conversation, and the community building that had been very successful all year (i.e., this was a class where children had a very close and trusting relationship with each other and the teacher).

At the end of the discussion, I asked the girls to stay with me, commented that I had noticed that they hadn't said anything, and wondered why that was. All three girls giggled a little and shrugged coyly, and María, the eldest of the girls, a very popular girl who had repeated an earlier grade when she was a newcomer to English, said, "I didn't have nothing to say." I asked the other two girls why they hadn't spoken up, and they agreed with María. "Well," I said, "so, what did you think of the book?" Very quickly, we were engaged in an animated conversation that touched on several themes in the book, including the wisdom of everlasting life (they couldn't decide whether Winnie, the main character in the book, should have drunk the magic water in order to remain with the son of the Tuck family with whom she had developed a special relationship). At the end of this conversation, I said that it seemed to me that they had a lot of very interesting things to say about the book, and I thought they owed it to both themselves and to the rest of the group to share their reactions to and insights into the book. I couldn't resist also remarking that, as a woman, it concerned me to see young women deferring to young men in this way, and that I hoped that they would speak up the next day when we would have a follow-up discussion. The next day, the conversation was remarkably different, as all six students contributed to the conversation.

This memory has remained quite vivid for me over the years, possibly because it acts as a reminder to me to be attentive to potentially harmful differentiated roles grounded in gender, as well as ethnicity, race, native language, and social class. I wondered if there had been other, less obvious, occasions when students had either closed down voluntarily or felt closed down by such contextually- and socially-constructed influences. I also began to wonder how this type of differentiated role taking might be reflected in writing and the kinds of writing experiences children have, particularly in schools.

I knew that writing had been the prerogative of upper class, wealthy men for centuries. This is reflected in Karen Cushman's popular historical novel for children set in the thirteenth century, *Catherine, Called Birdy* (1994), where the young heroine is able to read and write, a rare feat for a girl in those days, even for the daughter of a squire (an English country gentleman or a substantial landowner), as was Catherine. This gender- and social-class—mediated access to literacy continues to be true in many cultures where there are low levels of literacy, such as in Nepal, where only 40 percent of the population is literate and most teachers are men.

What of today's children in American schools? And what about writing? For example, do boys select different genres and topics, and confer differently than girls, when given choice over these elements? Do African American, Latino American, Asian American, Native American, and European American children approach writing similarly or differently? How do social-class and socioeconomic status (SES) affect the writing experiences of school children? How do race, ethnicity, social class, gender, and national origin affect teachers' expectations of and responses to young writers? And what of second language learners? After all, ELLs attend schools in 46 percent of all school districts in the United States, and in some states, such as California, Arizona, New York, Texas, and Illinois, large percentages of students are ELLs (National Center for Education Statistics [NCES] 2005). So, a huge question for me is, how do race, ethnicity, gender, social class, and SES intersect with the writing of children in grades K–8, particularly second language learners? Some of the questions I raise here have been addressed by research, whereas others have not.

The Influence of Gender on Children's Writing

Influences of gender on writing are often discussed in the context of teenagers or adults. However, there is research that indicates that gender is also a factor in the writing of younger writers. Guzzetti, Young, Gritsavage, Fyfe, and Hardenbrook (2002) conducted an extensive review of the research literature that focused on the impact of gender on literacy, and they found that gender both shapes and is shaped by writing, such as influencing topic, voice, and genre selection. Their book discusses some important findings, including the following:

- *Writing is a social practice in which gender plays a role.* Perhaps not surprisingly, given what we know about the social nature of writing, the social context of writing has an impact on the writing of girls and boys. Guzzetti and colleagues report on research into one genre, note writing, that revealed that the note is a medium through which membership in gender-specific social groups is marked, and the content of notes is often different for boys and girls. For example, whereas fifth grade boys tended to draw in their notes, and drew about sports, vehicles, and conflicts grounded in TV and comic books, fifth grade girls tended to write in their notes and their writing was about people, relationships, and looks. In all cases, note writing was an important way for students to negotiate, structure, and maintain social groupings and gendered identities.

- *Writing projects/classrooms addressing writing and gender forthrightly can have a positive impact.* Because girls often do not share their writing with or in front of boys for fear of being laughed at, some teachers have established writing circles for just girls so that they can establish their writing identities.

- *Some students dare to be different and cross gender-influenced lines.* Although there are many instances of gendered writing, there is also research that indicates that individual students do cross gender lines in their writing and "write against gender expectations."

Children Transforming Images of Power and Gender

Ann Haas Dyson is a thoughtful and detailed researcher who has investigated sociocultural influences on elementary-aged children's writing. In one study (Dyson 1994), she reports on how second graders in an urban, racially mixed and socioeconomically diverse classroom used superhero characters, Ninja Turtles and X-MEN, to expose and transform their images of power and gender. For example, the children sometimes acted out their stories in Author's Theater, and both girls and boys wanted to have parts in the superhero stories their peers had written. However, even when the more gender-balanced X-MEN cartoons with their powerful male *and* female characters became popular and children started to incorporate them into their writing, girls continued to complain that there were no parts for them or the parts weren't active. Some of the girls worked hard to be included, even writing their own X-MEN stories, and by the end of the semester, the children had reached an equilibrium whereby there was more balance in distribution of roles and the types of actions characters took. Dyson describes how Sammy, who was very popular in his class and wrote very well-received male-hero action stories about X-MEN, ultimately included girls by claiming that X-women were as strong as X-MEN. Dyson (1997) also reports on a third grader, Tina, an African American student, who was the only girl to write about superheroes, and who continually criticized the boys for making their female characters victims.

Gendered Character Portrayals in Children's Writing

Several studies have investigated the interplay between gender and the portrayal of male and female characters in young children's writing. For example, in a study investigating the writing of Latina/Latino American, Asian American and European American girls and boys in the primary grades, MacGillivray and Martinez (1998) found gender-specific roles in the children's free choice story writing. Typically, male characters were revealed as heroes, there were few female heroes, and female characters that were included were portrayed as either in need or as victims.

In a comparative study involving children in two very different countries and cultures, Harvey, Ollila, Baxter, and Guo (1997) investigated the influence of gender on the writing of Chinese and Canadian children in grades one, four, and seven. Children were asked to imagine that they were animals and write about the adventures of these animals. Colleagues of the researchers rated animals on three attributes that are typically viewed as culturally driven and reflective of sex-role stereotyping (i.e., weak versus strong, dangerous versus safe, and wild versus domestic). They found that girls in both China and Canada were more inclined to select animals that are safe, tame or weak (e.g., rabbits, cats, birds), whereas boys in the two contexts were more likely to select animals that are dangerous, wild, or strong (e.g., pandas, dragons, and cougars).

Gendered Meanings in Children's Writing

Barbara Kamler (1993) engaged in case study research focusing on two children, Zoe and Peter. She observed them for more than two years, from their first days in kindergarten to midway through second grade. In the kindergarten classes, the children wrote on self-selected topics, and their teachers conferred with them on a daily basis about the content of their pieces; the teachers also provided instruction about spelling and punctuation as needed and in the context of the children's writing. In contrast, the first and second grade teachers placed more emphasis on skills instruction, both in the amount of time that was devoted to decontextualized spelling and handwriting instruction, and in how they responded to the children's writing. As in kindergarten, the children wrote on self-selected topics, but in contrast with the kindergarten teachers, the first/second grade teachers conferred with the children only when they were ready to publish pieces, when the teachers would correct spelling and punctuation.

Kamler found that, although both children tended to write personal narratives, they produced "gendered meanings in their texts" (96), regardless of the type of writing classroom they were in (i.e., whether the teacher focused on content or mechanics). For example, Peter represented himself in his narratives as an active male, whereas Zoe constructed herself in a less active female role. One way in which this was revealed was in verb choice, such as when the two children wrote about receiving gifts for birthdays and Christmas. For example, Peter focused on himself, such as when he wrote, "I got a football from mum and dad," whereas Zoe placed the emphasis on others, such as when she wrote, "Grandma gave me some pretty ribbons" (100). Kamler argues that allowing free choice in writing topics tacitly encourages children to engage in culturally determined gender stereotypes. However, she does not suggest that children should not be given choice over their topics; instead, she urges teachers to monitor their reading of children's texts for gendered constructions, and engage children in critical conversations about gendered meanings that are taken for granted.

Gender and Children's Writing Topics

Although research indicates that there are differences in the content of topics that boys and girls select, there is variation in the findings. For example, Graves (1975) found that seven-year-old boys tended to write more often about "extended territories" than girls (i.e., settings far removed from anything familiar, and about violence, war, and aggression). In contrast, the girls tended to write about "primary territories" (i.e., topics that were familiar and closer to home, such as friends, family, and school). He also found that boys wrote more often than girls about events in the community and sports away from school ("secondary territory"). In contrast with Graves' findings, when Barbieri (1987) investigated the topic and genre choices of twelve-year-old girls and boys, she found that the twelve-year-old boys in her class didn't follow the trend identified by Graves. Instead, she found that 59 percent of the boys' writing was in "primary territory," 11 percent was in "secondary territory," and 29 percent was in "extended territory."

Gender and the Role of Play in Children's Writing

Daiute (1990) investigated a different element, the role of play in writing, and also found gendered findings. In this study, fourth and fifth graders wrote collaboratively on the computer, and Daiute found that play was a useful writing strategy for these students as they used it in a variety of contexts (e.g., with language, concepts, reality, and the writing instrument), and did so in approximately one-third of all utterances. She found that boys relied on play more often than girls when writing.

Gendered Audiences

Several researchers have reported on the way in which gender plays a role in audience, that is, for whom children write and with whom they are willing to share their writing. For example, Heather Blair (1998) found that eighth grade girls in an urban school district wrote a lot, wrote for other girls, and did not want to share their writing with boys (i.e., they were writing for a gendered audience), as they had found the boys to be an unsupportive audience in the past and "had had their voices silenced" (17).

The Influence of Gender on How Teachers Regard Children's Writing

Most teachers would probably assert that they are unbiased in how they view children's writing. However, there is evidence that teachers favor writing that is associated with writing that girls produce. For example, Peterson (1998) reports on the influence of gender in how fifty-five sixth-grade teachers evaluated students' writing submitted to a provincial Canadian writing competition. After rating narrative pieces written by five sixth graders, teachers were asked to determine the gender of the writer. Peterson found that teachers viewed writing associated with girls as manifesting more awareness of the needs of readers, and of being better developed and more sophisticated (e.g., writing well-developed characters, using more precise language, and editing more carefully). In contrast, teachers viewed boys' writing as being less well developed and relying too much on superficial superheroes and violence. When teachers (both male and female) thought a writer was a girl, they tended to rate it higher than if they thought the writer was a boy. That is, they privileged girls' writing or writing containing features of writing associated with girls' writing. This, of course, has implications for the veracity and impact of the results of large-scale, high-stakes testing, and also calls into question the heavy emphasis placed on comparative assessments.

The Influence of Ethnicity and Race on Writing

Just as gender appears to have an impact on children's writing, so do race and ethnicity. For example, in a study of eighth grade girls from different cultural backgrounds, Blair (1998) found that Native Canadian girls appeared not to value their writing and knowledge as highly as girls from other cultures. For example, in contrast with European Canadian girls, they tended to put fewer pieces in their writing folders, were more hesitant about sharing their writing with others, and were very quiet in class. Blair comments, "It was as though they had no voice" (16). Blair also found that the Native Canadian students bore major responsibility for negotiating the cross-cultural maze that often exists in schools and society. For example, there were no collections in the classroom of literature written by minority women, and there was no place for native languages in the school, inevitably reinforcing the notion that there was no place for native languages and cultures. Perhaps not unsurprisingly given this reality, the Native Canadian girls did not include their home cultures and worlds in their writing or use their writing to explore or explain their native cultures to and experiences with others, unlike other students. A similar reality existed for a Spanish-speaking girl from El Salvador.

Dissonances Between Home-Based and School-Based Literacy Practices

Since the late 1960s, many students have come to North American schools as refugees from war-torn Southeast Asian countries, such as Vietnam, Laos, and Cambodia. Although the first wave of refugees was made up primarily of highly educated families, later waves included many children from less privileged homes whose educations had been interrupted or limited. Ellen Skilton-Sylvester (2002) reports on the writing of a Cambodian American girl, Nan, who took part in a three-year participant-observation study that documented the literacy experiences and identities of seven Cambodian girls in Philadelphia. As part of this study, Skilton-Sylvester explored the home-based and school-based writing of the young women. Nan, a third, fourth, and fifth grader during the course of the study, was an active, prolific writer outside school, where her writing served several purposes and fell into many genres. For example, she wrote plays, poetry, multipage stories with pictures, letters, reports, and captions for pictures. She was a strong storyteller, artist, and orator, which were valued resources in her out-of-school environment. She expected to perform her writing, as "To her, writing was meant to be read orally for an audience" (67). At such times, she often strayed from the written texts and performed a more complex story than the one she had written. Skilton-Sylvester comments that this is similar to the Cambodian tradition of performance being an integral part of reading.

A focus in Nan's ESOL class was on oral language development, with reading and writing taking a secondary role. The attention paid to oral language development appeared to enhance her ability to integrate her learning of English with culturally familiar ways of using literacy, thereby allowing her to succeed. For example, when Nan read her journal aloud in her ESOL class, she was able to integrate a familiar practice (speaking) with a new practice (writing), which led to her being more engaged in her ESOL classes than in her mainstream classes. When writing, Nan also relied heavily on her artistic talents, and her drawings were more dominant than the words she wrote. According to Skilton-Sylvester, this emphasis on visual images is consistent with how Cambodians in the United States continue to connect with their native culture and homeland (e.g., one is often more likely to encounter videos, photographs of family members, and posters of Cambodia in Cambodian homes than print sources, such as books).

In contrast with the writing-related experiences that Nan encountered in her ESOL class, the academic writing that she encountered in her mainstream classroom did not allow Nan to draw upon or integrate her communicative strengths, her artistic skills, or her performance expertise to communicate her messages. Instead, she was required to rely exclusively on the written word and its form, and was unable to draw upon other language and communicative modalities to convey meaning. Skilton-Sylvester also points out that Nan experienced quite different roles at home and in school. For example, she had status at home as she was the most fluent speaker and writer of English, whereas at school, she had low writing status. This lack of status at school was apparent in circumstances such as when she had to write a report on the African American explorer, Matthew Henson, and struggled to write the following first draft based on some incomplete pages from an encyclopedia, which she had great difficulty understanding (73):

> Mattrew was born in 1837. he was an exporter he was black he was lucky because ~~it help him~~ every people thought he was their family. he explorer greenland North pol. Mattrew helped Aruther parory He was ~~Story~~ that people would Story ~~and~~ gave up and he dies in 1855.

After talking with Nan for a while about the piece, Skilton-Sylvester helped her to revise it, and the final version follows (73):

> Matthew was born in 1837. He was an explorer. Matthew helped Admiral Peary. Admiral Peary was a very famous explorer who discovered the North Pole. Matthew was black. He was lucky because the Eskimo people thought he was their family. He explored Greenland and the North Pole. He was strong. Other people would give up, but he didn't. He died in 1855.

Skilton-Sylvester points out that, in this type of academic writing situation, Nan had to rely exclusively on written language, and was not able to draw upon her strengths, such as performance and pictures, to convey her message, as she was able to in out-of-school writing contexts. Also, her writing in school often involved copying and was exclusively for the teacher (and to complete assignments), whereas her out-of-school writing was for many audiences and functions. For example, she maintained friendships through letters (which the girls in this study particularly liked as it was difficult for their parents to read English), and she wrote pieces that she gave as gifts, such as to Skilton-Sylvester at the end of tutoring sessions. The writing resources that Nan had access to were, unfortunately, not valued or visible in the school context, and Skilton-Sylvester concludes that schools are remiss in not providing students with opportunities to tap into their lived experiences and social identities.

Culturally Grounded Ways of Learning: The Case of Pedro

It is common for children from nonmainstream backgrounds to encounter dissonance in the types of literacy experiences they have at home and school, just as Nan did.

For example, Mary Jane Nations (1990) conducted an ethnography focused on the literacy development of Spanish-speaking children. Third grader, Pedro, was not a fluent speaker of English and he was not succeeding in school, in part because of the dissonance between the form of the mandated curriculum and his way of learning, what Nations refers to as "voice." At home, Pedro lived with seven adults and five children and almost all tasks, including literacy, were accomplished with others and accompanied by talk. For example, while making a shopping list, the women in his home talked with him about what they needed; he copied stories from a school library book after his uncle had read to him; he collaboratively played video games with family members; and, after learning about electricity in school, his aunt helped him to construct a battery-powered electric circuit that he said could "help your nerves" (6). In addition, Nations found that Pedro's literacy events at home were always purposeful and contextualized, and family members regarded him as competent.

In contrast with his literacy success at home, Pedro struggled with school literacy tasks, which were often decontextualized skills exercises that he was expected to complete alone at his desk, without talk, and without opportunities to collaborate. (The rigid, whole class, textbook-oriented curriculum was not compatible with the teacher's preferred style of teaching, but it was endorsed by the mandated curriculum.) Pedro delayed beginning assignments (e.g., making trips to the distant restroom), rarely turned in homework, infrequently engaged in center activities or independent reading, and appeared disengaged during whole class instruction.

Despite these disengaged behaviors, Pedro was not entirely disconnected from school literacy learning and frequently used his *cultural voice* to mediate events so that he could participate and succeed, albeit not in the ways that were necessarily viewed as successful by the dominant school culture. For example, although he appeared disengaged during whole class instruction, whenever he had an opportunity, Pedro would willingly join Nations and a handful of other students at a small table, where they worked together. At other times, he subtly altered the seating arrangement in the class, for example, saying, "It's too hot here," so that he was able to sit near another student and ask for clarification. Once, when asked to write a paragraph on "My Favorite Place," he clearly struggled with the unimodal task (just write) and his two-sentence paragraph included three repetitions of the designated title (see Figure 4–1). However, he sought out Nation's help and asked if he could draw. After completing his drawing, they talked about the picture, and then he labeled items and began to expand them into sentences (see Figure 4–2); he was not able to further develop it into an entirely written form due to time constraints. Nations comments that the labeled picture is like a visual paragraph. The creation of this piece underscores two conditions that supported Pedro's learning, and which are often missing from school literacy events, particularly in the upper grades: (1) opportunities to integrate oral and visual languages, and (2) authentic audiences and opportunities to collaborate.

Pedro's experiences as a writer changed markedly after criterion-referenced test scores were published in the spring and the classroom teacher had evidence that the skills she had taught had not been internalized by students such as Pedro. She

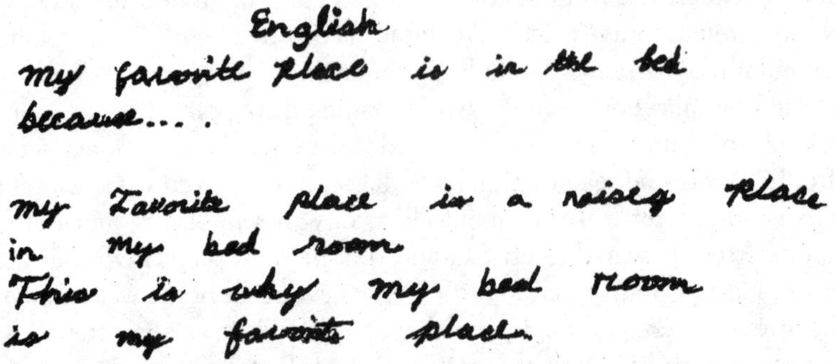

English

my favorite place is in the bed
because... .

my favorite place is a noisey place
in my bed room
This is why my bed room
is my favorite place.

Paragraph about Pedro's favorite place written without the
benefit of any drawing.

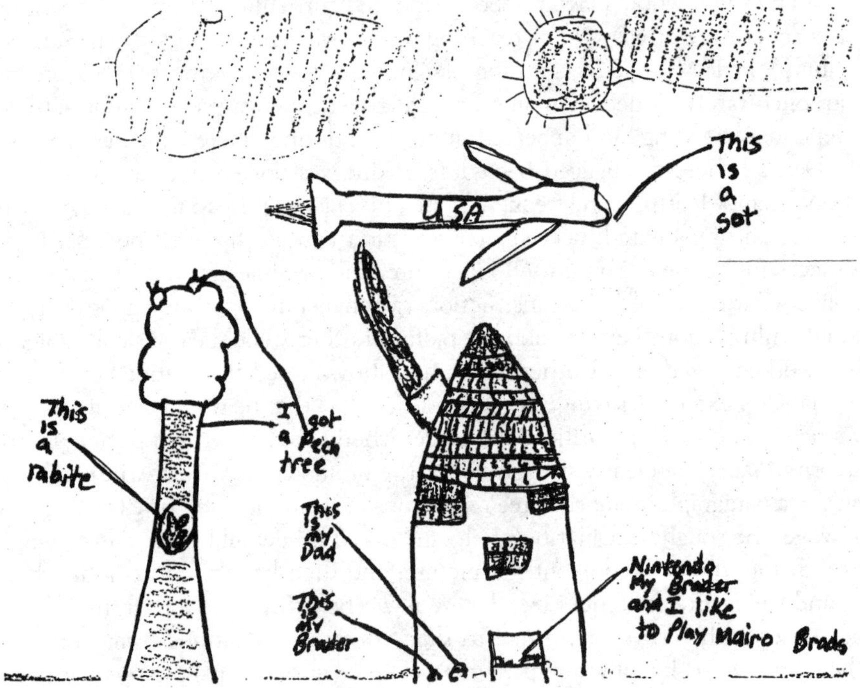

This
is
a
set

This
is
a
rabite

I got
a Pech
tree

This
is
my
Dad

This
is
my
Bruter

Nintendo
My Bruter
and I like
to Play Mairo Brads

USA

Sample of Pedro's writing when it accompanied drawings.

Figure 4–1. *Pedro's Writing: My Favorite Place and Labeled Drawing* believed that the mandated curriculum had failed the children, so she introduced a daily writing workshop, which she hoped would meet the needs of students such as Pedro by being more compatible with their learning styles and needs (as well as her own teaching style). This innovation on the part of the classroom teacher had an immediate and highly positive effect on Pedro. Whereas he had once resisted the writing exercises and assigned writing, which he thought "boring because they won't let you use your own words" (18), now he embraced and looked forward to writing. Instead of writing being an arduous task, he willingly wrote stories, which classmates and adults in the class read and appreciated. Another change was in Pedro's willingness to review his writing. With the writing tasks generated by the mandated curriculum, he would not revisit and revise his writing; now, after conferences, he revised his writing willingly, and his writing benefited from it. He also began to orally compose with peers, and then write.

A dramatic change in Pedro's in-school behavior also occurred, which Nations attributes to changes in the writing environment, activities, and expectations. Whereas he had once resisted speaking up in school, now he was assertive about sharing his writing with others. Whereas he once resisted school literacy tasks, now he was an enthusiastic and dedicated writer. Whereas he once rarely handed in homework, now he did so regularly. Whereas he once did not participate in science and social studies and did not read books independently, now he voluntarily participated in other curriculum areas and read library books. That is, he thrived in a collaborative learning environment in which there were authentic reasons to write. Nations comments that the writing workshop came too late for Pedro as he failed the criterion referenced test and had the option of either repeating third grade or being placed in special education; because he had already repeated first grade, his parents chose the special education placement.

This situation is still all too common with children who are acquiring English—they are assessed in a language in which they are not fluent and then they suffer the long-term consequences of invalid results. Many children whose home languages, cultures, and learning styles are different from those that schools endorse experience the same discontinuity that Pedro experienced until his classroom teacher introduced a writing workshop. Too often, few efforts are made to mediate the cultural differences, and children are seen as problems, their home lives as disadvantaged, and their parents neglectful (even though those making such judgments rarely know the families or have visited families in their homes and so have virtually no basis on which to make such judgments).

Writing as an Expression of Culture

As Franklin and Thompson (1994) point out, what one writes reflects one's culture and traditions, as well as one's expressive intentions. Over the course of a year, they collected the writing of seven Native American children in first grade who attended a tribal school on a Sioux Indian reservation. The children were bilingual

Dakota/English speakers. The children's classroom teacher (Thompson) is an enrolled member of the Turtle Mountain Band of Chippewa. She provided authentic reasons to read and write, opportunities for class members to collaborate with each other and adults, and units of study that were multicultural in nature, emphasized Native American issues and content, and built on children's interests. Franklin assisted in the class, and coordinated the data collection process throughout the year. When analyzing the data, Franklin and Thompson included several key people, including the children's parents or grandparents and a Dakota language and culture teacher, in order to more fully interpret the data.

The Case of Monica

One of the children that the study focused on was Monica, a first grader who was bilingual in Dakota and English. Over the course of the year, she generated 704 pieces that she wrote and/or illustrated, and these included personal narratives, fictional narratives, labels, responses to books, theme projects, and photograph annotations. Seventy-eight percent of these pieces were classified as self-selected; that is, Monica wrote them during free time or writing workshop. The remaining 22 percent were completed in response to the teacher's directions (e.g., write on a particular genre or topic, or work on a designated art project).

Data analysis revealed that the most dominant and richest themes in Monica's writing were about relationships (e.g., expressing feelings for family members and friends in order to strengthen bonds), cultural commitment, and romance. Relationships were explored primarily through three genres:

- Personal narrative (e.g., "Me and Julie went to the pow-wow and we got money from dancing," 494)[1]
- Fictional narratives (e.g., "Anna and Me and Julie, Dawn and Laura, we were going to the store and we bought some pop because we were thirsty. We went back to my treehouse," 495)
- Letters and cards

In the *personal narratives*, Monica related activities in which she was rarely alone and all participants were equal; often, these activities focused on physical activity, such as playing on playground equipment, being chased by boys, or making jewelry. Her illustrations reveal happy people. In fact, on only one occasion did she write a story about conflicts with friends. In her *fictional narratives*, Monica extended her geographic horizons and wrote about cooperative activities on the reservation (e.g., picking berries and going to the store) and elsewhere (e.g., going to Disney World). In her fictional narratives, she added drama and intensity to her writing (e.g., writing "Oh, no, oh, no!" to indicate concern when a character got lost). In her *letters and cards*,

---

[1]Franklin and Thompson (1994) edited the spelling and punctuation.

Monica expressed her feelings for family members and friends and, unlike other children, she didn't combine the functions of narratives with those of notes and cards.

About three-quarters of Monica's cards and letters were self-selected. A sample, a get-well card to a peer (Franklin and Thomas 1994, 497), follows:

> I miss you,
> too, Anna,
> very much,
> so much.
> And I love
> the stuff
> that
> you
> wear
> all the time.

Monica particularly enjoyed the note/letter genre, and she sent notes and cards on official holidays, such as Christmas, as well as birthday, get-well, welcome-back, and friendship cards and notes. In her writing about relationships, Monica learned to use the conventions of the genre, such as salutations and celebratory expressions (e.g., "Here's to you!" in letters, and the inclusion of dramatic moments in fictional narratives).

In the case of Monica, cultural commitment refers to her interest in the cultural and language practices that define a person as a member of the Dakota Oyate, which she explored through three genres/activities:

- Responding to specific books—these oral, visual and written responses were teacher planned. Children responded to nineteen books over the course of the school year, eleven of which were multicultural, and nine of which were on Native American themes.
- Writing an informational book about Native Americans—this was a teacher-planned activity.
- Writing in a notebook during writing workshop—this was self-selected writing.

When writing and drawing responses to books with Native American themes, Monica demonstrated understanding of the texts, but also added aspects of her Dakota experience. For example, she added a village of Dakota tepees to a mural of a Hidatsa village, which the class was working on in response to *The Mouse Raid* (Ward, Burr, and Ahler 1989). On other occasions, Monica used her writing workshop notebook to explore the spiritual life of the Dakota Oyate and in relating what she was learning to her Dakota heritage. For example, she wrote a poem that included references to Dakota content, such as eagles, tepees, and buffaloes.

The third theme that dominated Monica's writing was romance (e.g., love, courtship, marriage, princesses, castles). All of these pieces were self-selected and were written in her writing workshop notebook. These included illustrated short narratives, labeled drawings, and drawings without any writing; the illustrations generally took precedence over the texts. Written entries included, "Laura had a wedding. Me and Julie was a flower girl" and "Me and Laura were going to a castle. We were dressed for the prince" (502). In these works, her friends continued to be the main characters. The romance theme appeared to be influenced by popular culture (e.g., *Cinderella*) and popular movies, such as *The Little Mermaid*.

Individual Preferences

Franklin and Thompson point out that Monica's preference for particular themes and genres was a very individualized reality as other children in the class appropriated other themes and genres. For example, some children preferred the adventure theme and a subtheme of relationships, conflicts with friends, both of which provided them with opportunities to explore themes of conflict, struggle, and overcoming obstacles. Franklin and Thompson argue that it is important for teachers to provide multiple materials (e.g., note-writing materials), genres, and opportunities to respond to books, especially those that connect with the children's home culture, in order to provide students with writing experiences that tap into their strengths and interests. They also point to the importance of teaching children about multiple genres in meaningful ways in order to extend their repertoires.

The Dangers of Literacy Being Viewed Aculturally

Anne Haas Dyson has written extensively about her research into the writing processes and writing development of young writers in urban contexts, and she has expressed concern that culturally-grounded differences in the writing of young children are neither recognized nor valued. She refers to *stories* as the medium through which we judge children's language and literacy use and development, and points out how only some stories seem to be respected and valued (1990). For example, she remarks on how, if children don't come to school having experienced literacy practices that are valued by schools, such as having been read to widely, they (and their families) are often deemed lacking. She also laments the overreliance by educators and educational researchers on school-like literacy behaviors and how this leads to a very narrow view of what literacy is. She comments, "by focusing on child behaviors compatible with those already valued in schools (a particular storytelling style, a use of letter/sound correspondences), it presents an anemic—a too linear, too static, too narrow—view of literacy . . ." (197).

Dyson (1991) also raises the issue of whether we are guilty in writing/literacy circles of viewing literacy in an "acultural" way, that is, without any recognition of sociocultural influences. She points out that children come to school familiar with multiple genres (e.g., jokes, songs, stories) that are influenced by the folk traditions of their communities, popular culture that surrounds them, and written literature they have encountered at home, in the community, and/or at school. However, many of these familiar genres are not high status genres in schools (e.g., jokes and songs).

The Case of Jameel

Children live in many worlds and their language and literacy knowledge and use are often valued differently according to the values of these different worlds (and there are power differences, of course). To illustrate this point, Dyson refers to Jameel, an African American student in a K–3 urban classroom, who had lost his cat and, after an accident outside the school left a pedestrian injured, wondered if the same fate had befallen his cat. Later that day, he wrote a story that incorporated the familiar Dr. Seuss characters, Cat and Hat (28):

> Sat on cat. Sat on hat.
> Hat sat on CAT
> CAT GoN. 911 for CAT
> (*Punctuation added by Dyson to indicate Jameel's pauses while he read the story.*)

When Jameel read this story to his peers, one child, Edward, indicated considerable appreciation for it and commented that it sounded like a poem, but another child, Mollie, said that she didn't understand it. There ensued a bit of an argument as to whether it made sense, with Edward backing up Jameel and Mollie sticking to her position that it didn't make sense. Jameel's teacher asked the two children to try to sort out the problem on their own, so they moved over to a side table. Mollie continued to insist that it didn't make sense and suggested he write a story about his own cat, which frustrated Jameel. He said, "This IS about my cat. I ain't writing about no cat. I'm writing about MY cat cause I don't know if he died" (29). After Mollie left, Jameel said, "Why she tell me—I did it the way I wanted it. And now they want me to do they want it. But it's my decision" (29).

Dyson argues that Jameel's way with story was not recognized or respected by Mollie for the song-like piece he had written. She appeared to expect the labels of pictures and simple descriptive statements often found in young children's writing (and celebrated in many primary classrooms). Dyson argues that Jameel had another way of telling a story, another genre in mind. She writes, "Jameel, however, had another kind of story, another kind of sense in mind, one built with performance possibilities—the music of language" (29). Dyson also comments on how many picture book authors often use playful language that acts as "rhythmic accompaniments to, or complements of, pictures; their texts are neither explicit nor information-packed" (29). She points out how Jameel viewed an audience as made up of people who participate in, but do not control or offer explicit advice (i.e., peers could not be both audience and helper).

Social Class, Socioeconomic Status, and Writing

Social class is not an entity that people tend to focus on in the United States, where there is more emphasis on ethnicity and race, even though social class and race/ethnicity are often closely related. When reviewing the literature on the interplay of social class and writing, it is useful to begin with a broad focus, the intersection of social class and access to print.

SES and Access to Print

Imagine if the government were to suddenly decree that there would be no more libraries and bookstores, or that no magazines, newspapers, or books would be available for purchase. How would we respond? Concerned, perhaps? Possibly enraged? And why? Maybe because we know how important books, libraries, and bookstores are to us, our family members, and our friends, and we know that they have a profound impact on the literacy development and literacy habits of children. However, many children living in low-income neighborhoods experience a reality that resembles in some ways this imaginary scenario. That is, they frequently have very little access to books, libraries, and stores where books are sold, and their access is markedly more limited than that experienced by children in higher-income neighborhoods. Also, children from low-income classrooms often have much less access to books and magazines than those in high-income classrooms (e.g., Duke 2000).

Inequities in Children's Access to Print

Inequities in access to print is revealed in a very compelling study of low- and middle-income neighborhoods in Philadelphia (Neumann and Celano 2001). The researchers report that, in contrast with low-income neighborhoods, middle-income neighborhoods have:

- Greater availability and better quality of book collections in local preschools;
- Better quality of books, more days open, and greater computer availability in local school libraries; and
- Larger collections, more books per child, and more evening opening hours in public libraries.

It is telling that one of the low-income neighborhoods was home to many nonnative English-speaking immigrants, and the other was predominantly African American.

Access to Different School-Related Print Experiences

Although research indicates that access to print may be affected by income and socioeconomic status or social class, it would be a mistake to assume that this factor alone influences children's success with literacy. For example, Harste, Woodward, and Burke (1983) argue that socioeconomic status isn't what influences knowledge about print; instead, they point to how the experiences that children have with written language affect their knowledge about print. That is, the type of print experiences that children have in school and the availability of meaningful and comprehensible print in their schools and communities have a profound impact on children's literacy development and success as readers and writers.

Social Class Bias in Literacy Curricula and Learning Experiences

When discussing literacy success, it is important to consider what constitutes success and who determines successful behaviors, and to recognize that these are elements that are inherently biased (and that bias is influenced by multiple factors, including social class). Social class bias in schools is evident in literacy assessment and curricula. For example, McCarthey (1997) conducted research in a racially and socioeconomically mixed urban school and found that the school literacy curriculum was more congruent with middle-class, European American children's home experiences than it was for children from Latino and African American working-class backgrounds. Although the working-class families valued literacy for their children and used literacy in their home lives (e.g., reading newspaper advertisements to find jobs, reading invitations to social events, and memorizing passages from the bible), these activities were less closely aligned with school literacy events, and were often inadvertently ignored or undervalued in schools, in part due to teachers' ignorance of the lives and cultures of their working-class students.

McCarthey found that middle-class literacy values were routinely reinforced in the school and, although the teachers intended for all the children to draw on their home experiences in school-based learning, in fact there were marked social-class and ethnicity differences in the degree to which these connections occurred. For example, middle-class children tended to have more of a voice in whole class discussions and their contributions were often given special attention, such as when teachers commented favorably on colorful language or interesting words in students' journals and then displayed the terms publicly. When the teachers tried to include the more reticent children, including children from nonmiddle-class backgrounds, in these types of activities by explicitly asking them or requiring them to contribute, it often backfired as the students did not necessarily feel comfortable sharing in these contexts.

The students' classes incorporated literacy practices often considered to be inclusive and supportive of all learners, such as reading trade books rather than textbooks, teacher conducted read-alouds, writing workshop, cross-curriculum integrated projects, and literature response journals. However, students had few opportunities to share their work and experiences with peers, such as in small group book discussions and writing conferences. Also, the trade books that the students had access to were not reflective of diverse experiences. In addition, instead of whole class discussions being open-ended and fostering text-to-self and text-to-world connections, they were fairly traditional teacher-centered recitations in which the teacher initiates (often asking a known-answer question), students respond, and the teacher evaluates. This type of interaction is thought to reflect mainstream, middle-class discourse styles (e.g., Heath 1983; Pease-Alvarez and Vasquez 1994; Vasquez, Pease-Alvarez, and Shannon 1994).

In addition to describing general findings, McCarthey provides more detailed analyses through five case study students. The two case study children whose home literacy practices most closely resembled those of the school were Mandy and Andy, who came from middle-class homes; they were regularly read to at home, they had access to fiction and nonfiction books in the home, and/or they had access to technology. A third case study child was Matthew, a Latino child from a working-class background who was a passionate drawer, which was valued in school and provided one of the few points of intersection between his home culture and the school culture. The remaining two case study children's home and school experiences were the most disconnected. One was an African American girl, Sheila, who was very quiet in school and whose home life was marked by frequent moves. The other child, Eduardo, was a Spanish-dominant Latino boy whose mother had high academic aspirations for him; however, she had limited resources to help him at school because of her low-paying job, and diminished cultural capital due to her lack of literacy skills in Spanish and English.

McCarthey reports that the teachers in this study did not know about the working-class case study children's home lives and backgrounds, even when the children and their families were encountering difficult situations, such as those presented by repeated moves or a father returning to his home country. This was in stark contrast with how much the teachers knew about the two middle-class case study children and their families.

While recommending home visits, McCarthey recognizes potential deterrents (e.g., teachers already being overworked; some schools prohibiting home visits; and some parents not welcoming home visits). She also recommends that teachers modify learning experiences so that they are more culturally inclusive, such as replacing didactic whole class book discussions with open-ended small group book discussions, and substituting writing for only the teacher with writing for others and opportunities for peer writing conferences. She also recommends making sure that books read and discussed are culturally relevant and positively address a range of cultures, so that all children have the opportunity to see their life experiences in books at least some of the time.

The Drawbacks of Ignoring Culture

It is possible to ignore culture and its impact on learning and teaching in several ways. For example, Dyson (1991) suggests that educators often view literacy in an acultural way, that is, not being aware of different cultural norms, values, and means of expressing oneself and using literacy. On the other hand, McCarthey (1997) concluded that teachers were aware of cultural differences grounded in social class, but tended to ignore them because they believed that all children should be treated equally. She comments, "Instead of understanding and addressing diversity, the teachers believed it was necessary to treat all students alike" (167). Consequently, the teachers ended up treating the students inequitably, favoring the children whose home cultures most closely resembled that of the school and the teachers.

ELLs Do *Have Rich Literacy Experiences at Home*

Many teachers assume that their ELL students, particularly those from low-income homes, do not have rich or challenging literacy experiences at home. Also, they often assume a lack of family support for children's education and learning. However, researchers who have studied literacy experiences in homes have found that this is not the case, although the literacy experiences in the home may not be identical to those found in the school or in middle-class homes (e.g., Heath 1983; Orellana, Reynolds, Dorner, and Meza 2003; Schecter and Bayley 2002; Taylor 1983; Vasquez, Pease-Alvarez, and Shannon 1994).

Luis Moll and his colleagues have contributed valuable insights into the importance of connecting home and school practices and experiences through "Funds of Knowledge," which refers to socially and culturally accumulated, constructed and distributed areas of expertise among community members that can be drawn upon by teachers for pedagogical/curricular purposes (e.g., González and Moll 2002; González, Moll, and Amanti 2005; Moll, Amanti, Neff, and González 1992). This research challenges the deficit views of linguistic, cultural, and socioeconomic nonmainstream families and communities that so often dominates the discourse about ELLs and their families in schools.

In my own work with children in a Migrant Education Program in Western New York State, I learned firsthand that parents were very interested in their children's learning and school activities. Most of the families were native Spanish speakers, but some were African American, and a few were Caucasian. All lived on very low incomes, despite family members working long hours in frequently arduous conditions. Through getting to know families, primarily through home visits (which were extraordinarily invaluable), I learned why parents and guardians didn't attend the school-sponsored events, such as conferences and back-to-school nights, attendance at which teachers frequently used to gauge family interest in a child's education. Parents and guardians gave the following reasons for not attending school events:

- They felt inferior and unwelcome at the schools because they were poor and/or did not speak English well.
- They were not able to communicate with teachers when English was their nonnative language.
- They did not have time to go to school during the day for conferences as they had to work to put food on the table.

- They often had no means to get to school for evening meetings and conferences as they typically lived in rural areas at a distance from the schools and without evening bus service.
- They had difficulty reading messages sent home, particularly Spanish-speaking parents when notices were in English.
- They did not have child care for younger children when attending meetings.

Other researchers, such as Auerbach (1989), have documented similar realities.

What Does It Mean to Be a Supportive Parent?

A dissonance between schools and families grounded in national origin, race, and social class is unfortunately encountered frequently, and has been reported on in various immigrant communities. For example, Huss-Keeler (1997) reports that parents and teachers held quite different views about how involved and interested Punjabi-speaking Pakistani immigrant parents were who lived in the north of England. Huss-Keeler comments that the immigrant parents, who came from rural areas of the Punjab in Pakistan, were very involved and interested in their children's education, but this was manifested in different ways from how middle-class parents might express it, such as being very involved with school-sponsored events; when parents were not involved in such events, it was often misinterpreted by school personnel as a lack of interest on the part of parents.

Huss-Keeler found that Pakistani parents came to school events, such as a "Community Games Evening," even though translators weren't available, which she interpreted as a sign of the parents' interest in their children's education. However, because they were not involved in running the events, the school staff interpreted this as an indication of immigrant parents' lack of commitment to their children's schooling. Also, Pakistani parents came out in large numbers for culturally familiar and comfortable events, such as a "food bazaar" and a play put on by the school about the Muslim celebration of spring, Eid. In these events, the parents did not have to speak English with an authority figure, which can be very stressful. However, teachers did not highly regard this manifestation of parents' interest; instead they judged parental interest by attendance at the "Parents' Evenings," when teachers talked about the children's progress.

The Impact of Limited Communication Between Parents and Teachers

Huss-Keeler (1997) also found often-conflicting expectations on the part of teachers. For example, one teacher commented on how parents weren't using the same methods as those used in the school to support young readers and writers; however, the school parent handbook didn't include explanations of the reading and writing programs. In addition, the school did not send home report cards to the Pakistani parents, believing that the parents wouldn't read them, even though they sent them many notes in English.

Teachers also discounted parental ability due to a belief that mothers were illiterate. Although this was true for some Pakistani mothers, the teachers failed to realize that there were other family members present in the home who could and did help the children in their English-medium literacy learning. Also, because they did not think that the children were getting help at home, the teachers did not send home school work and did not allow the children to take home school books, which further distanced the Pakistani families from the school. After two of the teachers visited a home for the birthday party of one of the children, Huss-Keeler detected a marked change in the teachers' perceptions of the child's family life; instead of holding a deficit view of the family and their child that was grounded in a lack of information, after the visit, the teachers spoke positively about the child's loving family.

As a result of lack of communication between parents and teachers, Huss-Keeler found that there were several serious consequences that had an impact on the Pakistani children's literacy progress. For example, access to literacy information for parents and literacy learning experiences for the children were based on how teachers viewed parents' interest in their child's education. For the teachers, coming in to school to talk with them was the most powerful indicator of parental interest, which discounted the many ways in which the parents who were least fluent in English supported their children at home. Those parents who came in to school to meet with teachers at Parents' Evenings were more highly regarded and their children had the greatest access to literacy in the classroom (e.g., access to literacy groups and permission to take home school library books). There was clearly dissonance between the cultural norms of what parents were expected to do in England (come in to school), and in Pakistan, where respectful and interested parents were not expected to go in to the school, but support their children at home.

The Silencing of "Literacy Stories"

Ann Haas Dyson (1990) points out that not all children come to school with the same school-related literacy experiences and they are often prejudiced for that, and their "literacy stories" silenced. She argues for much more tolerance, careful observation of children as they engage with language and literacy, and the embracing of diverse literacy experiences and development. This means allowing space in classrooms for literacy-supporting activities that students engage in, but may not be so familiar to the teacher, such as playing with letters instead of writing a sentence, or acknowledging the importance of oral storytelling to support drawing and writing. Dyson argues, "while children benefit from our guidance in literacy activities that we think are important, they also need space for writing and reading that they think is important. Most critically, children need our skill as sensitive and willing listeners and observers, as readers of children. This child reading can be perplexing and challenging, so, as with any skill, practice, persistence, and caring matter" (203).

Implications of the Research for Teachers of Writing

Although there is often considerable dissonance between school literacy practices and those in the homes of ELLs, there are teachers who have successfully bridged the gap by becoming knowledgeable about their students' families, communities, and cultures. They acknowledge, respect, and build on the language and literacy practices and experiences with which children enter school.

English language learners come from homes that have established ways of learning and transmitting cultural and literacy knowledge. Sometimes, these practices and experiences are hidden from teachers, who then mistakenly assume that families do not value literacy. We need to find out what children do at home around literacy and what their areas of expertise are, through observing them, through talking with them and their family members, and through visiting them in their community and home environments.

We need to provide a variety of learning experiences and configurations that accommodate different styles of learning (e.g., independent and group work, quiet and less quiet places to work). ELL children need to be offered authentic writing opportunities and audiences, and multimodal writing experiences (e.g., opportunities to integrate oral, visual, and print literacies). They also need to have access to a wide range of books that reflect the diverse cultures in our society, including cultures and experiences that are familiar to the students.

As the research discussed in this chapter indicates, even when teachers institute learner-centered literacy experiences and curricula, there continues to be the danger of inadvertently favoring a particular group of children due to differing styles of response and interaction. This can occur, for example, when home experiences with literacy more closely resemble that of school, as often happens with many middle-class children. In order to avoid this phenomenon, we must make sure we are familiar with and respectful of the home and community-based literacy experiences of all children and ensure that they all have equal access to, for example, sharing their writing and responding to the writing of others.

The research points forcefully to the importance of educators getting to know families. Some years ago, I worked for a Migrant Education Program, in which all teachers were required to make home visits each week. Through these visits, we got to know parents, homes, and the kinds of efforts that families made to support their children, which eliminated the deficit views that still prevail in conversations about ELLs and low-income children from diverse linguistic, ethnic, racial, and cultural backgrounds.

It is also clear from this body of research that we need to have the same basic expectations vis-à-vis communicating with parents, but will almost certainly need to modify how we do this with ELL parents (e.g., sending home notices in the L1 and using translators). We also need to provide alternatives to traditional forms of expression of parental interest and involvement, and establish parent events that allow all parents to feel comfortable and involved.

5

Reading/Writing Connections

*"In the beginning of the books I pay attention to what kind of writing
that is . . . sometimes I try to use that kind of writing."*

HOMA, EIGHTH GRADE WRITER

"We are the sum of what we read."

CRISTINA GARCIA, NOVELIST

One day I was in a third grade classroom where I went on a weekly basis to help a
teacher implement writing workshop. Toward the end of the session, the entire class
gathered on the rug for whole group share (sometimes referred to as *author's chair*), a
time for children to share and receive feedback on their ongoing and finished pieces.
I had gone to bed late the night before, the classroom was very warm, and I was having a hard time concentrating on Eric's bed-to-bed story, which he was obviously very
proud of. When he finished reading it and had responded to the questions and comments of his classmates, he started back to his place on the rug. Before he could sit
down, though, he chuckled to himself softly, quickly returned to the chair where the
author sat, and said, "I forgot to tell you. I finished *Alice in Wonderland* at the weekend and I was trying to write like Lewis Carroll. In that strange way." I was immediately alert and listened to Eric talking about all the crazy things that happened in
Alice in Wonderland (Carroll 1865, 1981) and how he was trying to emulate this. It
didn't occur to me then to probe him further or help the rest of the class see how what
Eric did was something that writers do.

Just as this memory involving Eric is vivid, so is the day when I first became aware
that I was reading like a writer. I have loved to read for as long as I can remember,
finding books to be a wonderful means of escape, of being transported into new
worlds, and of learning. But I hardly ever wrote, except for school- and work-related
purposes, such as the mandatory essays at high school in England, the higher education term papers and theses in England and the United States, and the letters and
reports for work. It's true that I enjoyed writing letters to family and friends. It's also

true that I would write story fragments in my head. But I didn't put pen to paper to really write until I was in my late thirties (it's interesting that I don't associate *real writing* with my school- or work-related writing). One day, after I had begun to write for myself, I had been reading Gary Paulsen's *Hatchet* (1987), with its staccato-like writing style that conveys dramatic tension very effectively, and thought to myself, "He's using single word paragraphs very effectively in conveying tension. Hey, this is something I could use in my own writing." It was the first time that I was aware of having made a conscious connection between my engagement with a book, an author's craft, and what I could do as a writer. Although I don't think I have yet used a single word for a paragraph, I have written very short sentences and series of very short, somewhat repetitive sentences, and they have been influenced by Gary Paulsen's writing style, as well as other authors, such as Sandra Cisneros (e.g., *The House on Mango Street* [1989]), who use short sentences very effectively.

Focusing on the Craft of Writing Needn't Destroy the Reading Experience

In the past, I had wondered, even worried, that paying attention to a writer's craft might ruin the aesthetic experience of reading that I so much valued and looked forward to. Much to my surprise and relief, I discovered that I did not lose a profound appreciation for and engagement with the story, essay, or poem I was reading once I started to pay attention to how writers craft their pieces. Instead, I felt like I had won the jackpot. As a writer, I didn't fully understand this symbiotic connection between reading and writing until walking up the hill one day in our Oakland, California neighborhood, enjoying the soft evening light and thinking about a short story written by Nadine Gordimer (1991) that I had just finished reading. In this story, "Some Are Born to Sweet Delight," a young Englishwoman becomes pregnant by a young man from an undisclosed country who boards with her family. Upon hearing that she is pregnant, the young man asks her to marry him and arranges for her to visit his family before they marry. He buys her a plane ticket, she boards the plane, but she never makes it to her destination as the plane on which she is traveling explodes midair; her lover is implicated in the politically-inspired explosion. This story seemed very familiar, and while walking, it occurred to me that Gordimer may well have been inspired to write this story after hearing a news account of a similar story that I had read about in the newspaper. In this case, an Irish girl living in London had entered a relationship with a young man from another country. Like the girl in the story, she was killed in an airline explosion that was traced to her boyfriend.

It dawned on me then that part of Gordimer's gift as a writer isn't to invent everything, as I once thought, but to be able to use real life for inspiration. I realized that this was something that I could possibly do. In the past, I had steered clear of short story writing in part, I suspect, because I was intimidated by the writing of all those writers whose stories I so much enjoyed. I didn't think that I had enough imagination to write a short story. Upon the realization that writers may work from real events, I immediately rid myself of the notion that I couldn't write fiction, my favorite reading genre. This experience made me realize that the stories are out there to listen to, read about, observe, dream about, and borrow; that writing a story doesn't necessarily mean that one works without resources. And I began to write short stories. A short, thought-provoking, wordless cartoon from Czechoslovakia that I saw at a movie theater inspired the first one that I wrote. Although the inspiration for my own story was influenced by a nonprint medium, it reinforced the notion that it was okay to borrow ideas from other sources; this was a direct consequence of reading the Gordimer short story.

Now that I read like a writer, I notice and often borrow stylistic devices and other literary features that impress me, such as Mildred Taylor's rich use of dialect in her stories (e.g., *Roll of Thunder, Hear My Cry* [1976] and *Mississippi Bridge* [1990]). Taylor's books have inspired me to listen very carefully to and even takes notes of conversations on buses and trains. What I read has also inspired me to write in new genres, such as when I wrote my first narrative poem, *A Child's Christmas in England*, after reading Dylan Thomas' *A Child's Christmas in Wales* (1954, 1959). One of my sisters-in-law had given me a copy of Thomas' book, which was sold in a small egg-blue envelope and, although I had read this poem[1] year after year at the holiday season, I wrote my poem only after becoming fully aware of ways in which reading influences writing. Similarly, when I became aware of the interesting juxtaposition of alternating narrator's voices in, for example, Amy Tan's *The Joy Luck Club* (1989), Louise Erdrich's *Tracks* (1988), and Mette Newth's book for young adults, *The Abduction* (1989),[2] I was inspired to experiment with this narrative form in my own writing.

Ways in Which Reading and Writing Are Connected

Sometimes, when we read or hear people talking about the connections between reading and writing, we may be tempted to yawn. So, they're similar, we may say. So what? But, to ignore the relationship between reading and writing is to miss a powerful opportunity to help children become better writers (and, of course, readers). The most recent research literature discusses two broad areas relating to the interconnectedness of reading and writing: (1) ways in which reading and writing are similar processes, and (2) ways in which reading influences writing. These connections will be explored in more depth in the following pages.

---

[1]Although I always think of Dylan Thomas' *A Child's Christmas in Wales* as a poem because of the poetic quality of the language and how it is laid out in my copy, he didn't write it as a poem, but as a radio broadcast or essay.

[2]Mette Newth won the Mildred L. Batchelder Award for this historical novel, which is set in Greenland and Norway, and is about the kidnapping of two Inuit young people who were then enslaved in Norway. This award is made by the American Library Association (ALA) and the Association for Library Service to Children (ALSC), and is awarded to a U.S. publisher responsible for an English-language edition of a work originally published in a foreign language in the preceding year.

Reading and Writing Are Similar Processes

Even casual consideration of what is involved in reading and writing reveals that they share some similar processes, including the following:

- Both readers and writers assess meaning and revise meanings accordingly. For example, when reading, we revise thoughts and predictions. When writing, we revise words and longer chunks of language. Both reading and writing involve a great deal of questioning, much of it silent, but some articulated.

- Before beginning to write or read a text (and while we are writing and reading), we engage in a form of preparation, which can be either fleeting or span many days, depending on the context and circumstances of our literacy involvement. For example, when embarking on a new piece of writing or opening a book, note, or magazine to read, we engage in a stage that has been described as *prewriting* and *prereading*. For example, before putting pencil to paper or touching computer keys when writing, we may gaze out of the window while thinking, jot down notes, observe carefully, draw a sketch, or talk with someone, all preliminaries to the act of writing, as well as occurring throughout the writing of the piece. This process can take minutes or days, and is an act of idea generation and reformulation. As readers, we engage in similar processes. For example, we may glance at the title and/or pictures, read the back cover, glance at chapter headings and subheadings, or talk with others about the text. Sometimes we do this immediately before beginning to read, but other times, we may not read the text until much later, as often happens when one buys a book, either at a bookstore or on the Internet.

- Both readers and writers are involved in constructing meaning. In the case of reading, we make meaning based on the structure of the text, the language used, and our own background knowledge or schema. As writers, we need to consider our readers, and convey our intended meanings in the best ways possible.

- Both reading and writing often involve a public act of sharing. In the case of writing, this occurs when we confer with others about an in-process piece of writing or when we share a finished piece. As readers, we share when we talk together about books, discussing their meanings and affect upon us, as happens in literature study circles (e.g., Daniels 1994, 2002a, 2002b, 2002c; Eeds and Peterson 1991; Eeds and Wells 1989; Peterson and Eeds 1990; Samway and Whang 1996; Samway and colleagues 1991; Schlick and Johnson 1999).

- Both readers and writers benefit from engaging with complete texts, rather than with truncated and artificial experiences, such as one finds in reading and writing worksheets.

- Both readers and writers make errors that often reflect the developmental nature of literacy and language learning. The errors frequently illustrate the creative construction of language that typifies all aspects of language.

Reading and Writing Are Meaning-Making Processes

By the early 1980s, research suggested that reading and writing were parallel, meaning-making, text-related processes that rely on similar skills (mechanisms) that draw upon a common pool of cognitive and linguistic operations (e.g., Dyson 1982; Harste, Woodward, and Burke 1984; Teale 1982). Drawing on her extensive work in literary theory development, Louise Rosenblatt (1988) enumerated several ways in which reading and writing share similar processes, including the following:

- Both reading and writing are transactional processes. Just as "the writer is always transacting with a personal, social, and cultural environment" (9), so the reader taps into personal experiences when transacting the meaning of words on the page. Also, the writer engages in a transactional relationship with the text being composed, which involves ongoing reading and rereading of the text and revision.
- Both readers and writers have to rely on their "individual linguistic capital" (8). That is, past experiences with life and language provide the material with which to construct meaning.
- Both reading and writing involve the creation of an original text. While this may seem obvious for writing, it is also part of the reading process. As Rosenblatt comments, "when a reader describes, responds to, or interprets a work, a new text is being produced" (13).

Despite these similarities in processes, Rosenblatt cautions that reading and writing are not simply mirror images, and although they support each other, teaching about one will not necessarily enhance the other.

Differences Between Reading and Writing

While there is evidence that reading and writing are interconnected in terms of process, development, and instruction, there are also several marked differences, as the following observations made by researchers such as Goodman and Goodman (1983) and Goodman, Smith, Meredith, and Goodman (1987) illustrate:

- Although children are exposed to both reading and writing in literate communities, they are exposed to much more reading and more purposes for reading than they are for writing.

- Readers have a mechanism for judging their effectiveness right away (they do or they don't understand), whereas writers are often dependent on the feedback of others, and this feedback may be delayed.

- Readers do not have to write, but it is impossible for writers not to read, particularly as their texts become longer and more complex.

- As skills-based reading instruction and test scores have dominated reading instruction, less attention has been paid to writing.

This last point reminds me of the 1980s in New York State, when the State Education Department was concerned that students weren't writing and developed a writing test that required that students actually write (rather than, for example, completing a multiple choice or fill-in-the-blank test of writing features). However, when visiting schools and talking with teachers, I often observed that, once the test had been given, teachers retreated to the days of virtually no opportunities for students to write, little or no writing instruction, and a heavy emphasis on reading.

The heavy emphasis on reading continues to prevail in many schools today, and a comment that Charles Chew made over twenty years ago (when New York State was developing its writing test) about the way in which reading has dominated language arts instruction, research, and funding, could just as easily apply today. He wrote: "Reading has dominated the scene in language arts instruction, research, and funding. In most elementary classrooms, reading instruction dominates the day, starts the instructional agenda, controls grouping, and dictates schedules" (1985, 169). The same could be said for today, with the intense attention paid to reading instruction. Of course, given the nature of the debate about reading instruction, with its emphasis on (often decontextualized) phonics and skills instruction, one could be cynical and hope that those who are obsessed with reading skills instruction steer clear of writing, even as one recognizes the important role that writing occupies in overall literacy development, including reading.

Reading and Writing Are Meaning-Making Language Processes

Because both reading and writing are grounded in language, there has sometimes been an assumption that they are simply identical communicative processes, that of composing and meaning construction. As Judith Langer (1986) points out, reading and writing are markedly different endeavors in that they are used differently and for different purposes, and are much more complex acts than simply being acts of communication; she argues that they are a means for people to symbolize experience and knowledge. That is, they are meaning-making thought processes that are grounded in language. The understanding and production of language and meaning that are at the core of reading and writing respectively are both highly active, nonlinear processes, despite a popular myth, even among educators, that reading is a passive act. That is, reading and writing involve the active participation of readers and writers, just as listening and speaking do.

Langer's research (1986) has provided additional insights into relationships between reading and writing. She gathered data from sixty-seven children in grades three, six, and nine (aged eight, eleven, and fourteen, respectively), and asked whether, given that reading and writing are both meaning-making operations, there is a common core of knowledge and routines that students rely upon when reading and writing. She gathered multiple sources of data, including: (a) observations of children during writing and reading activities (e.g., writing to imaginative/story and informational/report writing prompts, and reading and retelling imaginative/story and informational/report texts), (b) tape recordings of students reflecting on what they were thinking while reading or writing, (c) interviews of students, teachers, and parents/caregivers, (d) retellings of reading passages, and (e) children's writing generated by prompts.

Awareness of Genre Differences When Reading and Writing

Langer found that there are both similarities and differences between reading and writing. She found similarities in processes in that both are meaning-centered activities in which young readers and writers are continually developing and refining meanings, and responding to the specific features of different genres. For example, she found that children as young as eight had a well-developed understanding of exposition as well as storytelling, and they used this knowledge when reading and writing. Also, they differentiated between the uses of story and exposition when reading and writing. That is, they were aware that written language serves different purposes and were able to use different genres for different purposes. When talking about story writing and report writing, they described them in different ways. For example, eight-year-olds described reports as providing information and stories as being *made-up*. This age group was also aware of linguistic formulae such as *the end*, which they recognized as belonging in stories, but not in reports. By the age of eleven, students were more aware of organization (e.g., the need for a conclusion in a report), and by the age of fourteen, students were making connections between writing and the way in which it helped them to remember and learn, a sociocognitive function of writing.

Reading and Writing Generate Different Emphases in Children's Thinking

Two main differences between reading and writing emerged in Langer's study: (1) reading and writing served different purposes in the children's lives, and were viewed by the students as being different in content, intentions, and properties, and (2) reading and writing generated different kinds of cognitive behaviors and drew upon different patterns of knowledge before, during, and after the activity. That is, reading and writing generated different problems and emphases in the children's thinking.

When writing, the children focused more on the form of their writing (e.g., word choice, grammar, spelling) than when reading, when they focused more on the meaning of words and longer sections of texts. Another difference that Langer found was that, when reading, the students focused more on specific content and validating the *text-worlds* being developed; in contrast, when writing, the children were more likely to focus more on the strategies that they could use in order to create their meanings. Also, Langer found age differences, such as older students tending to be more reflective and using more strategies when talking about their reading and writing processes than the eight-year-olds.

Reading and Writing as Social Acts

Reading and writing are both social acts whenever there is an author and audience. In a symbiotic relationship, writers take into consideration the needs of their readers, and readers take into account the author's intentions. In Langer's study, however, students did not overtly show a great deal of concern for audience or author, though they were aware of this type of partnership in communication (e.g., they recognized that if a piece had been written for a different audience, it would have been different). Younger children seemed to find awareness of audience to be a complicating factor (e.g., eight-year-old Jason commented that he didn't think about who he was writing for because he had so many ideas and didn't want to forget them). This may be a function of instructional/learning experiences and foci, of course. I wonder if the lack of explicitness in the comments of the students in Langer's study is connected in any way to whether they had opportunities to write for *real* audiences, such as peers in their own classrooms.

Processes of More and Less Proficient Readers and Writers

Instead of analyzing data generated by many children, Birnbaum's (1982) research exploring relationships between reading and writing behaviors and possible influences upon them developed case studies of four fourth and four seventh grade students. This study also looked at students' writing processes, and similarities and differences between the reading and writing processes of more and less proficient readers and writers. Four of the students were white, three were black, and one was a former English language learner who was by then fluent in English. The students engaged in videotaped oral and silent reading and composing events (referred to as *episodes*), followed by discussions with the researcher (there were three reading and three composing episodes). The silent reading was of realistic fiction, fantasy, and factual accounts; after reading, the students were interviewed (e.g., asked to retell the story and answer a set of comprehension questions). The three composing modes were expressive (write about a memory), poetic (write a poem or story), and transactional (write about a lesson she or he had learned); after writing, the students talked with the researcher about the text and the process of producing it.

Birnbaum found that, although all the students had been identified as good read-ers and writers, some of the students were more proficient than others; this may have been influenced by variations in teachers' criteria for assessing goodness. For exam-ple, some teachers associated good writing with neat handwriting and correct spelling, whereas other teachers equated it with "ideational fluency" and creativity. Major findings relating to reading and writing connections include the following:

- Proficient behavior was context-specific. For example, students could write well in one episode, but not well in another, and this appeared to be related to the circumstances, such as whether they were interested in the writing mode; sometimes they did better when they self-selected their topics and modes.

- More proficient readers and writers used a wider range of alternatives at each stage of the reading or writing process. For example, they took time to select a text; surveyed the alternatives; thought about and planned a piece before beginning to write rather than jumping into the writing immediate-ly; reread while composing; and revised the content rather than mechanical features.

- More proficient students' responses were more coherent, contextualized, and detailed, in part it seems because they took time to reflect upon what they were about to do.

- More proficient students took time to select texts to read, to select topics to write about, and to collect their thoughts before retelling the piece read.

- More proficient students were better able to talk about and explain their reading and writing behaviors. That is, they seemed more conscious of their behaviors and processes.

- More proficient students cited experiences in one mode as being an influence on the other mode, possibly a consequence of their ability and willingness to reflect upon their reading and writing processes.

It is compelling to me that many of the attributes of proficient writing that Birnbaum identified are able to be developed through demonstration, discussion of the writing of professional writers and other students, instruction, and meaningful practice. For example, if students have difficulty talking about their writing processes or noticing craft elements in familiar texts that can be used in their own writing, these are issues that can be developed through reading; contextualized, explicit teach-ing; writing; and focused talking.

The Influence of Reading on Writing

Published authors frequently comment on how their reading influences their writing. Is this also true of students in grades K–8? And, what about English language learners?

109

If there are influences, what form do they take? Several researchers have investigated these questions, both in experimental research (e.g., Bereiter and Scardamalia 1984; Crowhurst 1991; Dressel 1990; Eckhoff 1983) and more naturalistic research (e.g., Atwell 1987; Hudelson 1989; Jaggar, Carrara, and Weiss 1986; Lancia 1997; Samway and Taylor 1993a, 1993b).

Relationships Between Reading and Writing Persuasive Texts

In 1991, Marion Crowhurst reported on findings from a study investigating the inter-relatedness of sixth graders' reading and writing of persuasive texts. Students from two classes in two middle-class suburban schools were stratified by ability and gender, and then randomly assigned to one of four groups, a control group and three intervention groups. The project lasted for five weeks and each intervention group received instruction in ten 45-minute sessions. Students in the control group read novels and wrote book reports. The three intervention groups did one of the following:

> *Writing group*—students were taught about the structure of persuasive writing, read and discussed a piece of persuasive writing, and wrote four pieces of persuasive writing.
>
> *Reading group*—students were taught about the structure of persuasive writing, and read and discussed ten pieces of persuasive writing (five pro and five con pieces).
>
> *Single-lesson group*—students read novels and wrote books reports, and received one lesson in the final week about the structure of persuasive writing.

A writing prompt and a specially written piece of persuasive writing were used to assess students' pre- and postintervention competence in writing and reading persuasive texts, respectively. The students' writing was rated in two ways: (1) each piece was scored holistically for overall quality, (2) in a different rating session, each piece was assessed holistically for organization, and structural elements (e.g., reasons, elaboration of reasons, total number of words, and conclusions) were counted. Students' proficiency in reading persuasive texts was rated in two ways: (1) counting the number of propositions students recalled, and (2) a holistic assessment of reading recall protocols that included attention to content, organization, and general persuasiveness.

Crowhurst reports that the findings provided "modest support" for her hypothesis that reading persuasive writing improves students' persuasive writing. Although the reading group's writing showed significant improvement, she couldn't really control for the effects of being instructed about the structure of persuasive writing. However, the writing of the single-lesson group did not improve. Crowhurst concluded that a combination of reading and being instructed in text features influenced the improvements.

The Impact of a Short-Term Intervention on Writing Suspense

As part of a study investigating the capacity of people of many ages, from young children to adults, to extract knowledge of the rhetorical structures of various types of texts, Carl Bereiter and Marlene Scardamalia (1984) investigated the creation of suspense. The young participants were students in grades three through seven; the students in grades three through six came from a private school attended by children from high socioeconomic backgrounds, whereas the seventh graders attended a public school in a working-class neighborhood. The students were first interviewed about their knowledge of suspense, after which they wrote a suspense story. They were then given instruction (one of three instructional treatments) in suspense, rewrote their story to make it more suspenseful, and were finally interviewed a second time to determine principles that the students had tried to apply in order to make their stories more suspenseful. The three instructional treatments were:

1. *Principles*—being presented with five principles that generate suspense (e.g., scary words, danger appears), with explanations, examples, and practice in generating additional examples
2. *Reading*—participants read and reread model suspenseful stories with a researcher, and the reading stopped whenever the student noticed a suspenseful part or feature, and
3. *Reading plus principles*—a combination of (1) and (2), with students asked to locate examples of each principle in the text.

They found that, although students increased their use of the five principles of suspense across the treatments, the overall suspensefulness of the students' own stories was not enhanced due to the intervention. That is, short-term (single) instructional encounters in how to generate suspense did not lead to any marked gains in students' writing.

The Impact of Books Read Aloud on Children's Writing

Janice Dressel (1990) investigated whether the quality of children's literature read to and discussed by fifth graders would affect their narrative writing. One of her hypotheses was that children who heard literature of different quality would write stories that would be rated as different in quality. Forty-eight fifth graders from an upper middle-class community participated. After being sorted by reading ability (based on a norm-referenced, standardized reading test), students were randomly assigned to one of two treatment groups: hearing higher- or lower-quality literature. Both groups heard classical detective stories from one of two series that had been rated highly by respected review sources, such as *Hornbook*. Informed professionals rated the two series on genre and literary characteristics to determine that they were, in fact, of differing levels of quality.

Over the course of about ten weeks (forty-nine of fifty-two consecutive school days), Dressel met with each group on a daily basis. The first six sessions were devoted to writing a pretest detective story—she explored literary and genre traits with the students, they read a short story containing the traits of a classical detective story, and then they discussed how each of the genre characteristics was revealed in the short story through literary elements (e.g., character development, style of the story). Then the groups brainstormed possible detective story topics, and possible storylines. Students each generated four possible storylines for their own stories and then wrote until they were finished (all had finished within three sessions).

After completion of the pretest, sessions followed a predictable pattern—Dressel read aloud for half a session, then she spent the remainder of the period helping the children bring to a conscious level their "intuitive understanding" of literature in general, and the classical detective story in particular. This procedure continued until toward the end of the study, when time each period was devoted to writing a posttest detective story. Stories were typed up and spelling and punctuation corrected so that raters wouldn't be hindered from focusing on content and meaning. Experienced teachers who were knowledgeable about children's literature holistically rated the stories. Pretest data indicated that there were no significant differences between the two groups on either literary traits or genre traits. However, the posttest writing indicated that there was a significant difference in the students' writing according to treatment, with the group who heard the higher-quality literature being rated higher.

Borrowing Text Features

In classroom-based research that did not rely on an intervention, Jaggar, Carrara, and Weiss (1986) studied influences on fourth grade children's writing in Carrara's classroom. The classroom was a rich literacy environment (e.g., hundreds of books; frequent discussions and displays about books and literary elements; a heavy emphasis on different literacy events, such as sustained independent reading, reading conferences, daily writing and conferring, and writing in learning logs). The researchers collected student writing samples, field notes, audiotapes of classroom reading and writing events, interviews of the children about their writing (e.g., influences on topic choice and revisions, knowledge of narrative discourse features, self-awareness of writing strategies, reading/writing connections, and concepts of selves as readers and writers).

After only one month into the study, the researchers observed connections between the children's reading and writing, such as the use of a third-person narrator in fiction writing, and the incorporation of elements from familiar books. Sometimes children described how their writing was based on real events that they had experienced, but they had fictionalized and embellished it, as professional writers whom they liked did. They were aware of this writing strategy and used it. Based on their findings, Jaggar and colleagues commented that reading and writing influence each other in the following ways:

- When writing, children borrow text features from what they read (e.g., content, words, use of dialogue, and third-person point of view).

- Children need to write in order to become effective writers, even if they are exposed to lots of reading.
- Classroom context is vital. Authentic and meaningful opportunities to read, write, and talk about reading and writing are critical for children to become effective writers.

Borrowing from Established Authors

In a year-long study in his second grade classroom, Peter Lancia (1997) reported similar findings indicating that children borrow from their reading. He collected several sources of data, including all the writing his predominantly low-income students worked on over the course of the school year; "status of the class" records from writing workshop, which listed children's writing topics for each day; notes from writing conferences he held with students, when they often talked about the origins of the children's ideas; lists of books each child read; and reading conference field notes. Lancia found that the children borrowed from established authors in the following ways, in descending order of frequency of occurrence:

- Plot devices, such as language patterns and vocabulary, titles, and setting (43% of all borrowed elements). For example, one girl modeled a series of books she wrote on the *American Girl* series, and used descriptive language, events, and titles that were similar to those in the original books.
- Characters in books, such as Amelia Bedelia and Curious George (32% of all borrowed elements). Children either continued with the original story or wrote new material.
- Information from nonfiction sources (13% of all borrowed elements). For example, after reading many texts about dinosaurs, one boy included a lot of factual information in a fictional piece about dinosaurs.
- Genre elements, such as when one boy wrote a legend, "How the Leaves Change Color," and used a heroic animal to perform an important deed, a feature of many Native American legends (9% of all borrowed elements).
- An entire plot, including retelling events from an original story (3% of all borrowings). For example, one child retold *Henry and Mudge: The First Book* (Rylant 1987).

Lancia found that all but one child borrowed from established authors, suggesting that literary borrowing was an integral, accepted practice in this classroom.

The Impact of Reading/Writing Discussions on Young Children's Writing

Another classroom teacher, Ellen Blackburn (1985), investigated the reading/writing connections of her first grade students. She asked children to think about how professional authors of books that they knew and loved found topics, and how they made decisions about beginnings, endings, and details. They also talked about how stories could be changed or two stories combined. Blackburn found that children's writing began to show the effects of these discussions. For example, one child, Shawn, who knew only six letter sounds upon beginning school three weeks earlier, wrote a patterned story modeled after Bill Martin's predictable story, *The Haunted House* (1970). He did, however, use the model only broadly, adding his own words, events, and sentence patterns, and selecting an entirely different ending. That is, he used Martin's story to help him write, but was not dependent on it, as this copy (Blackburn 1985, 4) shows:

> I came upon a haunted house.
> I opened the door.
> I saw a goblin. A-A-A-A-A
> I went in the T.V. room.
> I saw a devil. A-A-A-A-A
> I went in the kitchen.
> I saw Daddy Frankenstein. A-A-A-A-A
> I went upstairs.
> I saw a witch. She went E-E-E-E-E
> I thought they were bad,
> but they were good.

Shawn's story evolved in a very different way from what often happens in primary and ESOL classes, where children read a patterned story several times and are then directed to write their own piece modeled on the adult piece. Often, it is more like an exercise than an authentic composing process, as Shawn's writing of "The Haunted House" had been.

The class also made connections between books, and talked about how one book reminded them of other books. For example, one day, after reading *The Clay Pot Boy* (Jameson 1973), the class discussed stories that this book reminded them of and ways in which they were similar (e.g., same author, or similar theme, topic, and language), which Blackburn then charted. This chart included books written by professional authors and stories that children in the class had written. Blackburn found that a child would often turn to several other stories (adult as well as child authors) for features to then incorporate into his or her own story. Several children would write their own version of a particular story (e.g., about a haunted house), but would also vary the genre, sometimes writing a fictional piece, a poem, or a personal narrative (e.g., about visiting a haunted house at Halloween). As Blackburn observed, "The children don't just replicate the story, they improve it" (9).

The Impact of Self-Selected Reading on Older Students' Writing

At the other end of the age spectrum, Nancy Atwell (1985) found that the extensive, self-selected reading that her eighth grade students engaged in influenced their writing. This was revealed through reading dialogue journal entries, which Atwell instituted to extend her students' thinking about books, "to go inside others' written language in written conferences" (152), and to see if what they read would influence what they wrote. Students were already accustomed to analyzing writing, as they did this with their own writing in writing workshop. Atwell encountered many instances where she suspected a connection between what children had been reading and what they then wrote.

The Case of Daniel

One example of this kind of connectedness between reading and writing is revealed in Daniel's writing, a youngster who had not read or written much before entering this class and did not view himself as a writer at the beginning of the year. He began the year writing short business letters to companies whose products he consumed, and to actresses. By the end of the fall semester, he had begun to write a series of nonfiction narratives about his adventures with two of his friends. Atwell believed that these were influenced by the stories that he had been reading, realistic fiction about boys on their own who are loyal to each other. As Atwell put it, "In December, Daniel was reading S. E. Hinton and *writing* S. E. Hinton" (156, emphasis Atwell's).

In the spring semester, Daniel began to read a new genre, survival-in-the-wilderness novels. He also began to write "Trapped," a fiction piece about two boys trying to make it out of the woods after their motorcycle breaks down in a snowstorm; this was the first piece of fiction that he had written in Atwell's class. At one point, he wrote in his dialogue journal, "*Two for Survival* (the book he was reading) is getting to sound like my piece in parts" (157). Many of his dialogue journal entries talked about the ways authors of novels he was reading concluded their stories and was very proud of his ending to "Trapped." By the end of eighth grade, Daniel had begun to see himself as a writer, and wrote, "I have said all along that to write well you have to like it. Well, I like it. Yes, I am a writer" (158).

The Case of Tara

Another of Atwell's students was Tara, who was an avid reader but, like Daniel, did not see herself as a writer at the beginning of the year. In her dialogue journal entries, she enjoyed exploring what she did as a reader and comparing it with what her teacher, Atwell, did as a reader. But she didn't initially connect the perceptive insights she had into an author's craft with her own writing. So, in December, Atwell, began asking Tara to think about what authors did to generate the feeling that she had about the books she read.

Gradually, Tara began to incorporate elements into her writing that she had noticed and appreciated in her reading. For example, in March, she wrote the following entry about the impact of a very popular book by S. E. Hinton, *The Outsiders* (1967).

> I loved <u>The Outsiders</u>! I can't believe Hinton was only 15! It's really
> interesting the way she asked her friends for help. . . . My latest poem
> ("Sleep") I thought of on the way to Sugarloaf. I planned out just
> what to say. In the part where I repeat myself I did that because of
> <u>The Outsiders</u>. The only reason I thought of doing it this way was
> because of the book. (161)

In this kind of entry, Atwell didn't have to rely on inference to gain insights into the influences of reading on her students' writing.

Also in March, Tara wrote the first piece that she thought was good, "Beautiful Mountains," about an occasion when she saw an apparently dead woman pass her on a rescue sled when she was skiing. Later, she reflected upon why it was that she loved to read, but didn't like to write. She commented:

> I just realized I'm starting to like books with points: books that make
> me think, that have meaning . . . One of the best things you've done
> for me is you've opened books up, almost like dissecting something in
> science. I think I enjoy them more now that I can understand and
> appreciate what the authors have done.
>
> For me, writing and reading are starting to combine. The other
> night my dad and I were talking about me and why I love to read
> but don't enjoy writing. "I think it's because I can't write the kinds of
> things I like to read." This was the night before I wrote "Beautiful
> Mountains." (162)

In May of that year, Atwell invited Tara to write a report about their reading dialogue journals (which Atwell refers to as letters), and her development as a reader and writer. At one point, Tara's report explored influences on her writing, most specifically "Beautiful Mountains." She wrote:

> I also learn from other people's work. My one "good" piece ("Beautiful
> Mountains") was written the way it was because of a few good sto-
> ries by other authors.
>
> I kept "Beautiful Mountains" in my head (without much conver-
> sation) because of a piece I really liked by Justine Dymond, entitled
> "A Night in the Life." I made a point with my piece because of <u>The</u>
> <u>Outsiders</u> by S. E. Hinton. I added and took out certain details
> because of other students' stories I've heard that have too many, not
> enough, or the wrong details. (163–164)

So, Tara's writing was influenced by the writing of professional writers, but also by the writing of her peers.

The sentiment shared by Tara about being intimidated by one's favorite writers and feeling one can't reach their standards is one I have felt myself. When I first started to write, I wrote professional articles, then I branched out and wrote poetry, short stories and picture books for children. But writing short stories and poetry did not come easily or quickly to me, and I realized one day that it was because I was intimidated by the kinds of writing I loved so much as a reader.

The Impact of Textbook Reading on Children's Writing

Many children do not have the rich reading experiences in school described in the preceding research reported on by Atwell (1985), Blackburn (1985), Lancia (1997), and Jaggar, Carrara, and Weiss (1986). Instead, their reading in school is grounded in textbooks, and it is worth looking at how these types of texts influence children's writing.

The Influence of Different Basal Writing Styles on Children's Writing

Barbara Eckhoff (1983) looked at the influence of reading basal textbooks on the writing of second graders in two classrooms. One series, Basal B, contained a simplified style typical of many basal readers, whereas the other series, Basal A, contained more complex literary language, longer sentences, longer T-units and more subordinated clauses than Basal B. Both series contained expository, narrative, and fairy tale pieces. The children were asked to write to two prompts, one narrative and the other expository.

Eckhoff analyzed the style, format, and frequency of occurrence of linguistic structures. She hypothesized that, although children may read a lot of other books, in addition to their basal text, the basal text would exert considerable impact on their writing because they spent so much time reading it. Though there was variation across children, she found that there were noticeable differences in the writing of the children according to their basal text. Major findings included the following:

- Basal A children wrote more words per T-unit than children from the Basal B group.
- The sentences of Basal A children incorporated more elaborate structures, such as subordinate clauses, participial phrases, and infinitive phrases (e.g., "The robin came back to the tree *carrying a straw in its mouth*" and "*When I wear the gown*, I will look so beautiful *that everyone will admire me*"), which they were likely to encounter in their reading text. In contrast, the Basal B children used simpler sentence structures (e.g., "She could fix the insides of clocks").
- Basal A children used more complex verb structures overall, although both groups of children used about the same number of verbs. For example, Basal A children used auxiliaries, such as, "This lady *has* just boght (bought) some tomatoes."

117

When looking at format and style, Eckhoff found similar differences, again closely related to the writing in the basal reading texts. Preprimers in the Basal B series tended to have one sentence per line, such as the following (612):

Ben said, "Stop, ducks!
You can't eat this.
No, you can't!
No, ducks! No!
You can't eat this."

This pattern continued into the second grade texts, though to a modified extent. In contrast, very few of the Basal A texts had this type of one-sentence-per-line format. Eckhoff found that more Basal B children wrote in this format. In fact, 85 percent of the Basal B children reading below grade level (and who encountered a lot of one-sentence-per-line texts) wrote like this; in contrast, only one Basal A child wrote in this way.

Even when Basal B children were exposed to more normal print formats, as happened with children reading at or above grade level, some still continued to be influenced by the one-sentence-per-line format. For example, they put periods at the end of lines and capitals at the beginning of every line, even when their sentences continued onto another line. This suggests that their reading influenced their use of punctuation.

Eckhoff recognized that factors other than the basal text may have influenced the children's writing and the results of the study, including differences in teaching methods, linguistic abilities of the children, and time spent on writing and outside reading. She therefore investigated the children's knowledge of children's literature by administering Huck's Inventory of Children's Literature (1960). She found that the two groups of children had equal knowledge of children's literature, indicating that outside reading was not likely to have influenced the differences in writing that she found.

ESOL Children's Writing Influenced by Their Reading Textbooks

Similar findings indicating that the type of texts that children read in school can exert a powerful influence on their writing is reported on by Hudelson (1989). In a participant-observation research project that lasted a year, Hudelson worked with two native Spanish-speaking students, Roberto and Janice, who were emergent speakers of English when they entered second grade and she began to work with them. Both children had been assessed as beginners on an English proficiency test, and were in the same second grade classroom; they also received ESOL instruction from a different teacher.

In their second grade and ESOL classes, the only writing experiences the children encountered involved copying letters, syllables, words and sentences, and a modified cloze exercise in which the children had to complete sentences using one word from a selection of words. The children never had opportunities to write for authentic purposes, what Hudelson refers to as "original writing." This was grounded in the teachers' beliefs that the children needed to know how to write letters, words, and sentences before they could be expected to write on their own.

In contrast, Hudelson believed that children learn to write through writing original messages, even when their control of the language is emerging. She gained permission to work with the two children about twice a month, and in these meetings, the children selected what they would draw and write about. Hudelson found that the children were severely constrained by their regular and ESOL classroom writing experiences and expectations, and appeared to view writing as the reproduction of sentences that they had read in their basal reading program or encountered in locally produced materials. For example, one day, Roberto had been telling Janice and Hudelson about how he came to the United States on a boat. After the conversation, Janice drew a picture of a boat on some waves with a child next to it, but she then wrote the following (Hudelson 1989, 91) (the right column indicates what Janice read aloud):

Do cat si durinking	The cat is drinking
DodsiTiffsitting	Dog sit Tiff is sitting

As Hudelson points out, Janice did not write about what she had drawn and expressed quite effectively; instead, she reproduced sentences that were totally unconnected to her drawing that she had encountered in the *Miami Linguistics Readers* (Robinett, Rojas, and Bell 1970).

The Impact of Nontextbook Reading on ESOL Children's Writing

What happens when ELLs *do* have opportunities to write authentically and read non-basal books, such as trade books? A few years ago, I was involved in a multiyear collaborative research project with an ESOL teacher, Dorothy Taylor, and her students in grades four through eight. This project investigated ESOL children's ability to reflect in writing on their growing literacy and to examine the influence of adult correspondence on their writing processes (Samway and Taylor 1993a, 1993b).

As a pullout ESOL teacher, Taylor incorporated a process approach to learning, and stressed the interrelatedness of all components of language (e.g., Atwell 1987; Calkins 1986; Graves 1983). She offered many opportunities to use language for authentic purposes. For example, students chose the books that they read, and reflected upon them in writing; they selected their writing topics, conferred with their peers and Taylor, and revised them as they saw fit; they corresponded with Taylor in literature dialogue journals, in which they reflected upon literary aspects of the books that they had been reading, asked questions, and made connections to their own writing.

I also corresponded with Taylor's students about their reading and writing habits and processes. In these letters, the students and I talked about ourselves and what we had been reading and writing. I embarked on this study in order to investigate what children said about connections they made between their reading and writing, rather than having to rely on inferences.

Major findings indicated that, when writing, the students got help from many sources, not just literature. They got help from their environment and real life situations. They got ideas for stories or plot from TV. They got help and inspiration from their teachers. However, students were deeply influenced by their reading, and they talked about the following categories of influence: (1) content (what the story was about, in general or in detail), (2) literary techniques (e.g., genre, humor, plot, leads, ambiguity), (3) mechanics (spelling, punctuation, capitalization, paragraphing), and (4) process (how they viewed the process of being a reader and writer).

Content Influences

The children read fairy tales and they sometimes modeled the content of their own stories on content that had captivated them in the fairy tales. For example, after reading *Cinderella* stories, eighth grader, Shanti, wrote a story about Madonna becoming Michael Jackson's wife. The first paragraph of her final draft follows:

> *When Madonna was eight years old her father died. Then her mother got married with another man because her mother wanted Madonna to have a father and sister and brother. But when Madonna got older her stepfather and stepsister and stepbrother didn't like her because she was so beautiful. And her stepbrother and stepsister were so ugly and mean to her. They never let Madonna go anywhere. But one time her stepbrother and stepsister went to the park, and Madonna said, "Can I go with you?" They said, "No, you can't go with us." She said, "Only one time, then I won't go anywhere else." They said, "O.K., we will let you got with us only one time. Then you can't go anywhere else." She said, "O.K."*

Shanti went on to describe how Madonna met Michael Jackson in the park. He asked her to marry him, but her stepfather refused because he wanted his own daughter to marry Michael Jackson, and Madonna was made to return to her life of drudgery, hard work, and ugly clothes. That night, Michael came to their house, recognized Madonna and told her he wanted to marry her. The stepfather called the police, who eventually took the stepfather to jail, after which Madonna and Michael Jackson married . . . and lived happily ever after. In a conversation with Taylor about influences on her writing, Shanti commented on the influence of the *Cinderella* stories, as the following conversation excerpt illustrates:

TAYLOR: What about in Madonna, how did the *Cinderella* stories that you read influence your writing of the Madonna story?

SHANTI: Well, like, same thing happen in *Cinderella*, like the stepsister or step-father, stepmother, they always treat her like in, not kind way, but they always tell her to do work and Madonna book doesn't take her anywhere until like she just said, "Let me, can you take me one time to park and then I won't go anywhere?" And they say, "Yes." And in *Cinderella* story this one happen. The fairy god-mother helped her.

As can be seen from this short excerpt, Shanti borrowed plot elements, characters, and themes (rejection and evil being punished) from the *Cinderella* stories.

Influence of Literary Techniques

A more skillful writer than Shanti, Homa was a very astute, avid reader who routine-ly tapped into what she had learned about writing from authors she read. One day, she commented, "In the beginning of the books I pay attention to what kind of writing that is . . . sometimes I try to use that kind of writing." And that is exactly what she would do. For example, she had been impressed by stories beginning with dialogue and began her own story, *Bad News*, in the same way:

> "You know who just called?" Mom asked.
> "I don't know. Who?" I answered.
> "Just take a wild guess," Mom replied.
> "I don't know. Did Grandma call or something?" I asked, not too interested.
> "No but you say you were at the library doing your homework after school?" Mom questioned.

This story is about an occasion when the narrator deceived her mother and her moth-er finds out. She was caught up in self-pity when she was called to her parents' room because they had bad news for her. She was sure that the bad news concerned her punishment, but instead she discovered that her great grandfather had died. It is a very poignant story in which dialogue in the form of telephone calls builds suspense and is integral to the plot.

Influence of Mechanics

At times the children were aided in their use of mechanical conventions by books they had read. Fourth grader, Rubén, commented on this phenomenon, and how reading *Hoops* (Myers 1981) had helped him:

> I think reading, it helps me, you know when I write my sentences, like the punctuation, instead of putting comma or something like that or new paragraph or like semi-colon or where to start to putting capitals or organizing the paragraphs . . . I think now what I write I

know how to, to order the paragraphs . . . I just did how Dean Meyers [the author] organize them . . . like when the idea is over, like putting everything on, like I go a something, something, something, comma something, something, something and . . . period.

These inspirations from literature came unexpectedly, as other types of influences did, too. Homa captured the unexpectedness of this phenomenon when she commented "that night, when I was reading that word came up and I was like, 'Oh, that's how you spell it,' so sometimes that helps with spelling."

Process Influences

Comments in the process category indicate that the young writers were taking an author's stance as they got lost in the interdependent processes of reading and writing. They compared authors as they talked about books and their writing, and they recognized attributes of good authors. For example, Rubén said of Donald Honig:

I think Donald Honig is a professional for that. He knows how to write. He knows how to order his ideas. He knows how to introduce a book and then everything.

Because he wrote, Rubén could better appreciate and critically analyze another's craft.

Implications of the Research for Teachers of Writing

As the data that I have shared illustrate, the writing of nonnative English-speaking children, as well as native English-speaking children, is influenced by what they read. When given opportunities to discuss connections between what they read and what they write, ESOL children are able to do so.

Although researchers indicate that adult writers, such as college students, often feel intimidated by professional writers (e.g., Foster 1997), this feeling stands in marked contrast with many young children (e.g., Blackburn 1985). It is as if children, once given opportunities to make explicit connections between reading and writing, aren't particularly intimidated. Also, it would seem that the adult writers whom Foster wrote about interpret the question, "What can you transfer from this writing to your own writing?" in an unmanageable way (e.g., How can you write like Annie Dillard?)" rather than as a potential tool, a craft strategy to draw upon.

Children need to be participants in discussions about connections between reading and writing so that they may be fully literate people. This can be fostered in a variety of ways, including:

- Reading and being read to often, followed by discussions about what has been learned about writing from the texts just read (e.g., students commenting on what the piece reminded them of, which often leads children to their own topics).

- Demonstrating how reading influences one's own writing (e.g., "I was reading Sandra Cisneros' *House on Mango Street*, and I'm now going to write a short, short story.").
- Reading about professional writers and influences on their writing (e.g., in autobiographies, articles, interviews, and on websites).
- Writing and reading minilessons focused on reading-writing and writing-reading connections. Minilessons can also focus on how particular writers are influenced by what they read.
- Using part of whole group share time at the end of a reading workshop for students to share what they have learned from their reading that they can take with them as writers.
- Writing notebooks in which students list words, phrases, and longer pieces of text that resonate with them, and that they might like to use as resources in their own writing.
- Using mentor and touchstone texts in writing conferences to teach about craft elements.
- Introducing reflection logs and dialogue journals in which students comment on and correspond about reading-writing connections.
- Gathering data through informal interviews and questionnaires in which students comment on how their reading has influenced their writing.

We need to talk explicitly with children about these issues and connections, to teach them about other writers' craft, and to help them build the repertoire of writing strategies that they have access to. So, after reading a Mildred Taylor short story or one of her books about her family's experiences in the segregated south (e.g., *Mississippi Bridge*), we may talk about how these books have inspired us to write about family stories or write more authentic-sounding dialogue. Or, we may talk about the possibility of rewriting a first-person narrative in the third person so as to be able to provide readers with more insight into the thinking of several characters. Similarly, after reading Beverly Cleary's *Dear Mr. Henshaw* (1983) or Karen Cushman's *Catherine, Called Birdy* (1994), we may talk about writing a piece in the form of journal entries or a series of letters. Or, the staccato-like language use in Gary Paulsen's *Hatchet* (1987) may inspire us to try a more direct style of writing with truncated sentence forms that suggest an immediacy and urgency that description may not be able to convey. And, after reading Arnold Adoff's poetry, such as *Sports Pages* (1986), we may decide to experiment with the layout of lines and the font size.

I have found that many inexperienced writers, both adults and children, think that to learn from others and to borrow writing strategies and ideas is somehow cheating. In fact, I can remember thinking this myself, that somehow I had to have a completely original idea, one that wasn't influenced by others, or I would be cheating. It took me a while to realize that I was avoiding a splendid resource if I ignored what admired writers do and what they say about how reading influences their writing. One of my favorite authors, Cristina García, the Cuban American author of novels, such as *Dreaming in Cuban* (1992) and *The Agüero Sisters* (1997), spoke at a local college one day (1998), and in just a few words captured the powerful role of reading on writers. In describing her work as a writer, she said, "We are the sum of what we read." This is true for both acclaimed adult writers and relatively unknown young writers.

6

Reflective Writing

"Dear people, I'm not a number I'm a person."

CLARA, FIRST GRADE WRITER

"How can a snake hold a cupcake on his head. That's silly."

PHUONG, FIRST GRADE WRITER

A few years ago, while I was sitting in a hospital room outside of Newcastle, England, where my mother was dying from bronco-pneumonia, I discovered a writing function that I had never considered. In the quiet of the night, when I sat by her bedside and was not holding her hand, I wrote. Not to solve problems, not to make lists, not to write articles, chapters, stories, or poetry, but to soothe myself. I knew that she was dying, though none of the medical personnel actually said that (they simply said she was "very poorly"), and I found it very soothing to write about the moment, and my increasingly vivid memories of Mum from when I was just a child to earlier in the year when I had made another visit under more positive circumstances. It was soothing to write in my spiral-bound notebook as I listened to Mum's increasingly shallow breathing. Sometimes I sat quietly with my sister and niece, sometimes I was alone with my mother. When on my own, I felt an urge to talk to Mum, to let her know how much I loved and appreciated her, but decided that it was likely more calming for her if I were quiet. So when I was not holding her hand, I wrote.

Incorporating Reflective Writing in the Classroom

Written reflection is the opportunity to use writing to think about, clarify, explain, and internalize information, experiences, insights, beliefs, and learning processes. It is an important path on the road to knowledge. As written reflection can be enormously helpful to the academic and affective development of students, it is important that children have opportunities to engage in this kind of writing. This is particularly true for ELLs, as reflective writing is typically first draft writing and the presence of written mistakes is very normal, but isn't the focus of attention or instruction; instead, the content of the message is paramount.

Reflective writing can also provide teachers with insights into a multitude of important issues, including students' understanding of content (e.g., when they explain magnetism or long division in science and math logs, respectively), their opinions about class activities and class dynamics (e.g., when responding to a questionnaire about the effectiveness of peer conferences in writing workshop), life experiences (e.g., in open-ended journals) and their learning processes (e.g., when writing a letter to readers in which they describe their writing goals, struggles, and accomplishments in the process of writing a published collection of poems, or an essay, nonfiction picture book, or memoir).

Different Forms of Written Reflection

Written reflection comes in many forms and serves many purposes. See Figure 6–1 for an overview of different types of written reflection, and the purposes and features of each one. Written reflection can provide students with opportunities to clarify thinking, identify and solve problems, prepare for learning experiences, record knowledge and learning processes, share knowledge, foster interpersonal communication, and build community. Also, this type of writing can provide teachers with important assessment data. A discussion of some of the most frequently occurring forms of reflective writing follows.

Logs and Journals

One of the best-known forms is the individual log or journal, in which students reflect on their learning and learning processes, comment on their reactions to events and experiences, and ask questions. For example, students in Angie Barra's newcomer ESOL class responded in writing to books. In Figure 6–2, one of her middle school students succinctly and incisively responded to a humorous Shel Silverstein poem, "Memorizin' Mo," about a person who memorized the dictionary, but wasn't very successful at finding a job or a partner.

Sometimes, teachers introduce reflective writing as a means to address interpersonal conflicts. For example, when students in one of my son's sixth grade classes had arguments, the teacher would ask the students involved to independently write about what had occurred. The students then exchanged entries, read them, and responded to them in writing. Often, the act of writing clarified the genesis of the conflict and enabled students to resolve their differences with minimal intervention from the teacher. In a similar way, second grade teacher, Heather Juhl, introduced her students to a *complaint book*, in which individual class members wrote their names, the situations that were bothering them, and who was involved. Juhl then checked it each day to see if she needed to intervene (see Figure 6–3 for sample entries).

Types of Written Reflection	Purpose	Features
Logs and Journals	• Provide important assessment data on an individual learner and/or an entire class (What do learners know/understand? What are learners confused about? What do I need to go over again/teach?) • Provide learners with opportunities to clarify their thinking • Provide learners with a record of their learning and learning processes	• Learners report and reflect on issues that they are studying, are interested in, or are dealing with (e.g., the outcome of a science experiment, family language patterns, interpersonal conflicts) *and/or* • Learners focus on their learning processes (e.g., how they selected their independent reading books, which books influenced their published pieces of writing, how they figured out the answer to a math problem) • Learners and/or the teacher may choose the subject and topic. If selected by the teacher, topics should be selected carefully, and written in an open-ended manner (e.g., Describe the steps you went through to research your history inquiry study versus Did your research plan work?) • May be used on an ongoing basis or at the end of a unit of study
Dialogue Journals	• Foster teacher/learner communication • Provide learners with individualized mentoring • Provide learners with an opportunity to reflect on their experiences, knowledge, and learning • Provide teachers with assessment data	• Two or more people correspond in the journal (e.g., student-teacher, student-student) • Content may be entirely open-ended or focused on a particular topic (e.g., What learners are learning in a given subject/class *or* what is being studied on a particular day) • Staggering the handing in of journals can make the response to them more manageable for teachers • Teacher responses should follow the lead of learners (e.g., in content), be substantive (versus "interesting entry"), and model content vocabulary and use of language

Figure 6–1. *Types of Written Reflection (continues)*

Questionnaires and Interviews	• Assess students' knowledge of content, learning processes, and/or attitudes to a learning event (e.g., reactions to a speaker, feedback on the structure of a writing workshop)	• May be completed at the beginning and end of a unit of study in order to note changes over time • Generally focused on content, processes, and attitudes/motivation • Questionnaires require that learners can write • Questionnaires may be followed up with a class or group discussion and/or a brief individualized interview • Content may be entirely open-ended or focused on a particular subject (e.g., a reading log)
Field Notes	• Support students in reporting and reflecting on issues that they are studying (e.g., the behavior of animals or language use in the community)	• Learners report and reflect on events that they are studying (e.g., the behavior of an animal, family language patterns, the literacy development of a younger learner) • Similar to the notes that ethnographers and anthropologists keep
Book Reviews	• Provide students with opportunities to reflect upon books, synthesize their responses to books, and make book recommendations to other readers (i.e., an authentic response to literature)	• In order to distinguish between book reports and book reviews, learners need to be immersed in the book review genre • Learners write concise, substantive reviews, which are then published so other learners can have access to them (e.g., in a class newsletter, on a bulletin board, via the Internet)
Idea Bookmarks	• Help learner prepare for book discussions	• On strips of paper divided up into boxes for comments, learners write words, quotes, questions, short comments or predictions that strike them as important, such as the following example

Figure 6–1 (*continued*). *Types of Written Reflection*

		Idea Bookmark Name: *Angelina* Title: *The Great Gilly H* Date: *10/7* *I bet the next person would find a sticky surprise* Pg. 3 *Right here you can tell that Gilly is a different child* Pg. 4 *Gilly put her left hand on the door knob and the right hand on her hip . . . I think she was telling is Mrs. Trotter to bit it* Pg. 8

Double-Entry Journal	• Provide learners with opportunities to:
	  • Connect with a text and its content
	  • Clarify understanding
	  • Assess their learning over time
	• Provide teachers with insights into learners' thinking about and understanding of a topic being studied
		• Learners keep a two-column journal/log in a notebook
		• In the left column, learners write words, phrases and longer quotes from the text that strike them as important, intriguing and/or confusing.
		• In the right column, learners write thoughts about the responses to the entries in the left column
		• Teacher can suggest a minimum number of entries (e.g., one per page of text or every two paragraphs with shorter texts). However, it's important to keep it from becoming too prescriptive, and to focus on the importance of quality (i.e., thoughtful) entries

Letters	• Provide learners with authentic opportunities to reflect upon their experiences and learning *and/or* identify and solve problems	• Learners write to authors and/or experts about compelling issues *or* • Learners write to others (e.g., peers) about problems they have identified and wish to solve *or* • Learners write letters to readers of their pieces of writing, describing their writing goals and accomplishments

Figure 6–1 (*continued*). *Types of Written Reflection*

MEMORIZIN' MO

memorized the dictionary
just can't seem to find a job
anyone who wants to marry
neone who memorized the dictionary.

> 11/16/98
>
> The tittle of the poem is "Memorizin' MO" and the outher is Shel Silverstien. I like his poem and I think is stuped memo-rized the dictionary, I think the best is underland the words.

Figure 6–2. *Literature Journals: A Response to "Memorizin' Mo"*

Dialogue Journals

When journals involve a written response, for example, from either another student or a teacher, they become dialogue journals. Dialogue journals can be open-ended (i.e., including any topics that students select, including personal experiences) or can be geared to a particular area of the curriculum, such as math or reading.

Teacher-Student Dialogue Journals Sometimes, when teachers respond to their students' dialogue journal entries, their comments are very cursory (e.g., "Interesting," or "Nice entry"). However, in order to develop a true correspondence and mentor learners, we need to invest ourselves and make substantive and personally meaningful comments, as Chinese English bilingual teacher, Siu-Mui Woo, did when responding to Phuong, one of her first grade students. Phuong had reflected upon a book that her teacher had read to the class, *Oh, A-Hunting We Will Go* (Langstaff 1974), and her entry consisted of a question about the plausibility of the snake being able to put a cupcake on its head, as well as an evaluative statement (see Figure 6–4). Woo responded by acknowledging the child's insights and then offered an inference about the author's intention ("It is silly but funny. I think the author intends to make this a silly book so people can laugh.").

Kevin
Charles don't listen to Mr Z.

Xavier
Billy not let me B₂ he fen

Kevin:

Charles don't listen
to Mr. Z.

Xavier:

Billy not let me be
his friend.

Figure 6–3. *Reflective Writing: "Complaint Book" Entries*

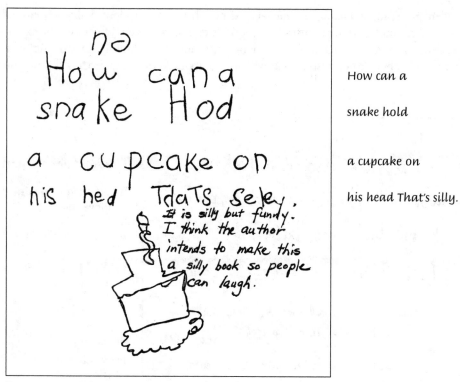

no
How cana
snake Hod

a cupcake on
his hed ThaTs seley.
It is silly but funny.
I think the author
intends to make this
a silly book so people
can laugh.

How can a

snake hold

a cupcake on

his head That's silly.

Figure 6–4. *Dialogue Journal Entry: Snake and Cupcake Entry*

When I visited this class, I also responded to some of the children's dialogue journals, and it was clear to me that they were accustomed to having substantive written, book-based conversations with their teacher. For example, as Figure 6–5 shows, May wrote about the play, *Rumpelstiltskin,* which she had seen with her class and had enjoyed; however, she was critical of one aspect of the play, the baby not being real. I was intrigued by May's comment and wondered how she knew the baby was a doll, and so I asked her about this in my written response. I moved over to read another child's journal entry, and after a few minutes, May sought me out to share her journal response, in which she explained that the lack of any movement had alerted her to the fact that the baby wasn't real.

This type of reflective writing allowed all of the children to share their responses to literature with their teacher, something that would have been difficult to accomplish if left to the oral mode only. It also provided the teacher with insights into the children's engagement with books, as well as their language development and cognitive processes.

Student to Student Dialogue Journals Although teacher-student dialogue journals are most common, student to student journals can also be very effective. For example, fifth/sixth grade teacher, Gail Whang, introduced her immigrant students in a year-round school to corresponding with peers about books, which they did on the

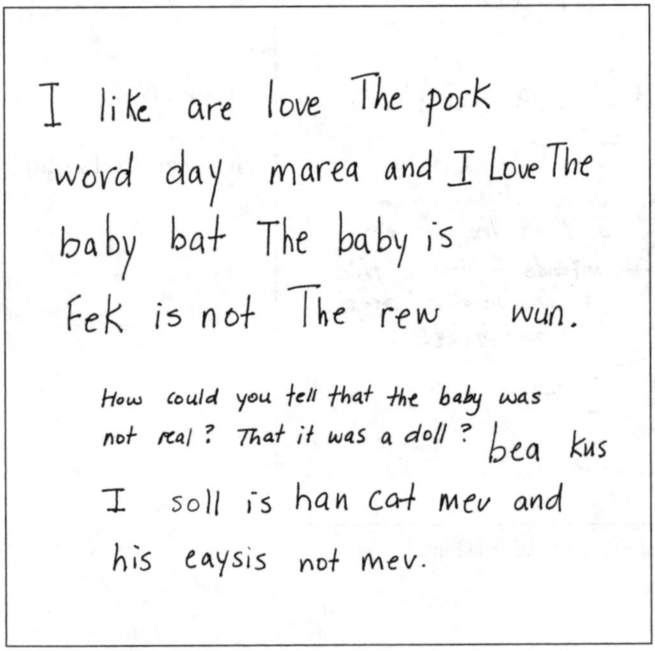
I like are love The pork
word day marea and I Love The
baby bat The baby is
Fek is not The rew wun.

How could you tell that the baby was
not real? That it was a doll? bea kus
I soll is han cat mev and
his eaysis not mev.

I like and love the part
where they marry and I love the
baby but the baby is
fake is not the real one.

Because
I saw his hand can't move and
his eyes is not move.

Figure 6–5. *Dialogue Journal Entry: Rumpelstiltskin*

computer. In the following series of entries written just before a four-week break, Billy and Nan discuss the books they have read, make text-to-self connections, comment on the experience of corresponding across genders, and commiserate over a shared family experience, being made to help out at home (which they referred to as being used by their parents):

DEAR NAN:
     MANIAC MAGEE IS A VERY GOOD BOOK. I KNOW YOUR READING IT SO YOU MUST KNOW SOME THING ABOUT IT. I LIKED IT BECAUSE IT REMINDED ME ALOT OF THINGS LIKE WHEN MAGEES AUNT AND UNCLE WAS ARGUEING. THAT'S WHAT MY AUNT UNCLE WAS DOING TO BECAUSE OF MY LITTLE BROTHER. ANY WAY DID YOU LIKE IT? IF YOU DID CAN YOU TELL ME WHAT YOU LIKE ABOUT THE BOOK TOO? IT AMAZED ME WHAN MAGEE RAN AWAY FROM HIS AUNT AND UNCLE BECAUSE I WAS GOING TO RUN AWAY FROM HOME TOO!
     WELL I HAVE NOTHING ELSE TO SAY SO HOPE YOUR RESPONSE TO ME QUICKLY?!.....
     SINCERELY BILLY

DEAR BILLY,
     THANKS FOR YOUR LETTER.
     I DID LIKE THE BOOK ALOT. IT MADE ME THINK OF THE TIMES I WANTED TO RUN AWAY FROM HOME. I THOUGHT IT WAS GROSS HOW MANIAC ATE WHAT THE ANIMAL ATE. HOW DID YOU FEEL ABOUT MANIAC?
     HAVE YOU EVER FELT YOU HAD TO RUN AWAY, BUT WAS SCARED? I DID. IT WAS WHEN I WAS STILL 9 OR 10 YEARS OLD. MY MOM KEPT ON USING ME. I WANTED TO GO OUT AND PLAY AND SHE STILL WOULD USE ME. I DID'NT LIKE IT ONE BIT.
     THAT'S ALL I HAVE TO WRITE FOR NOW.
     THANKS,
     NAN

DEAR NAN,
     THANKS FOR WRITING BACK SO QUICKLY! I THOUGHT MANIAC MAGEE WAS DUMP (DUMB) TO RUN AWAY FROM HOME, BUT IT WAS RIGHT DOUGH (THOUGH). THERE WAS ONE TIME I WAS GOING TO RUN AWAY FROM HOM BECAUSE MY PRARENTS WAS USEING ME TOO!
     I WONDER WHAT BOOK YOUR READING NEXT. I WANT TO KNOW BECAUSE I MIGHT GET THE SAME BOOK AS YOU. AND IT WILL BE BOR-ING IF WE RESPOND BACK TOGETHER IN THE SAME BOOK LIKE WE DID ON MANIAC MAGEE. AT FRIST I THOUGHT IT WILL BE DESAISTER BEING PARTNERS WITH YOU. BUT IT IS VERY FUN NOW THAT WE ARE

RESPONDING TO EACH OTHER A FEW TIMES. I KIND OF LIKE WORK-
ING WITH YOU.
    SINCERELY BILLY

DEAR BILLY,
    I KNOW WHAT YOU MEAN. I THOUGHT THAT WRITING TO A BOY
WOULD BE A TOTAL DISASTER. BUT I GUESS WE WERE BOTH WRONG.
BUT I GUESS I STILL FEEL UNCOMFORTABLE WRITING AND RESPOD-
ING TO A BOY. WHEN I FIRST HEARD OF THE IDEA, I THOUGHT MRS.
WHANG WAS GOING TO LET THE BOYS WRITE TO BOYS.
    RIGHT NOW I AM READING FREEDOM TRAIN. IT IS GOOD SO FAR.

Questionnaires and Interviews

Teachers with whom I have worked often find questionnaires to be very helpful in
assessing students' learning and knowledge about, for example, writing. At the end of
the school year, fourth grade teacher, Sonny Kim, used a variation of a questionnaire
when he asked his students to evaluate their writing, select the two pieces of writing
that they thought were best, and explain their thinking. He asked his students to
respond to the following questions:

1. Why did you select this piece?
2. What do you see as the strengths in this piece?
3. If you could work on this further, what would you do?
4. What have you learned to do as a writer?
5. What should next year's teacher know about you as a writer?

Students began going through their folders, glancing at their stapled drafts and final
copies. After a while, I moved around the classroom, checking in with individual students, asking them why they had selected these particular pieces.

    The most common reasons students gave for selecting pieces were grounded in
the effort they put into the writing, themes interesting them, and/or topics being per-
sonally meaningful. For example, Felicity selected a poem she had written, "My
Dream 2000," because she "wanted everyone to know I cared about the world.
Everyone should have peace. Way back, whites and blacks didn't like each other."
Cameron selected her biography about the San Francisco Bay Area Indians, the
Miwoks, because of the effort involved. She said, "I had to do a lot of work (research).
I did my best effort. I really worked hard on it. I took some time out from DEAR time
to write it." These written reflections allowed the children to process a year's worth
of writing and evaluate its relative worth; it also provided Kim with valuable insights
into his students' writing processes.

    Questionnaires can also provide important insights into students' reactions to
particular aspects of school. For example, Whang and I discovered through a ques-

tionnaire that asked questions such as, "What did you like best about literature study circles?" and "What did you like least about literature study circles?" that her fifth/sixth grade students did not like having to write regularly in reading journals, and they overwhelmingly advised us to drop the daily literature journal. (When we had time to respond, they liked the journals and were engaged, but when there was no response, they saw it as busy work, and were much less happy.) As a consequence of this feedback, Whang altered the expectations—the students prepared for the discussions with idea bookmarks, and instead of writing regularly in the reading journals, they wrote a single entry for each book finished, so that they would have a record of their reading.

Interviews can supplement questionnaires in valuable ways. For example, after children have written responses to questionnaire prompts, I read them and, if I am confused or have additional questions, I briefly interview students to clarify their messages and gain additional information and insights into their thinking.

Idea Bookmarks

Idea bookmarks serve a similar purpose to double-entry journals, which are most frequently found in secondary English classes, in that they invite succinct responses to literature. Whang's students used Idea Bookmarks extensively in preparation for literature study circles (Samway and Whang 1996); in fact, one student, Angelina, designed double-entry bookmarks as she found this tool to be particularly helpful to her (see Figure 6–6). On these bookmarks, students commented on parts of the book that had resonated with them, expressed opinions, identified terms that confused them, raised questions, made predictions, and made text-to-self, text-to-text, and text-to-world connections. Some students referred often to their bookmarks in the literature study circle discussions, as if to jog their memories, whereas other students, including Angelina, rarely read them when discussing the book. It was as if the writing had prepared her for the discussions and she no longer needed them as a visual prompt.

Letters

In schools, children are frequently taught how to write letters, but it often resembles an exercise, rather than an authentic opportunity to communicate one's thoughts and feelings to others. In Jennifer Jones-Martinez's bilingual primary classroom one semester, most of the students had been very unhappy about the high-stakes, standardized reading test that they had just taken. After the class had expressed their concerns, Jones-Martinez suggested that they write to the test designers, which some of the children did, including Clara (see Figure 6–7). In her letter, Clara's voice is palpable as she berates the test designers (*pepol*/people) for how the test doesn't tell them much about her or what she has been learning in school. Through letters, these students had an opportunity to reflect on their test-taking experiences and convey to the test designers their reservations about a system that they essentially considered an invalid

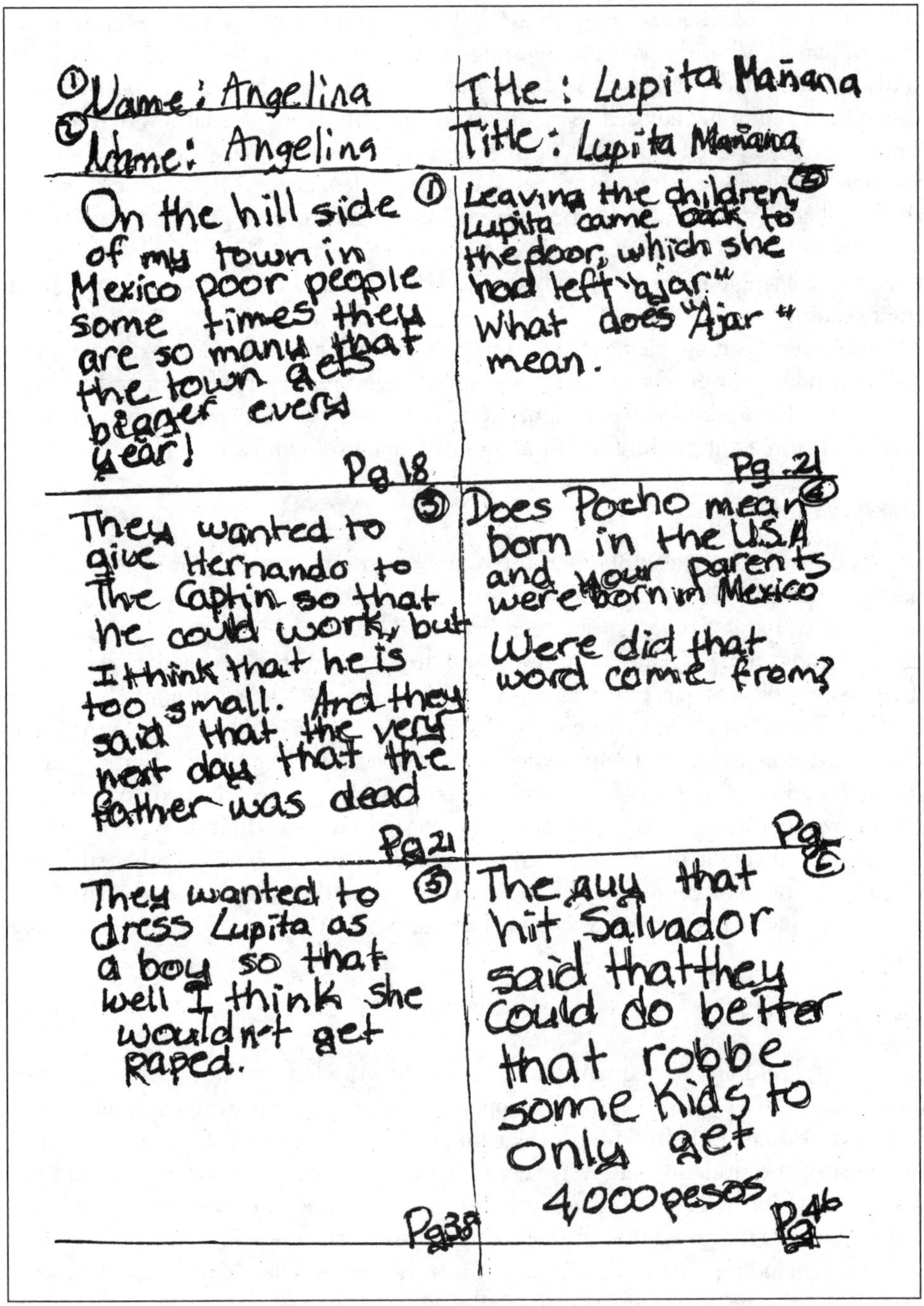

① Name: Angelina   THle: Lupita Mañana
② Name: Angelina   Title: Lupita Mañana

On the hill side   Leaving the children,
of my town in   Lupita came back to
Mexico poor people   the door, which she
some times they   had left "ajar."
are so many that   What does "Ajar"
the town gets   mean.
bigger every
year!
                Pg 18   Pg 21

They wanted to   Does Pocho mean
give Hernando to   born in the U.S.A
The Captin so that   and your parents
he could work, but   were born in Mexico
I think that he is
too small. And they   Were did that
said that the very   word come from?
next day that the
father was dead
                Pg 21   Pg

They wanted to   The guy that
dress Lupita as   hit Salvador
a boy so that   said that they
well I think she   could do better
wouldn't get   that robbe
Raped.   some kids to
                         only get
                         4,000 pesos
                Pg 35   Pg 46

Figure 6–6. *Reflective Writing: Angelina's Idea Bookmarks*

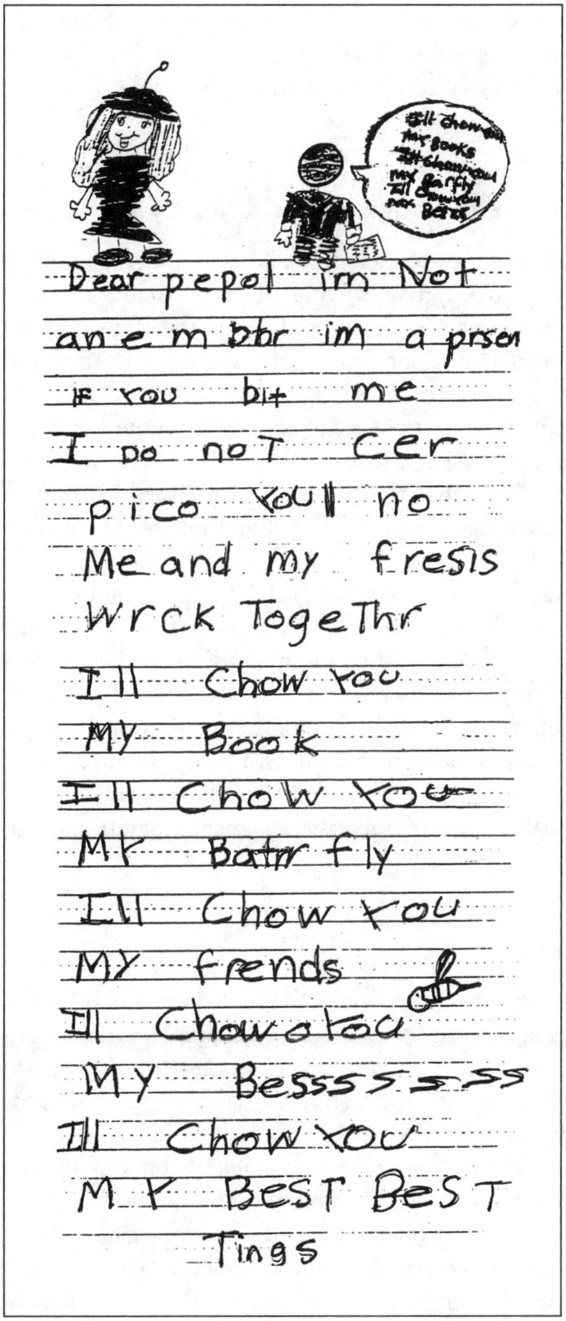

Dear pepol im Not
an e m bbr im a prson
iF you bit me
I Do noT cer
pico youll no
Me and my fresis
Wrck TogeThr
I ll Chow you
MY Book
I ll Chow you
MY Batrfly
I ll Chow you
MY frends
Ill Chow o you
MY Besssss ss
Ill Chow you
M Y BEsT BesT
Tings

Dear people, I'm not
a number I'm a person.
If you invite me
I do not care
because you'll know
me and my friends
work together.
I'll show you
my book.
I'll show you
my butterfly.
I'll show you
my friends.
I'll show you
my bees.
I'll show you
my best best
things.

Figure 6–7. *Clara's Letter to Test Designer*

measure of their knowledge (e.g., Clara knew about bees and butterflies, which the class had been studying) and interpersonal skills (she was able to work collaboratively with her peers and make friends). Regrettably, the test designers did not respond to the letters that the children wrote.

The Role of Reflective Writing in Language and Literacy Development

Reflective writing can serve many purposes, including affective, pragmatic, intellectual, and academic. It is known to improve writing fluency, stimulate cognitive growth, reinforce learning, and foster problem-solving skills. In the 1980s and 1990s, reflective writing became increasingly popular with teachers as they heard about the power of journaling on learners, and how it can support learning about language and literacy processes, about concepts in a particular subject, about oneself and others, and about the world at large (e.g., Atwell 1985, 1987; D'Arcy 1987; Hall and Robinson 1994; Kooy and Wells 1996; Parsons 1994; Peyton and Reed 1990; Samway and Taylor 1993a, 1993b; Staton 1980, 1985, 1987; Taylor 1990; Wollman-Bonilla 1989, 1991).

Toby Fulwiler's 1987 edited volume, *The Journal Book*, captures the broad scope and potential of journals, dialogue journals, learning logs, and other forms of reflective writing across the grades, for primary-aged children to adults, and across a wide range of content areas, from literacy and literature to history, music, mathematics, physics, sociology, geography, and the arts. Although journaling is typically found in mainstream K–12 and university classrooms, teachers have also used journals to build relationships with parents (e.g., Finnegan 1997), to enhance the learning of students with special needs (e.g., Staton 1985), and in university teacher preparation programs (e.g., Gannon 2001).

Journals as a Record of Experiences

Journals can provide a record of experiences, which the writer and others have access to later when reflecting upon an experience. For example, when Marjorie Faulstich Orellana, Jennifer Reynolds, Lisa Dorner, and María Meza (2003) investigated the interpreting work that Spanish/English bilingual children did for their immigrant families, journals generated important data. In the journals, the children recorded their experiences as the interpreters or language brokers of written texts for their families. The children translated a range of genres, including letters, forms, advertisements, labels, news, and reference materials; sometimes the texts that the children translated were very convoluted and full of bureaucratic language, and the children and their family members co-constructed the texts' meanings. Through the journals that the children wrote in, the researchers gained insights into the collaborative nature of the translating that the children did and how they felt about it (e.g., although they sometimes found the task tedious, they felt a great sense of accomplishment that they could help family members). The researchers comment that, when translating, the children had and were viewed by others as having considerable expertise, not an experience they typically encountered in school.

Reflective Writing Supporting ELLs

Reflective writing has been found to be very beneficial to ELLs, both those living in countries where English is not the dominant language and those living in English-speaking countries.

Reading Response Journals in an English as a Foreign Language Setting

Emma Rous (1993) used reading response journals when she worked with thirteen- and fourteen-year-old English as a foreign language (EFL) students one summer in Estonia. She took suitcases of paperback novels and picture books and, after giving a brief book talk on each book, invited students to select books to read for about an hour at home each day; the students also wrote journal entries on what they had read. Rous found that the students who responded best were those who had been able to personally connect with the content of the books. Sometimes, this was because the books addressed topics about which they were relatively unfamiliar, such as Hiroshima. Other students identified with the plight of oppressed people, such as Native Americans. Still other students connected with a book that reminded them of a personal experience. For example, Kaidi had longed for a puppy and read *Where the Red Fern Grows* (Rawls 1974). She loved the book, and wrote: "Billy is infected with puppy love . . . I like this book because I have had also such disease. When I read this book, I live with Billy and remember my stories, when I was ten years old." Through the books and the reading response journals, these EFL students were able to develop their fluency in English.

Role of the Teacher in Dialogue Journals with ELLs

In a study investigating the role of the interactive strategies employed by a sixth grade teacher, Mrs. Reed, on the participation of her ELL students in dialogue journals, Joy Kreeft Peyton and Mulugetta Seyoum (1989) found that the teacher assumed a supportive and co-participant role in her interactions. For example, she was more likely to respond to topics initiated by the students, rather than initiating her own. Also, rather than responding with cheerleading types of comments (e.g., "interesting entry") or with questions intended to elicit more writing, the teacher contributed substantive, on-target information and opinions. Also, the teacher's questions were authentic and grounded in the students' comments, as the following excerpt from an interaction with Claudia illustrates (320, 322).

Claudia's entry:
oh Mrs. Reed what do you feed chickens here? We have a hen that layd & egg.

Teacher's entry:
Chickens will eat scraps of bread, wheat, seeds, water and some insects.

Claudia's entry:
oh but the hen has some white lines in her dirt of her body that throws up by a hole. I don't know what you call it. She has wat it looks like worms, but little worms those white ugly worms & they are very skiny, what are they? do you know how to get the hen of her stomach sickness or is it usual for her to be like that because she is layng eggs & she could even lay 30 eggs so I don't know if it is usual or if it is a sickness of her.

oh poor hen she cooks and coocks when I say pretty hen in a low low voice & she looks like she is used to children because she is cook & cooking when I say pretty things, oh she's so nice!!!!

Teacher's entry:
It is normal for the feces (the waste from your hen's body) to have white lines in it. I've never heard of a hen having worms—but it is possible. Go to a pet shop and ask them or to a veterinarian. Who gave you the hen? Maybe they will know.

We say a hen clucks. It is a pleasant little sound as though they are happy. They cackle when they lay an egg. That is usually loud! Does your hen cackle?

I think hens like having people or other hens around, don't you? (320, 322)

The interactive strategies that Mrs. Reed used appeared to have a positive impact on her students, who were enthusiastic dialogue journal writers.

Impact of the Teacher's Interactions on the Quality of Students' Reflective Writing

Peyton and Seyoum (1989) also investigated the role of the teacher's interactive style on the quality of the students' responses. Although it is reasonable to assume that ELLs may write more and/or attempt more complex grammatical structures when writing on a topic that they initiate, Peyton and Seyoum did not find that syntactic complexity or length of entries was affected by whether the students initiated or responded to journal topics; this appeared to be more related to the students' proficiency in English and their engagement in a topic. It is interesting to note that the researchers did not find that the teacher varied her use of interactive strategies according to the English proficiency of the students but, as Peyton and Seyoum point out, this may have been due to their analysis being limited to broad-based strategy categories. However, in a series of more detailed analyses involving the same teacher and ELLs, the researchers found that the teacher did vary her strategies according to the students' proficiency (see Kreeft, Shuy, Staton, Reed, and Morroy 1984).

Variations in ELL Children's Responses to Dialogue Journals

As part of an observational study of the writing processes of four intermediate grade Southeast Asian children classified as transitional ELLs, Carole Urzúa (1987) investigated the role of dialogue journals in the children's writing development. The students corresponded with their ESOL teacher, Sue Braithwaite, on self-selected topics twice a week. Although the journals provided an authentic audience, there were pronounced individual differences in the students' recognition of audience. For example, Vuong appeared to approach the dialogue journal writing as an assignment rather than an opportunity to collaboratively explore issues that were of interest to both him and his respondent, his ESOL teacher. He wasn't sure what to write about and after the teacher had suggested that he could write about what he did over the weekend, he wrote about this for several weeks, without really having a written conversation with his teacher. The following is a fairly typical entry that he wrote:

> It was Saturday I woke up and I took a shower. And after a shower then I watched cartoon with my mom. My dad wasn't home. He went somewhere. When he come back he took us to my uncle house. We had dinners there. And came back to our house. (303)

After struggling to find a way to engage Vuong in a written conversation, the teacher eventually succeeded when she asked Vuong about something that was important to him, his violin playing. She wrote, "Vuong, what is the name of your favorite violin piece? How long have you been playing the violin?" For the first time, Vuong responded to his teacher and wrote back, "My favorite piece is called Lightly Row that my favorite piece I been playing for three year" (304). Urzúa concluded that the dialogue journals allowed the students to experiment with language, take risks, and develop their voices as writers.

Differences in ELLs' Responses to Dialogue Journals and Interactive Reading Logs

Two forms of reflective writing most frequently found in schools are dialogue journals and responses to literature (e.g., literature logs). In an October to May study, María de la Luz Reyes (1991) investigated the effectiveness of a process approach to writing on ten middle school Latino students who wrote in dialogue journals and interactive literature logs (they corresponded with their teacher about books they were reading). The sixth grade children all spoke Spanish as their native language; seven were classified as dominant in Spanish, and three were classified as bilingual. The language arts teacher who worked with these children, Mrs. Sands, was fully bilingual/biliterate.

The children were encouraged to write in their dialogue journals on a daily basis and were required to write in their literature logs once a week; they could write in either language in the dialogue journals (five students preferred to write in Spanish), but they were expected to write in English in their literature logs as a consequence of a district policy. Mrs. Sands matched the child's language output in the dialogue journals by responding in the language used by the child. The students could select the topic for their dialogue journal entries, but in the literature logs, they were obliged to keep a "businesslike diary of what you are reading" (300). In addition to the journal and log entries, Reyes collected observational data and teacher interviews.

Reyes found that the dialogue journals offered students a more authentic, supportive experience for becoming writers. For example, in the dialogue journals, students elaborated and they were able to draw on culturally relevant experiences and knowledge, such as incidents involving family members, as Sara did when she wrote the following entry about witchcraft, a fairly common experience in many traditional Hispanic families:

> *Maestra perdoneme porque no le escribi su carta pero yo perdi la carta. Mestra usted gre en brujerias. Yo si. Porque las brujas an quedrido hacerle brujerias a mi mama.*

> *Teacher forgive me for not writing you a letter but I lost the letter. Teacher do you believe in brujerías (witchcraft). I do. Because the witches have wanted to cast spells on my mother.* (301)

In contrast, in the literature logs, the entries were much shorter and more functional, and lacked substance (e.g., "I am reading *(book title)*. It is about *(character)* who does XYZ. It is a good book. I like it" [298]).

Choice over topic also affected the quality of the children's writing, as well as how much they wrote. For example, when topics were imposed, their writing often lacked the vitality, engagement, and confidence of their self-selected writing. After Sara and Mrs. Sands had exchanged several entries about witchcraft (a cultural experience with which Mrs. Sands was familiar), and Mrs. Sands had steered Sara to another topic because she was concerned that her student was too focused on this topic, Sara's writing became much more sparse (e.g., writing just, "Si maestra/*Yes teacher*" in response to a suggestion that she write about ghost stories at Halloween). Although Sara had been writing almost a full page in Spanish each entry up to that point, her entries diminished to two to three lines and eventually she stopped writing in her journal. Mrs. Sands then suggested that they correspond in English, which Sara did, but her writing lacked the fluency and substance of her earlier self-selected entries in Spanish, and she became a cautious writer who focused on grammatical correctness.

Reyes reports that the interactive literature logs did not provide Mrs. Sands' students with a successful writing experience. Of the ten students, only one student responded personally and substantively to books. Reyes concludes that the district policy that the bilingual program's language arts classes be conducted in English was a major influence as the students were not able to use their strongest language to fully understand and write about literature. Also, the students lacked strategies for selecting books that they could relate to and/or understand, and their teacher did not give them much guidance. Interestingly, when Mrs. Sands abandoned her own admonition to write in a businesslike fashion (e.g., when she included personal greetings and maintained social interactions in the log), it seemed to support the writer.

ELLs Reflecting in Writing on Their Literacy Development and Processes

In a two-year collaborative research project with Dorothy Taylor, an ESOL teacher-researcher, we investigated the writing processes of nonnative English-speaking students in grades four through eight, and their ability to reflect in writing on their growing literacy (Samway and Taylor 1993a, 1993b). The students with whom I corresponded had a rich literacy experience in their ESOL class. For example, they read real books (i.e., trade books and books authored by students, rather than controlled readers); they wrote on topics of their own choosing, conferred with their peers and teacher, and published their writing; and they corresponded with their teacher about books they were reading in a dialogue journal. The students and I corresponded about reading and writing in letters. In addition to the journals and letters, Taylor and I also collected interview data and our adult correspondence over the two-year project.

Variations in Students' Responses

Analysis of the data revealed that there was great variation in the types of responses that the youngsters engaged in as literary correspondents and this appeared to be related to how experienced and engaged the students were as readers and writers, as well as how accustomed they were to reflecting on books, writing, and their reading and writing processes. For example, Homa, an eighth grader, was an experienced and enthusiastic reader in both English and her native language, Farsi, and corresponded from the beginning about her reading and writing. In contrast, another eighth grader, Shanti, was a very reluctant and inexperienced reader and writer who steered the content of the letters away from a strictly literacy focus to one that included personal elements, as she was much more at ease discussing friends, work, and family members than she was discussing books and writing.

Teachers Investing Themselves

As a written relationship with the students developed over time, Taylor and I assumed more natural, less traditional *teacher* or *researcher* roles and invested ourselves in ways that we had not initially anticipated (e.g., including personal information about family members and activities, sharing our own reading and writing processes, and soliciting feedback on drafts of our writing). The modeling of literary discourse was therefore grounded in a genuine attempt to have a dialogue, rather than to model an artifact of language and thinking, and this appeared to have an impact on the students' entries, which became more engaging.

Questions are an integral part of correspondence, but we found that when they are not grounded in an entry that reveals something of the writer, they tend not to enhance the correspondence. Although Taylor and I tended to ask most of the questions, over time the students began to ask questions, although the degree to which this occurred varied from student to student.

Students and Teachers Following the Lead of Each Other

Both adults and children initiated topics, both literary in nature (in reading journals and letters) and personal (in letters), and incorporated elements present in their respondents' writing into their own writing (e.g., salutations in letters, vocabulary, and topics). That is, we followed the lead of each other.

The Impact of Dialogic Writing with Children on a Researcher

An unexpected result of the project was the influence of the students' letters on my reading and writing, and the way that I came to view myself (and act) as a reader, writer, teacher and researcher. When I analyzed the letters, I became aware of three stages in my developing role as a correspondent: (1) Objective Researcher, (2) Emergence of New Role, and (3) Personal Investment, and these stages were very much influenced by the stances that the students took as correspondents. Although Homa had greater facility expressing herself in English than the other intermediate grade students, there were some shared features, and I will refer to my correspondence with Homa to illustrate points.

Stage I Correspondence: Objective Researcher When I first wrote to Homa, she was a seventh grader. She had come to the United States from Iran the previous year. At the beginning, I approached the correspondence as a distant researcher keen to know about her language and literacy development. My demeanor or role changed over the course of the two years that we corresponded, and to a large extent, Homa initiated the changes, whether consciously or unconsciously. At the beginning of the project, in Stage I correspondence (Objective Researcher), I quite deliberately assumed the role of inquiring researcher. I expected to encourage students to write about things that they may not have considered otherwise, that could be helpful to them as learners, and that were interesting to me as an educator and researcher.

In this stage, my letters were long, entirely focused on the students' literacy experiences and processes, and filled with questions and requests, albeit very genuine ones. This stance is reflected in the following excerpt from my first letter to Homa:

> I was talking with Ms. Taylor about the possibility of you becoming a fellow researcher with us. That may sound very scary, but I think you will find it enjoyable. What it would involve would be writing letters to me describing what you do when you write. To begin with, you may find it easier if I ask you some questions, which

you can think about and answer. I bet that you will quickly find other questions that you would like to talk about in your letters. What I promise to do is to answer your letters and read any writing that you would like to share with me. You can send xerox copies. Here are a few questions that I'd like you to think about:

1. How often do you write in your native language?
2. What do you like/dislike about writing in your native language?
3. How often do you write in English?
4. What do you like/dislike about writing in English?
5. How is writing in your native language the same as writing in English?
6. How is writing in your native language different from writing in English?

I am looking forward very much to hearing from you. I hope that you will decide to write back. If you have questions, please ask them. Good luck with your writing!

As the following excerpt shows, Homa dutifully responded to these questions and requests:

> I don't write often In my native language because I just write when someone writes a letter to me. Also I like writing in my native language because I like writing in a nother language and I dont want to forget it. I write in english most of the times exept the letters that I write to my Grandma and grandpa for example I do my home workes, I write letters, I take notes and other things that I don't remember right now. I like writing in english because of the way its written and I think it's kind of fun too. Writing in my native language has nothing to do in writing in English. The alphobets are different ant every thing else that you think is different about it.

In her response, Homa also expressed pleasure that I had written to her and shared some personal information, much as one would in a letter to a family member or friend (e.g., "When you send you letter I was so excited for reading it and also thanks for writing to me. Thanksgivings comming and my mothers sick. I hope she gets better till then so we can do something. I hope you have a nice Thanksgiving and I've looking forward to reading your next letter."). Homa's personal response demonstrated what it means to be a correspondent, that one must establish an identity. It was almost as if she were saying, "OK. I've answered all your questions, now let's write real letters." But, it took me a while to internalize this message.

Stage II Correspondence: Emergence of New Role After a while, and with prodding from Homa's ESOL teacher, I realized that I needed to modify my stance, and I made an effort to put more of myself into the correspondence, a characteristic of Stage II correspondence (Emergence of New Role). I began to shed the guise of the strictly objective researcher, and allowed my own style of inquiry and interaction to develop. I did not abandon a questioning stance, but my questions were now more firmly rooted in what Homa had written. For example, I wrote the following note.

> It was very interesting to read about what helps you to learn English . . . not being afraid to ask questions and listening to other people speaking English etc. There was something in your letter, though, that confused me. You said, " . . . it's boring to write and sometimes I like writing because I have a lot to write about a subject and I don't want to stop writing." Could you explain what you mean? For example, what do you find boring about writing? When do you have a lot to write about? It would be very helpful to me if you could give examples. Thank you.

In addition, I began to share personal information, such as telling her about my plans for a family vacation. In this way, we began to build upon each other's content, taking the lead from each other.

Stage III Correspondence: Personal Investment Still later in this project, I learned to share my own reading and writing processes and preferences, a characteristic of Stage III correspondence (Personal Investment). For example, I sent a draft of a memoir I had written in a summer institute about one of my sons being hit in the head by a very hard-hit baseball. When I wrote to Homa, I asked for help with this piece:

> I had a hard time working out the story and wrote many drafts. I wasn't sure how to indicate the sequence of events, the passage of time and the fear that I experienced. I'm still not satisfied with that. In fact, I hate the title [I called it 'Concussion' then, 'Vigil' now] as it doesn't capture the substance of the story; however, I haven't been able to come up with anything else yet. I have asked several friends to help me by reading it and making suggestions. I would really appreciate it if you would do the same.

In this letter, I came very close to corresponding as I would to another person with whom I shared common interests. But, in my attempts not to write down to Homa, I had apparently frustrated her, at least at first. When she wrote back about a month later, she commented on how she had not understood the story when she received the letter, but had returned to it later. She commented on what she had liked in the memoir and what had confused her, and offered some suggestions:

> I recieved your letter a few weeks ago. I'm sorry that I didn't get a chance to answer it right away. At first when I got your letter I lost it for a week or so but, when I found it, I didn't know what to write to you. I didn't underestand your story so I put it off. . . . When I finaly decided to answer your letter I read your story again and I understood it more and I liked it. What I liked about it was the second part of your story. The way you made it interesting for the readers, like I kept on wondering what was going to happen to Patric. was he going to loose his memory or what. What I think I would change about the story would be, I would explain more about Patrick hitting his head. What he hit it with and. . . . Also the other thing that confused me was that you jumped from being in the baseball field to being at home. The last thing that I would say that you should write more about is that, you didn't say anything

about Patric being those peoples son or what ever. Other than that it was a very nice story and I enjoyed reading it.

Write soon

Despite having difficulty understanding my story, Homa persevered and gave the kind of feedback that is useful to a writer. In fact, she devoted half of her one-page letter to giving me feedback. She expressed herself succinctly and directly, and I wondered how I could effectively share my writing with youngsters. This memoir had not been written for children, and I did not want to compromise myself as a writer, yet I wanted to be able to share my writing with children. When I write I do not want everything to be explicit, but it was clear to me that Homa had not been able to understand who the characters were, their relationship to Patrick, and how he was hit. In later drafts, I took her suggestions into consideration. This was the first time that I really sensed the degree to which I, as an adult and teacher, could learn from a younger reader and writer.

What I Learned from the Correspondence About Homa (and Myself) Careful examination of our letters persuades me that this correspondence gave Homa many opportunities to use the letter genre in authentic ways. It clearly gave her exposure and opportunities to write in a particular style (e.g., "I would appreciate it if you would write comments . . ." or the salutation "Best wishes."). She was a thoughtful reader and writer who was quite capable of communicating her thoughts in English, even though she did not have native-like fluency. She expressed opinions, and explained and defended her position. She challenged me, her correspondent, in a feisty, energetic way. She was both dependent and independent as a writer—she complied with my requests, but she also initiated topics. Through this correspondence with Homa, I became more aware of my own reading and writing preferences and their role in my literacy experiences and processes. I learned from her how to improve my writing. I also learned how important it is to share the human side of me in literary-oriented letters.

A Change in Roles Over the two years of the project, our roles changed dramatically. For example, whereas I was once the all-knowing questioner, I became a learner and responder. I continued to ask Homa questions about the evolution of her writing over several drafts, but I also began to share my own writing and talk about what and who influenced it. Also, whereas I was once the only person to ask questions or make suggestions, Homa began asking questions of me relating to my literacy and offered help to me as a writer. Once I started to share my reading and writing experiences, goals, and struggles, the correspondence seemed to take on a new life.

This development suggests a very important finding as, despite the advice of educators who have explored dialogic writing extensively, many teachers continue to respond to their students in a strictly questioning mode, rather than investing themselves. Homa's responses nudged me to invest increasingly more of myself, which underscored the meaning-making and potentially revelatory process that is embedded in writing. This reality is reflected in the following letter from Homa, in which she hypothesized about my reading and writing preferences:

> Well enough about that junk!! The story I sent you with my last letter is long gone. Now I'm working on writing ssay (essay) tipe things. I think I have the same problems you're having with your writing. What I hate the most though about writing stories is starting and ending them. That's the hardest!! I read your story. I thought it was really good. You like writing mystory stories. Don't you!! Is that the kind of books you read? Have you written a ending for it yet? I wander what's going to happen! I thought the story was funny too. You explained things very well. and I have no questions except that what happened in the end. Well, I can't wait to read the ending of your story.

Homa had read some of my short stories and memoirs and, based on these pieces, she inferred that I liked writing mysteries. This was a revelation to me and, although I didn't read mysteries and wasn't attempting to write mysteries (what Homa referred to as *mystory*), I did like unresolved, ambiguous endings, both as a reader and as a writer. Until Homa made this comment, however, I wasn't particularly conscious of such a preference.

Implications of the Research for Teachers of Writing

As the research discussed in this chapter indicates, reflective writing can be a very beneficial experience for ELLs. This type of writing can provide a permanent record of students' experiences, knowledge, thinking, and learning processes. Particularly when an authentic dialogue between students and teachers is developed in reflective writing, the teacher can become an influential collaborator, mentor, and teacher—the quality of the teacher's response is critical to these exchanges. Teachers also need to exert great care in selecting the kinds of reflective writing experiences they offer their students. For example, several researchers report that journals and logs that do not incorporate a written response are less effective than reflective writing that has a dialogic component.

There are many ways of integrating reflective writing into the lives of children. For example, students may write in journals or logs on a daily basis or once or twice a week. They may write in journals for five minutes at the end of the day (e.g., to reflect upon what they have accomplished that day and as preparation for sharing their activities and learning with family members when they go home), or at other times during the day (e.g., after returning from a cross-age/buddy reading meeting with a younger or older student). They may write reflectively in one or more content areas (e.g., during language arts, math, science, or social studies classes). They may write with and without prompts. Their reflective writing may not be shared with others immediately or it may serve as the lead-in to other activities, such as a whole class discussion or the introduction to a new unit of study. Students may share journal entries, logs, and reflective letters with one or more peers, the teacher, or family members (e.g., as in a weekly record of class activities and individual progress and goals for the next week).

Although there are many, many ways of using reflective writing effectively, it is important to avoid overdoing it. I have found that it is a good idea to monitor very carefully how much reflective writing we ask students to engage in, as we can easily turn a very good idea into a chore. By being very clear about our goals when using reflective writing with ELLs, we can avoid tedium, and introduce students to a process for clarifying thinking, communicating with others, sharing opinions and emotions, deepening understandings, and supporting each other, as eighth grader Homa did when she identified and elaborated on writing processes that we shared.

7

The Influence of the Environment on Children's Writing

"I'm going to be a writer when I grow up."

Pablo, Third Grade Writer

One cold winter day in upstate New York, I walked with ten-year-old Pablo from his ESOL class in the school's basement to the nearby boiler room where I was going to interview him about his writing. The heat from the furnace kept us warm, and the rumble of the engine made it hard for us to hear each other unless we spoke more loudly than usual. But, Pablo was an enthusiastic writer who loved to talk about himself and his writing, and as I was a captivated audience, the unusual interview conditions did not hinder us. I asked him whether he thought he was a good writer. He nodded and said, "I'm going to be a writer when I grow up." When Pablo spoke these words, I was struck by their power. In my many contacts with children in schools in those days, I had only rarely heard children refer to themselves as writers. It had been rarer still for me to hear nonnative English-speaking children refer to themselves as writers, particularly if they were viewed as struggling readers and writers, as Pablo was. When I first interviewed him, I did not know him well, but I did know that he had been retained and that he was self-conscious about the form of his writing (peppered with reversals and misspelled words), which caused him to stand out uncomfortably from other children in his grade. I would not have been surprised, therefore, if he had said that he hated to write. But, he thought of himself as a writer. Why was this? I wondered.

Over the next four months, I was able to observe Pablo and fifteen other nonnative English-speaking children in grades two to three and four to six two to three times a week when they met with their ESOL teacher, Jean Olsen, after lunch each day in their respective classes. In that time, short though it was, I was able to gain a better understanding of these children's writing processes and begin to identify key elements that influenced their attitudes toward and understanding of the writing process (Samway 1987a, 1987b). I was interested in investigating this topic because there are so many children in our schools whose native language is not English and who have been classified as limited English proficient (LEP), and I had noticed that they were rarely expected to write, especially writing as a means of conveying meaning. Also, I had been profoundly influenced by the research of Donald Graves and his research team in New Hampshire with native English-speaking children (e.g., Calkins 1983; Graves 1975, 1982, 1983). This research revealed that children are capable of writing superbly when placed in an environment that stresses content over form, that gives time to writers, that teaches children writing skills and strategies according to their needs and in the context of their writing, and that acknowledges the important role that peers play in writing development. I wanted to know whether the same held true for nonnative English speakers, particularly as approximately thirteen percent of school children between the ages of five and fourteen were ELLs as a consequence of foreign birth or ancestry.

One ESOL Teacher Who Established a Workshop Approach to Literacy Learning

Olsen was one of only two ESOL teachers in the region that I could identify who used a learner-centered, workshop approach to writing; in fact, she was relatively new to writing workshop, having recently read the first edition of Lucy Calkins' book, *The Art of Teaching Writing* (1986), a copy of which she gave me as a gift and that is now weathered and kept together with tape that has yellowed over the years. The rest of the ESOL teachers either did not focus on writing at all or they used workbook pages with fill-in-the-blank sheets that are really grammar and/or vocabulary drills. Olsen talked enthusiastically about her ESOL program and the degree to which she was integrating literature and writing, she talked with animation about writing and conferring, and she talked about the need for children to read literature in order to become better writers.

Impact of the Workshop Experience on the Students

I found that the classroom environment had a marked impact on the children's writing and attitudes to writing. It was clear that the reading and writing experiences that Olsen offered her ESOL students, which were very different from what they encountered in their mainstream classes, affected the children very deeply. She believed that the children could succeed and conveyed this to her students through her interest in them, her encouragement of them, and her advocacy on their behalf with their mainstream teachers. Instead of focusing on their limitations, such as their nonstandardized oral and written English, she focused on their accomplishments and development, such as their writing of a compelling draft or thoughtful response to a peer's writing. The classroom was invitingly filled with books, children's work, and objects from around the world, and it often seemed that this ESOL class was the only time in the school day that the children were seen as having expertise. The children looked forward to their class, would burst through the door enthusiastically, and were engaged readers and writers, particularly once they had figured out that they could write about familiar content, such as personal experiences.

Influence of School and Community Writing Experiences on Children

Over the years, I have surveyed K–8 children about what writing is through questionnaires and interviews and have found that, unless they are in classrooms where children are writing for meaningful and authentic purposes, they invariably respond that writing is correct spelling, good handwriting, completing worksheets and, sometimes, writing a lot. The environmental influences on child writers are varied and profound. When children see others around them writing, whether at home (e.g., adults writing bills, lists, and notes, or on the computer seeking out information), at the store, in movies, or in school, they receive early messages about the role and importance of writing. All children who live in communities where there is a written language receive these messages, and children come to school having been exposed to a great deal of writing.

Influence of School Curricula on Children's Writing

More than a quarter of a decade ago, a team of researchers in the United Kingdom attempted to find out if there were qualitative and developmental differences in the writing of British students aged eleven through eighteen (Britton, Burgess, Martin, McLeod, and Rosen 1975). One of their most compelling findings was the huge influence of the school curricula, including exams, on the children's writing. For example, although the researchers found some developmental evidence that the young writers paid increasing attention over the grades to the needs of a wider audience, what they found more evidence of was writing for the teacher as examiner. They also found that, with greater age, the writers moved from relatively "undisciplined" *expressive* writing to *transactional* writing to *poetic* writing; curiously, *poetic* writing diminished in the writing of the oldest students, which the researchers attributed to the influence of the examination system, the highly competitive O-level and A-level exams that determine if students will go on to advanced study, and college/university entrance.

The Interplay Between Children's Understandings About Writing and School Writing

More recently, in research lasting two years involving much younger children in the United States, Purcell-Gates and Dahl (1991) investigated the literacy development of children from low-income homes who entered kindergarten in three inner-city schools in a large midwestern school district. Twenty-four children were African American and twelve were Caucasian. The literacy curricula in all three schools were traditional and focused heavily on skills development (e.g., letter recognition, letter formation, letter-sound correspondence), and the completion of many worksheets (e.g., of the 1,203 artifacts collected over the course of the two-year study, 986 were workbook pages or dittos).

In first grade, all the children were in a recently adopted basal reader program that used graded preprimers and primers, and writing involved copying words or sentences from the board. The researchers found that children who entered kindergarten with more fully developed schemata about written language were the most successful readers and writers at the end of first grade. They had a sense of the big picture for written language, that is, that it isn't just something you do in school, but serves to communicate in real world contexts, such as through signs, in books, and on games. Also, the most successful readers and writers did not rely on the school curricula, but independently experimented with print. They took the initiative and actively constructed their own knowledge about print.

Purcell-Gates and Dahl concluded that the experiences that children had had with written language was a major, defining factor in their literacy development. Also, the children who did the best in reading and writing in these skills-based classrooms were those who were self-directed in figuring out literacy; the least successful were those who were compliant. High levels of prior experience with literacy also appeared to support self-directed, independent learning. However, this wasn't always the case, as one of the children altered her stance over the course of the study. Whereas she entered kindergarten with considerable prior knowledge about print, she deferred completely to the curriculum in first grade and did not trust her prior knowledge to figure out the literacy system. Though Purcell-Gates and Dahl encountered only one child in their sample of thirty-five children who demonstrated this type of behavior, they expressed concern that it may reflect a sizable number of children with similar outlooks and behaviors.

Based on their findings, Purcell-Gates and Dahl argue on behalf of the following:

- Children should be taught about written language through meaningful, functional literacy events, and not through decontextualized skills instruction.
- All classrooms should be print rich, literate environments that facilitate self-sponsored learning and authentic opportunities for engagement in literate activities.
- Learning environments and curricula need to facilitate active learning on the part of students.
- Families should be meaningfully involved in the children's day-to-day lives in school.
- Instruction should be provided according to the individual child's conceptual development and needs.

The Influence of the Teacher: The Case of Tommy

First grade teacher, Mary Ellen Giacobbe (1986), described how environment influenced writers in her classroom. Unlike many teachers, Giacobbe did not demand accurate spelling in the early stages of writing and emphasized the importance of students writing messages that were important to them and that they would like to share, which the children began to internalize. For example, at first, Tommy wrote pieces using words that he knew how to spell, that is, safe words (e.g., I LOVE MOM). He continued writing messages (116) with safe words and then began to integrate unsafe words and inventions:

    I LOVE MES.   *(I love mice.)*
    CAT SI MES.   *(Cat is mice.)*

In the process of reading this piece, Tommy realized that it didn't make sense and inserted two words (MI/my and CANE/chasing) on the second line and a downward pointing arrow (117):

    I LOVE MICE.   *(I love mice.)*
    MI CAT SI CANE MES.   *(My cat is chasing mice.)*

When Tommy began to revise his writing, he tended to add information to the beginning of the story. By doing this, he demonstrated awareness of his audience, indicating that he was cognizant of their needs, and trying to answer their questions in his revised text. In one piece, *I want a parakeet*, which is about a time when he had thought about hurting his cat in order to get a parakeet (he was limited to two animals and already had a cat and a dog), he had clearly anticipated his audience's needs when he wrote at the end of the story, "Know why I wanted to get a parakeet?" As he became increasingly more aware of his audience (and the kinds of questions they would be likely to ask), Tommy began to write longer pieces, to write all he knew about a topic. Then, as he began to delete text that didn't belong, he didn't simply discard it, he incorporated it into a new piece.

Over the year, Tommy developed from a writer who wrote only for himself to one who anticipated the questions his audience might have. He realized that his writing needed to make sense to his audience. At first, his revisions were intended to make the text more understandable to himself, but as he developed as a writer, he revised to make his stories more understandable to others. Giacobbe comments that the attributes of writing that she valued freed the children to explore ideas, and they responded with much more fluid, interesting writing that was not controlled by the words they knew how to spell.

Influence of School Experiences on the Writing of ELLs: An International Perspective

The kinds of writing experiences offered to ELLs can have a profound impact on how they view writing, how they approach writing, and what they write. This is true regardless of whether the children are living in countries where English is the dominant language, such as the United States, or in countries where English is not the native language of many people. As with native speakers of English, offering authentic reasons and opportunities to write supports ELL writers.

A Case from Soweto, South Africa

In the mid-1980s, during apartheid in South Africa, a group of educators established an English language development project for children living in Soweto, a high-density black community on the outskirts of Johannesburg (Stein 1993). This was at a time when black South Africans experienced extreme discrimination, and one of the goals of the project, in addition to enhancing the children's English language development, was to help them find their voices through reflecting critically on the conditions surrounding them. Although the native language of most Sowetans is one of several African languages, English is the language of education. Originally, the Schools' English Language Research Project (SPEAK) focused on oral language, but almost immediately, the project staff realized that it needed to incorporate a writing component. The children began to write and talk about their daily life experiences, such as bus, school and consumer boycotts called to protest apartheid. For example, one group of students wrote about an incident in which a Soweto woman broke the consumer boycott by buying groceries from a white-owned store.

When the teachers talked with the children about what they would like to read and write about, the children repeatedly asked to know more about their own history, the history of African people in South Africa. This led to the development of an oral history project that culminated in students writing and publishing a book, *My Own History Book*. Although the project arose out of students' interests, it sometimes encountered resistance from parents. For example, some parents were not comfortable being asked to recall "the bitterness of the past" or to discuss "family secrets" with their children. Project staff called a meeting with parents to explore these concerns, and ultimately the parents decided that the project was sound and supported it. Project staff report that motivation levels increased dramatically, and students became much more interested in learning English because the oral and written content of their learning experiences were of interest and importance to them.

A Case from a Refugee Camp in the Philippines

Lauren Hoyt (1993) worked in another non-U.S. context, that of a Southeast Asian refugee camp in the Philippines, and she described the role of *process writing* in an elementary program for Southeast Asian refugees living in a camp in the Philippines. The camp served refugees who were to be resettled in the United States. Instead of the typical EFL curriculum, with its emphasis on workbooks and oral and written exercises, Preparing Refugees for Elementary Programs (PREP) focused on hands-on experiences and meaningful language and literacy experiences, many of them taught in the context of content areas such as math, science, drama, and cooking.

Literacy instruction drew on the children's personal histories, and the use of their native language was encouraged and respected. Teachers used Language Experience Approach (LEA) extensively to introduce children to written English, and as students became more proficient in English, they took on more responsibility for the writing of their texts. About halfway through the eighteen-week course, teachers introduced their students to a process approach to writing as described by Graves (1983). Students wrote, conferred with peers and adults, revised their pieces, and published them for other students and family members to read.

Over the course of the eighteen weeks, students responded positively to these experiences and their writing showed remarkable development. For example, Somlith, whose writing development was discussed earlier, in Chapter 2 (Figures 2–5 to 2–8), wrote lists reminiscent of workbook exercises in the first two weeks in the program, but by the sixth week he was writing more complex sentences and locating them on the page as a narrative. By the end of the project, Somlith was writing stories, which included more complex grammatical structures.

A Case from Estonia

When Emma Rous (1993) visited Estonia one summer to teach English to Estonian thirteen- and fourteen-year-olds, she took suitcases of paperback novels and picture books so that students could choose their own books, write in reading response journals, and talk about books in class. For writing, students selected their own topics, conferred with peers and adults, revised their writing, and published some of their pieces. They wrote about personal experiences and concerns, something that they were not accustomed to in their Soviet-era schooling, but something that they reveled in. They worked hard to express themselves in English, even when they lacked the complex language they needed to explore meaningful issues such as suicide, pollution, the divorce of parents, and the death of friends. The students also wrote about happier topics, such as travel and music.

Although the program lasted only two weeks, students read and wrote a lot, and learned to express themselves in English with remarkable skill and effectiveness. For example, Annika wrote the following second draft of a piece (127) about her fear of war:

> I fear war because it is a horrow, and angry people. I fear stay alone here world without a friends. I not want be outcast. Still I fear dark

and between too large expanse. Also own impending life, as I no know what me before expect. I desire these fears not at all know.

This piece is clearly not that of a native English speaker and contains multiple errors that are often found in the writing of ELLs, such as in how she expresses negation (e.g., *I [do] not want be outcast*), word choice (e.g., *outcast* for *alone*), and the absence of articles (e.g., *Still I fear [the] dark*). However, Annika is very successful at conveying her fears and her message is very evocative, despite her still limited command of English.

A Case from England

Rebecca Huss (1993) conducted a year-long participant observation study into the beginning writing development of Punjabi-speaking Pakistani students aged five to six in a multiethnic elementary school in the north of England. Huss found that having control over what to write had a profound and positive impact on the ELLs. For example, one student, Saira, indicated that she disliked *Monday News* as she wasn't taken places on weekends, and therefore didn't feel that she had anything to write about. However, when given opportunities to select her own topics, she wrote about her friends in school and school events, and also began to write fictional pieces. Huss found that when children had freedom over their writing topics, their writing became more expansive and less stilted.

In a later report on this research, Huss (1995) explored the role of talk in the children's writing development. The classroom teacher believed that ELLs needed to be given both topics and language models during prewriting group discussions in order to be able to write. Huss found that, although some children benefited from these group discussions prior to writing, this was not true for all children. She found that talk was very important in the process of writing a piece, but not in the way that the teacher intended. For example, talk was important to the children as part of the ongoing process of writing, as when they asked for help with spelling a word, drawing an object, or clarifying events that they were writing about.

Influence of School Experiences on the Writing of ELLs in the United States

There is considerable evidence that the writing development of ELLs in the United States is affected by the kind of classroom environment in which they are placed, whether they are placed in bilingual or English-medium classrooms. For example, Townsend and Fu (1998) documented an immigrant Chinese boy's writing development in his first year in the United States. The researchers attributed his rapid development to the kind of interactive classroom in which he was placed and in which he had multiple opportunities to interact meaningfully with others and with native English speakers.

Similarities and Differences in Classrooms That Foster Writers

There is evidence that, although environmental factors, including teachers' expectations, can have a profound impact on students' writing, there isn't a single type of classroom environment that fosters effective writing. For example, Ammon (1985) identified two classrooms where gains in writing were markedly better than in other classrooms. One of the classrooms was made up of Chinese-speaking children, and the other was made up of Spanish speakers. Ammon observed surface differences in these two classrooms. For example, the Chinese-speaking children were in a classroom where they tended to stay at their seats, and where most instruction was whole class. In contrast, the Spanish speakers were in a classroom where they moved around more freely, and where their teacher was more likely to teach groups of students.

Ammon also noted similarities in how the two teachers approached writing, including the following:

- They regarded writing as an act of communication about important content (and students often had choice over topics).
- They responded to the content of the writing and expressed interest in the content, which appeared to enhance students' sense of authorship.
- They paid attention to the form of written language through providing targeted feedback. The teachers also expected students to apply what they had been taught and make appropriate revisions.
- They provided time for students to write. Students wrote often, usually every day, and they wrote a lot. Ammon suggests that this led to a level of automaticity that is particularly helpful to emergent writers, including those writing in a nonnative language.
- They facilitated rich oral input in English through teacher talk, student talk, and reading (which involved a lot of talk in order to clarify meaning).
- They engaged students in rich reflection on and talk about language.
- They individualized instruction (e.g., through one-on-one writing conferences).

Lots of Writing, But Not Much Authentic Writing

In a four-month observational study involving nine teachers, McCarthey, García, López-Velásquez, Lin, and Guo (2004) investigated the writing opportunities offered to fourth and fifth grade ELLs in three distinct instructional contexts in one school: English-medium classes, English as a Second Language (ESL) classes, and native language classes (Spanish or Chinese [Mandarin]). The ELLs' daily schedule included

30–160 minutes of ESL instruction, 125–225 minutes in an English-medium class, and 45 minutes of instruction in the native language—students who were newcomers spent more time in ESL classes. That is, the students had at least three teachers each day. Also, the teachers had many students, and they did not meet to discuss their respective classes or students.

The researchers observed in classrooms, followed students through an entire school day, interviewed teachers and students, and collected writing samples representative of the kinds of writing found in the various classrooms. Although students were exposed to writing experiences often associated with a writing workshop (e.g., drafting and revising), none of the teachers had established a writing workshop and they did not incorporate minilessons, conferences, or authors' chair, and students rarely had choice over what they would write about. In fact, many writing assignments were aligned with the state test, which emphasized a five-paragraph essay.

Writing experiences in the English-medium classrooms included integrated reading and writing activities across the curriculum (e.g., research reports and book summaries), and journal writing. In ESL classes, students engaged in a variety of writing-based activities, including content-area writing (e.g., science worksheets, summaries of what they had learned, and observational logs), book reports, essays, and journals. They were allowed to write in their native languages, but were encouraged to switch to English as soon as possible. In native language classes, writing was not a priority, and writing instruction reflected "cultural definitions of writing" (367), such as correct formation of characters and pointing to passages in Chinese language textbooks that could be used as models. In Spanish language classes, students' writing was corrected for grammatical and spelling accuracy. In all cases, the teachers were very aware of the state-mandated testing requirements.

Students' comments indicated that they understood their various teachers' writing-related expectations, but they did not appear to understand the purposes for writing that they encountered. For example, one student from Taiwan, Paul, expressed confusion over being asked to write a thank-you note after a field visit. He said, "After our visit, don't we applaud? In that way we can show appreciation" (371). That is, writing was not seen as serving an authentic purpose, except to complete a school assignment. Students, particularly those born outside the United States, often did not understand the purpose of dialogue journals, in which they corresponded with their teachers, and in which the teacher often asked questions. In cases where the ESL teacher did not speak the language of the students and students wrote in their native language, there were instances of miscommunication (e.g., a student writing about Thanksgiving and the teacher responding with questions about how the student was adjusting to school).

Although there were variations in the number of opportunities students had to read (and respond to) peers' writing, overall students wrote for their teachers and they tended to consider that they were writing for only their teachers, even though they shared writing done at home with their family members. This may reflect the children's cultural backgrounds and previous school experiences (e.g., in China and

Taiwan, children were required to think through their writing carefully before actually picking up a pen, and in Mexico, children tended to ask for help that focused on mechanics rather than content).

The students actually had many opportunities to write, but most of it consisted of summaries of what had been learned or experienced in class. Despite a lack of understanding of many of the writing activities they were asked to engage in, the students successfully negotiated the varied expectations and activities of their many teachers; however, they did not appear to enjoy writing, and sometimes resisted it, often subtly (e.g., writing very little in journals). McCarthey and colleagues conjecture that this may be due to several factors:

- Lack of understanding about why they were writing (purpose)
- Absence of a writing workshop environment in which students would have many opportunities to share their writing with peers and talk about writing with both peers and teachers
- Limited opportunities to write in the native language, which suggested a devaluing of the native language

Most of the writing was expository and did not draw on the students' experiences or allow them to write about their identities. Sometimes, students used writing assignments as a means to do so, as when Manuel, a student from Peru, wrote about his Peruvian origins in response to a prompted journal writing assignment (see Figure 7–1); open-ended journals appeared to be the most effective writing in allowing the students to make connections between their experiences and their writing. The researchers found that students had few culturally responsive writing experiences.

Peer Support and the Role of Audience

In participant observation research, Carole Urzúa (1986, 1987) investigated how children used a process approach to writing, particularly ways in which children helped each other as writers and the impact of audience on the children's writing. Urzúa and an ESOL teacher, Sue Braithwaite, met with groups of intermediate grade transitional ELLs who were considered orally strong in English, but reading below grade level. They met once a week for fifteen weeks with four students, two sixth grade boys (one Cambodian and one Laotian) and two Cambodian fourth grade girls (three of the children were in one class and one child was with another group of children). The children were not literate in their native languages and their only previous formal schooling had been informal language classes in Thai refugee camps.

The structure of the weekly meetings embodied some of the features of a writing workshop that Donald Graves had explored and developed in the course of his seminal longitudinal research into children's writing processes (e.g., 1982), and then wrote about for teachers in such publications as *Writing: Teachers and Children at Work*

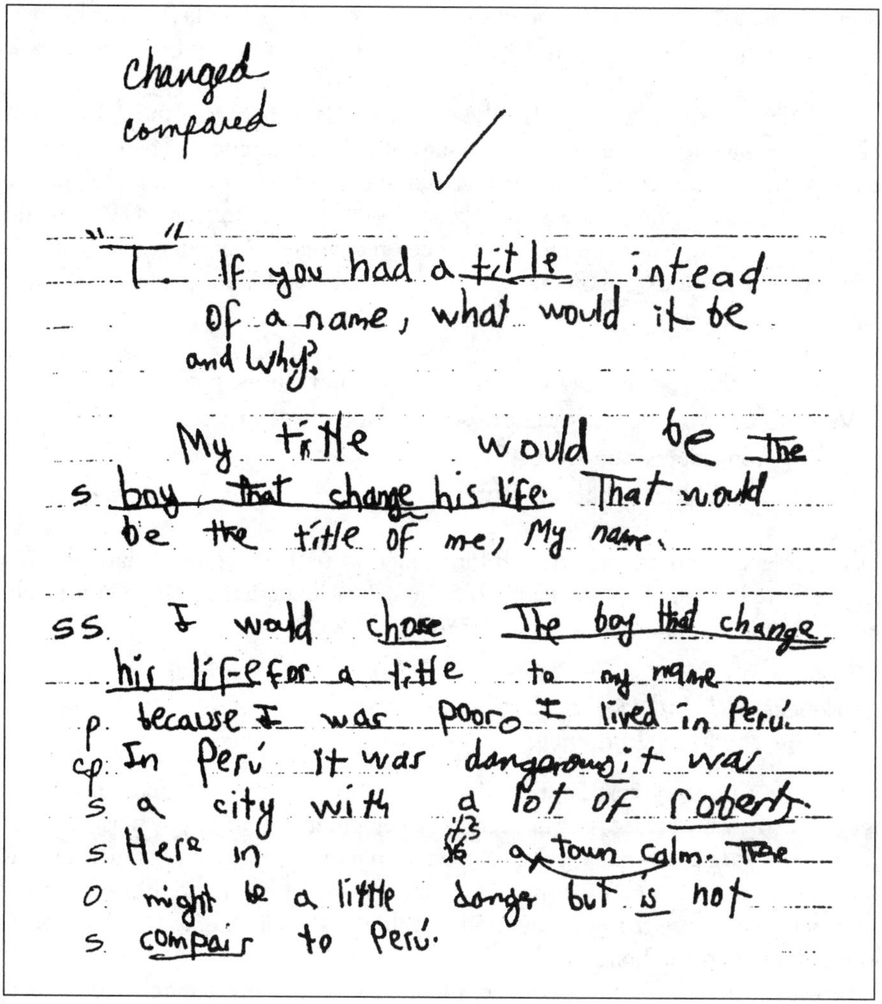

Changed
compared

" "
I. If you had a title intead of a name, what would it be and why?

My title would be The boy that change his life. That would be the title of me, My name.

ss. I would chose The boy that change his life for a title to my name
p. because I was pooro I lived in Perú.
cp. In Perú it was dangarous it was
s. a city with a lot of roberts.
s. Here in is a town calm. The
o. night be a little danger but is not
s. compair to Perú.

Figure 7–1. *Manuel's Writing About Peru*

(1983). Because the groups met only once a week, the children generally wrote at home. In the writing class, they conferred on their pieces with their peers, their ESOL teacher, and Urzúa, and all provided both oral and written feedback to the writers.

Urzúa found that the students learned to take the needs of their audience into account, developed a sense of voice, and acquired language that enhanced their writing. She found that questions from peers in group writing conferences had a profound impact on students' revisions, and this appeared to be related to a second influence, writing for an authentic, interested audience. The degree to which the students revised their writing varied according to the student. For example, Vuong rarely made changes to his writing until the end of the project, whereas Khamla frequently revised his writing in quite major ways in response to the feedback he got from his peers and the adults.

Children borrowed from each other (e.g., words, sentences, and format), and took into consideration what their peers suggested in conferences. The children also used oral language to refine their writing, asking each other the meaning of unfamiliar words, such as, "I don't know what a *laser* is" or "What is *fast food?*" (293). At first, the adults tended to exert the most influence on changes in language use, but eventually the students took a more active role. For example, Cham made the following suggestion to Vuong (294):

CHAM: In the beginning of the third paragraph, it can be put together.
VUONG: Oh, you mean, "I went to school. Nobody was there"?
CHAM: You stopped too soon.
VUONG: Yeah. Make that one sentence.

In this project, even though the children met with the teachers relatively infrequently, there is compelling evidence that the writing experiences offered to the children had a noticeable impact on their writing.

Experiences with Literacy at Home and School: Which Has the Most Influence?

I often hear educators commenting that home literacy practices have a profound impact on the school success and literacy development of children, suggesting that what they do as teachers has very little impact. In particular, there is a much-referred-to belief that children from low-income homes (many of whom are ELLs) do not do well in school because their families do not value or support literacy or model its use and importance in the home.

Research suggests that this is a very incomplete, if not inaccurate, view of reality (e.g., Taylor 1983; Orellana, Reynolds, Dorner, and Meza 2003). For example, Urzúa (1986) investigated the print experiences of four Southeast Asian, nonnative English-speaking students in their homes, and found that the amount of print in the home did not appear to have influenced the writing achievement of the children. The two students who struggled most as writers in English actually lived in highly literate homes (e.g., lots of printed materials, such as books, newspapers, brochures, maps, calendars, and newsletters in the native language and English). In contrast, the two students who made excellent progress as writers lived in homes where there was not very much print, either in the native language or in English, with the exception of a telephone book, Cambodian calendars, a few letters from relatives, and school books belonging to siblings.

Urzúa also visited the mainstream classrooms of these four students and found that the two students who struggled the most to write and find their writing voices were in classrooms where writing was almost nonexistent. For example, they completed workbook pages, copied dictionary definitions, and highlighted spelling words in word search puzzles. Urzúa did not observe any opportunities for students to share pieces of writing that were of importance to them, something that they responded to with enormous enthusiasm in their pullout ESOL class. In contrast, the two students who were much more successful writers were in mainstream classes where writing was much more a part of the school day. For example, in one class, the children wrote for at least an hour a day and had experience writing in multiple genres (e.g., fables, poetry, autobiographies, journal entries, and information pieces). Urzúa argues that the school environment exerted a very profound influence on how the students approached writing, viewed themselves as writers, and developed as writers.

Influence of the Environment on Children Writing Bilingually

Many myths surround the teaching of ELLs, including the notion that teaching them in their native language will impede their development in English. In the United States, ill-informed policies have often made it difficult to educate children bilingually, that is, teach them in their strongest language (their native language), while also teaching them English. This is true for several states, including my own, California, which has large numbers of ELLs. Nevertheless, bilingual programs still exist and there are efforts amongst bilingual and nonbilingual educators to enhance the underdeveloped national resource of bilingual/biliterate people.

In some cases, English-medium teachers express their appreciation of and respect for the home languages of their students through displaying bilingual signs and by purchasing bilingual books, and books in languages other than English for their classroom libraries. Sometimes they encourage their students to write in their native languages and to collaborate with other students in writing bilingually, particularly when one of the students is an emergent writer in English. In pointing out the importance of encouraging students to use their native language as they figure out how to write in English, Hudelson (1989) comments:

> If children feel free to use their native language, they may write more than if they feel constrained not to use it. Feeling comfortable narrating stories in a language children speak fluently provides a natural and authentic opportunity for fluent speakers to repeat their words in English, thus providing a model of fluent English and needed comprehensible input, which may later be used for further production. Allowing the native languages may make children feel comfortable and give them access to more input than they would have otherwise, thus contributing to, rather than retarding, their growth as users of English. (96)

The Impact of Holistic Approaches on Kindergarteners' Writing

Kuball and Peck (1997) investigated the impact of whole language instructional approaches on the writing development of Spanish- and English-speaking kindergarten children in bilingual classes in a year-round, multitrack school. The three elements investigated were:

- Children's self-concept as writers. For example, could the children write their name, a story, and a book?
- Compositional skills. They identified four stages, beginning with "writes a one-word statement" and ending with "writes a long story of four or more sentences with a plot, or a long letter that focuses on a single subject."
- Grapho-phonemic development. They used an eight-stage scale to assess this category.

The researchers found that the writing skills of the Spanish-speaking children were as developed as those of the English-speaking children, although there were slight differences across categories of writing. For example, the Spanish-speaking children tended to outperform the English-speaking children in the grapho-phonemic category. In contrast, the English-speaking children performed a little better than the Spanish-speaking children in compositional skills and also displayed a slightly higher self-concept as writers. They also found no evidence that the Spanish-speaking children were linguistically deficient, as is often claimed. For example, there were no occasions when the children used *cosa*/thing in place of a specific noun. Clearly, when provided with meaningful opportunities to write, the children were able to write, whether in their native language or in English.

Children Mediating Their Learning Experiences

Hudelson (1989) worked with two native Spanish-speaking students, Roberto and Janice, who were emergent speakers of English when they entered second grade. In their mainstream class, they had no authentic opportunities to write; instead, writing involved copying letters, syllables, words and sentences, and completing modified cloze exercises. However, over the course of the year, the children worked with Hudelson about twice a month, and here they had support in writing original messages. Although they were initially constrained by their classroom writing experiences, they began to respond favorably to Hudelson's invitations to be writers. For example, toward the end of the year, Janice was able to work for over half an hour writing a story to accompany a wordless picture book by Mercer and Marianne Mayer, *A Boy, a Dog, a Frog, and a Friend* (1971). She asked for translations of words she did not know in English (e.g., *tail, fishhook, die*), and sounded out unfamiliar words as she drew on her developing awareness of English spelling. Janice frequently used her native language to query Hudelson about how to write words and expressions in

English. This is very similar to what adults may do when speaking a nonnative language, for example, when we turn to someone and ask, "How do you say . . . ?" and then incorporate that information into our next utterances, whether oral or written.

In contrast with Janice, Roberto's writing remained limited (e.g., labels for pictures, phrases, and lists of words), and he was reluctant to write his own messages (as opposed to copying or writing from memory). Also, unlike Janice, he rarely interacted with Hudelson about his attempts at English writing, appearing to believe that what he wrote must be correct, and not realizing that he could avail himself of his and Hudelson's knowledge of Spanish. These two children point to how differently students mediate the learning experiences that teachers provide them. Had Roberto had more exposure to an environment where his native language was viewed as an asset and a resource for learning English, it is possible that he may have been able to respond to invitations to write more readily.

The Impact of Teachers' Beliefs and Behaviors on Children's Writing

In one of the first longitudinal studies investigating the writing and writing processes of bilingual children in nontest settings, Carole Edelsky (1986) and her research team collected data four times over the course of a school year. They collected multiple sources of data, including the writing of first, second, and third graders, interviews with teachers and instructional aides, and classroom observations. Edelsky found that the environment influenced the children's writing as a consequence of how teachers' beliefs about writing informed the learning activities they provided for their students. She comments that this influence was direct, such as through the beliefs and values they held (e.g., valuing and encouraging length and sound-based spelling strategies); and through the modeling and coaching they engaged in (e.g., requests to "Tell me more" led to add-on revisions). Edelsky notes that the influence of the teachers was also indirect, for example, through the materials they provided (e.g., unlined paper seemed to encourage children to number lines), and through their beliefs and values (e.g., believing it best to leave children alone while writing seemed to lead to children struggling repeatedly with their self-invented problems).

Although the district's bilingual program endorsed a whole language approach to literacy development, with an emphasis on meaning-making and writing complete texts (as opposed to more traditional school-based writing activities, such as completing worksheets and writing paragraphs), there was considerable variation in the degree to which teachers offered children meaningful writing experiences, and this was reflected in the children's writing. For example, Edelsky reports that, whereas children in one class, where the teacher let the children choose their own topics and genres, wrote jokes, songs, and movie summaries, the children in a phonics-oriented class wrote basal-like texts, such as *amo a mi mama*/I love my mother, and *papa oso casa*/father bear house (122).

In a related report, Edelsky and Jilbert (1985) found that children's writing plateaued when they lacked guidance from adults, such as when they (a) did not have meaningful and authentic opportunities to write, (b) were not taught increasingly more complex skills and strategies, (c) did not have conversations about literature to learn about writers and writing, (d) did not have opportunities to confer about their writing, to revisit, revise, and edit, and (e) did not publish their writing. Edelsky and Jilbert concluded that, without continuing guidance from others about why we write, thereby expanding our options and writing repertoires, children's writing can stagnate. Also, they argue that writing exercises, which many of the children had lots of experience with, don't take the place of real writing accompanied by good, focused instruction.

The researchers found evidence of the impact of teachers' beliefs and values about writing on the children's writing. For example, one teacher valued length, and this was reflected in the children writing long pieces with large print, big spaces, and multiple repetitions of words. Another teacher believed that children could not write until they had mastered spelling, and she provided considerable phonics instruction to her first graders before finally allowing them to write. Their (stylized) writing resembled their phonics workbook exercises, as the following example illustrates (65, 66):

As written by child	Standardized version	English translation
Es un corro	Es un carro	It's a car
Le niño no ida	El niño no iba	The child didn't go
La casa de mamá	La casa de mamá	Mama's house
Le corro de papa	El carro de papá	Papa's car
Tony ida a su casa	Tony iba a su casa	Tony was going to his house
mama ama a papa	Mamá ama a papá	Mama loves papa
Es una niña	Es una niña	It's a girl
Es una mamá	Es una mamá	It's a mama

In contrast, another teacher believed that children could write, and her students wrote songs, jokes, and poetic pieces, including the following (the researchers standardized the mechanics) (66):

Todos los días cae nieve en todas las partes. Y también caiá lluvia en todas las partes y un señor se robó y la policiá iba. La policiá agarría al señor y lo llevó a la cárcel y allí se estuvo todos los días. Era cuando estaba cayendo nieve.

Every day snow falls everywhere. And also it was raining everywhere and a man robbed and the police came. The police got the man and took him to jail and there he stayed for evermore. It was when the snow was falling.

As these examples show, teachers' beliefs about writing and how to support writers can have a profound impact on what and how children write.

Benefits of Teachers Adjusting Their Instruction to Students' Needs

In research conducted in the same state almost a decade later, Serna and Hudelson (1993) reveal the role of the environment in supporting the writing development of Spanish-dominant children who attended kindergarten and first grade in a bilingual school that had adopted a whole language approach. In case study research, they followed the literacy development of several children identified as at risk. They found that writing development was highly idiosyncratic and the children developed at different rates. Also, the children benefited from the teachers adjusting their instruction to meet the students' individual needs. Although the children entered kindergarten with different literacy experiences, their teachers responded to their individual needs. For example, whereas Cecilia quickly became an independent writer who was not dependent on an adult to transcribe her messages for her, Diana needed this kind of support more and for a longer period of time. However, she did become more independent, passing through stages in which the entire text was transcribed by the teacher, to jointly writing the text with the teacher. Serna and Hudelson concluded that the classroom environment and adjusted learning experiences allowed the two girls to construct meaning as writers (and as readers).

What Do ELLs Need to Become Successful Writers?

When children have meaningful, purposeful reasons to write, which often involve having an authentic audience, their writing is affected. For example, compare the following two pieces of writing, both of which are on self-selected topics. The first (Figure 7–2) is an excerpt from a six-page letter written by first-grader, Clara, to her teacher, Jennifer Jones-Martinez, after she had been doing somersaults in the classroom and her teacher had suggested that she think about why that may not have been a good idea. These two pages are the first and last pages of Clara's response, a letter of apology/explanation . . . and an accusation!

The second piece, "If I were a Popsicle" (Figure 7–3), was written by second grader, Patricia. This piece by Patricia, who attended a different school, resembles prompted writing, but was, in fact, a self-selected topic and was written during the one time a week when students had free choice over their writing topics. As can be seen, Clara's letter has an energy and purposefulness to it that is missing from Patricia's piece of writing. Whereas Clara wrote on a daily basis, wrote for multiple audiences (including the designer of the standardized test that she and most of her peers hated), and conferred regularly with her peers and teacher, Patricia had few occasions to write or to write for meaningful purposes.

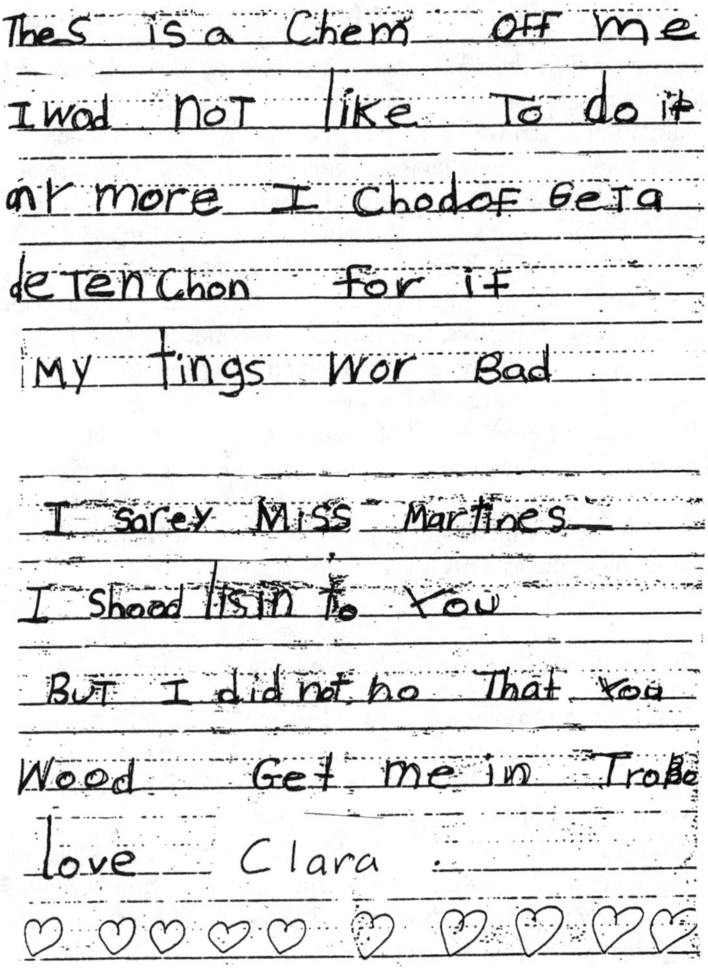

Thes is a Chem off me
I wod not like To do it
any more I chodof beTa
deTenchon for it
My tings wor Bad

I sorey Miss Martines
I shood lisin to you
BuT I did not ho That you
Wood Get me in TroBo
love Clara

This is a shame of me. / I would not like to do it / any more.
I should have got a / detention for it. / My things were bad.

I'm sorry, Miss Martinez. / I should (have) listen(ed) to you, /
but I did not know that you / would get me in trouble /
love, Clara

Figure 7–2. *Clara's Letter to Teacher (First and Last Page)*

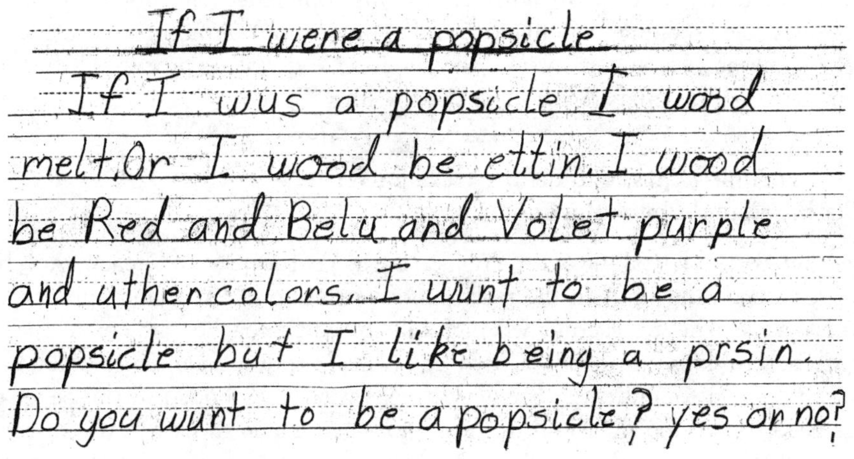

> If I were a popsicle
> If I wus a popsicle I wood
> melt. Or I wood be ettin. I wood
> be Red and Belu and Volet purple
> and uther colors. I wunt to be a
> popsicle but I like being a prsin.
> Do you wunt to be a popsicle? yes or no?

If I were a Popsicle / If I wus a popsicle I wood / melt. Or I wood be ettin (eaten). I wood / be Red and Belu (blue) and Volet (violet) purple / and uther colors. I wunt (want) to be a / popsicle but I like being a prsin (person). / Do you wunt to be a Popsicle? Yes or no?

Figure 7–3. *Patricia's Piece About a Popsicle*

What Type of Writing Program Is Best for ELLs?

Since the 1980s, more attention has been paid to teaching writing in American classrooms than was the case in the past. There is considerable variation, however, in how writing is taught and the kinds of writing experiences that children are offered. In some classrooms children are invited to generate and write about their own topics, whereas in other classrooms teachers always provide prompts. In some classrooms children write on a daily basis for 45–60 minutes each day, whereas in other classrooms children write sporadically, when there's time or when the teacher remembers. In some classrooms writing and content area subjects are naturally integrated, whereas in other classrooms writing is treated as a separate discipline from other content areas. In some classrooms children write to inform and entertain many audiences (e.g., peers, teachers, family members, and unknown readers), whereas in other classrooms children write primarily for the teacher and a grade.

In some classrooms children are taught how to improve their writing in contextualized ways (e.g., during a writing conference or in a class minilesson whose focus is selected based on needs the teacher observes or students request), whereas in other classrooms children complete skills sheets that are rarely grounded in the students' observed needs. In some classrooms writing conferences address a wide range of writing-related issues (e.g., craft elements, mechanics, processes; problems and accomplishments), whereas in other classrooms conferences are limited to writing mechanics (e.g., spelling, punctuation, and paragraphing). And, in some classrooms teachers talk about and demonstrate their writing and writing processes, whereas in other classrooms teachers never share their writing.

So, answer your own question

Opposing Approaches to Teaching ELLs to Write: Skills-Based and Communicative

Over the years of working with English language learners and teachers, I have observed trends and shifts in the teaching of writing to ELLs. Trends appear to fall into two approaches to teaching writing: skills-based approaches and communicative approaches. In skills-based approaches (see Figure 7–4), it is common to find limited, if any, attention to authentic, actual writing, which is grounded in the belief that ELLs need to develop their oral fluency before being able to write. Also, there are underlying assumptions that writing is made up of many grammatical subparts, which need to be taught sequentially in order for students to be able to use them accurately—inevitably, correctness often becomes the goal, rather than the content of the message. Skills-based approaches continue to dominate instruction, particularly where teachers and districts rely on published writing programs.

In communicative approaches to writing instruction (see Figure 7–5), the goal is one of expressing ideas and emotions in print. Hence, although it is recognized that writing is made up of skills, they are taught as needed, rather than in a predetermined sequence. There is an underlying assumption that children learn to write through the act of writing. Since the mid-1980s, a communicative approach to writing instruc-

Approach to Writing	Features of the Approach	Underlying Philosophy
Delay writing until oral language is developed	• No writing	• Written language is predicated on fully developed oral language
Focus on teaching writing skills	• Worksheets (e.g., practicing a grammatical structure) • Sentence-level writing • Error correction • Filling in missing words • Commercial writing programs with a skill and sequence progression	• Writing is made up of subskills that need to be taught sequentially • Only when the component parts are under control can ESOL students be expected to write longer texts

Figure 7–4. *Skills-Based Approaches to Writing*

tion has been most often articulated in some form of a writing workshop (with varying degrees of learner-centered instruction, self-selection of topics, and writing across genres and content areas). There have been several manifestations of this type of

Approach to Writing	Features of the Approach	Underlying Philosophy
Language Experience Approach (LEA)	• Teacher writes down exactly what students dictate • Patterned writing • Written texts are used to develop reading • Skills are taught based on the features of the text	• Students need considerable support to become writers • Students' messages and intentions are valued • Reading and writing are interconnected
Free write	• Students write single drafts • Some of the writing is published • Minimal attention is paid to teaching skills and strategies	• Having opportunities to write is the best way to become a writer
Writing workshop	• Students select topics and genres • Students confer with each other and the teacher • Teachers teach about writing skills and strategies in mini-lessons and conferences • Students are urged to revise their writing • Students publish their writing	• The message is the most important aspect of writing (versus mechanics) • Writing is socially constructed • Writing is developmental in nature and teachers should respond to the needs of students
Updated writing workshop: Unit of study	Similar to writing workshop above, but: • Inquiry approach to studying key topics (e.g., a genre or an author) • Reading literature to inform writing (touchstone and mentor texts) • Immersion in a topic before writing	• A very strong connection between reading and writing—studying the craft of writing • Too little attention has been paid to writing well and learning from accomplished writers

Figure 7–5. *Communicative Approaches to Writing*

communicative approach to writing instruction, and it continues to evolve, as the reference to "Updated writing workshop: Unit of study" at the bottom of Figure 7–5 illustrates.

A Unit of Study Approach to Teaching Writing

The most recent iteration of a communicative approach to teaching writing, a unit of study approach, has only recently been described in work with ELLs. Karen Smith, Cecilia Espinosa, Ernestina Aragon, Rebecca Osorio, and Nora Ulloa (2004) report on a collaborative effort they engaged in to better support fifth grade writers in dual-language classrooms; they embarked on a memoir unit of study. They describe how, at the beginning of their work together, the students had access to a writing workshop experience (e.g., they selected their own topics, were engaged and enthusiastic writers, willingly conferred with peers and their teacher, were taught through minilessons, and finished pieces were published). On the surface, things seemed to be going well with these predominantly Latino/a students whose native language was Spanish and who were reasonably literate in both Spanish and English, but the teachers were concerned by what appeared to have become a routine without room for growth. They found themselves wondering, "Is this all there is to writing?" (3).

An Alternative to a Routinized Writing Workshop

The authors subsequently embarked on curriculum development focused on units of study, such as author studies and genre studies. After extensive reading and talking together, they decided to focus on a memoir unit of study because the students came from a marginalized group and use of their native language in schools was being attacked by a proposition banning bilingual education in Arizona. The group of educators felt that a memoir study might be the last opportunity for the students to talk and write about their lives in their native language in school.

Teachers Immersing Themselves in the Memoir Study

Both the adults and the students immersed themselves in the study, which was often revelatory. For example, two of the adults, both Latinas, appreciated having opportunities to read memoirs that were grounded in similar experiences that they had had, and commented on how in their own schooling, they had grown up reading and valuing mainstream cultural experiences; they vowed to provide their own students with a different experience, an opportunity to see themselves in books, as well as an opportunity to encounter the lives of other cultures. Their goal in this unit of study was to give voice to their students and an opportunity to write effectively, to "write in order to speak personally and truthfully about their lives in thoughtful and skillful ways" (9).

A Successful Unit of Study

The memoir unit of study experience was successful. By the end of a three-week immersion in and discussion about books, students had each generated about twelve to fifteen seed ideas in their notebooks, and together had come up with a working definition of what a memoir is. They also tried techniques they had noticed in the books they read, such as what they called *getting to the point*, in which a writer transports readers through a long trip without including all the tedious details. For example, Antonio used this technique when writing about a trip he made, and wrote (14):

> Empezamos el viaje por la mañana, miramos el sol mover por el cielo y el cielo cambió de color. La alegría se convirtió en aburrimiento.
>
> We began our trip in the morning, we watched the sun move across the sky and the sky changed color. Happiness turned into boredom.

Students also incorporated a technique that allows writers to capture the voices of bilingual people in very specific contexts, code-switching. When Irma wrote her memoir, she included a leave-taking involving a monolingual, Spanish-speaking aunt, and wrote: "We had fun, fun, fun for the rest of the time. At noon we had to leave. When we got to my aunt's house, we thanked her, but she said, 'No te apresures. No es todo. Espera hasta mañana/*Don't hurry. There's more. Wait until tomorrow*" (15; translation mine).

Validating Students' Lives

One goal of this unit of study was to validate students' lives and give students an opportunity to make them public and "visible to others," and many of the students wrote memoirs that were specific to a Latino/a experience and perspective. Smith and colleagues comment that, even though not all children wrote about a "culturally relevant" experience, all students "bought into the value of telling their story and making some aspect of their life visible for others to read" (17). An example of a culturally relevant memoir is Jennifer's, "When I Was Young in Mexico," which is about growing up in Mexico (see Figure 7–6). When writing this piece, Jennifer used a technique that she had learned from Cynthia Rylant's *When I Was Young in the Mountains* (1982), a vignette-to-vignette pattern of organization.

Profound Changes in What Teachers Taught

Another development was in what the teachers focused on when teaching. Whereas in the past, they had focused on mechanics, now they focused more on revision and taught about a range of writing issues, including point-of-view, how to reveal characters, narrowing the story to the most important part, and story structures (e.g., circular

When I Was Young in Mexico

When I was young in Mexico, Abuelito would come home in the evening sweaty and tired. He would go to bed without saying a word to anyone. We thought that was funny.

When I was young in Mexico, Abuelita would have cups of atóle waiting for us in the morning. Sometimes it was too hot to drink, so we would sit and talk until the atóle cooled.

What I was young in Mexico, my family would go to the canal. Sometimes bees would swarm around us, but we would run around and jump in the water.

When I was young in Mexico, we would feel the chickens and the dog on my grandparents' farm while Abuelita went to the Mercado to buy food for dinner.

When I was young in Mexico, Abuelito would go in the chicken coop to catch a chicken. Abuelito would kill it. I had never seen anything like that before!

" . . . and then it was time to come home. I wished we had never left. I miss my family in Mexico very much.

Figure 7–6. *Jennifer's Writing*

texts, and connecting a series of vignettes with a repeated line or phrase). They also taught mechanics in their minilessons, and decided on topics based on the needs they observed in students' writing (e.g., punctuating dialogue differently in English and Spanish, and using ellipses). The authors conclude that they made substantive changes in how they taught writing in the following four dimensions.

- Authenticity—students were invited to write a memoir in order to "make their lives visible to others" (23). Instruction in and learning about writing elements and processes were all geared toward this goal, rather than as goals in and of themselves in a disconnected way.

- Explicit Content and Instruction—instruction was focused on features of and skills inherent in good memoir writing; in the past, teachers had given little attention to teaching about the particulars of the genres that students were writing. Now, the students "apprenticed themselves to writers of memoir and came to understand the power of memoir to speak to and make sense of their own lives" (23). Minilessons were connected to the needs of the students, rather than being randomly selected.

- Flexibility—instead of devoting most of the writing workshop time to independent writing, as had been the case in the past, they adopted a more "flexible" structure so that, in the beginning of the unit of study the classes spent a great deal of time reading and discussing memoirs, with writing being devoted to capturing memories and trying out writing techniques. However, in the last four weeks of the study, a lot of time was devoted to independent writing. The authors describe the change in this way: "We were now controlling the structure of writing workshop and not letting it control us" (24). Also, although students were obliged to write a memoir, they had choice over the topic.

- Inquiry and dialogue—through the memoir unit of study, teachers were able to investigate ways of supporting their students as writers, and their students were able to make their lives and life experiences public.

Features of a Unit of Study Approach

The unit of study approach that Smith and colleagues (2004) describe emerged from The Reading and Writing Project at Teachers College, Columbia University (see, for example, the August 1999 issue of *Primary Voices K–6*), and has been embraced by other writing teachers and organizations, such as the Noyce Foundation, which supports writing teachers in the San Francisco Bay area. In this approach, it is common for students and their teachers to engage in the following experiences as they explore how to become better writers of, for example, a particular genre (the steps are similar regardless of what the focus of inquiry/study is):

- *Best-Guess Gathering*—gathering books that represent the genre. Nia (1999) compares the process to a treasure hunt. The responsibility for gathering these books can be assumed by the teacher, can include the students, and can include the entire school community in searching out books that may represent the genre. Family members and friends may also participate.

- *Immersion*—through reading lots of books and talking about them, the students begin to identify craft elements that seem to be central to the genre (e.g., how a genre is structured and the kind of language that is used in the genre). Both reading and talk are critical to this stage so that students have opportunities to explore the veracity of the craft elements they are beginning to identify. That is, they individually and collaboratively begin to create a working definition of the genre.

- *Sifting*—the class identifies books that do two things: best represent the group's definition of the genre and can support them as writers. It is possible that texts that do represent the genre will be rejected because they are not like the texts that the students will write. Similarly, texts that represent the genre and *do* look like the kinds of texts that the students write may be discarded because the class does not think they are well written (or the teacher does not think that the content is appropriate). Teachers who have experience with a unit of study approach to writing find that it can take approximately two to three days to complete this process.

- *Second Immersion*—immersion in the books selected as best examples of the genre, and that most closely resemble the kinds of writing they will be doing; close attention paid to the craft details, such as leads and a simple but evocative style. At this stage, the teacher seeks out a *touchstone* text, a particularly well-written book she or he is likely to return to over and over again to demonstrate multiple features of writing. At the same time, each student is looking for *mentor texts*, those that they will probably refer to again and again and probably use as models (e.g., of text structure, language use, leads). In some cases, a particularly well-written touchstone text may be referred to over several units of study, for example, an initial author study and then studies on memoir writing and poetry writing. See Nia (1999) for further guidance on how to select touchstone texts.

- *Touchstone Try-Its*—the class rereads and talks about the touchstone text on several occasions in order to understand what the author did to write in such a compelling way (e.g., using short sentences for emphasis or using colloquial language in dialogue), so that they have access to additional strategies for their own writing. Through minilessons and conferences, the teacher encourages students to try out the "writing moves" that they have observed accomplished writers using. The students write these *try-its* in their writing notebooks and in their drafts, and if they like the outcome, they may incorporate one or more of them into their published writing.

- *Writing*—throughout the study, students are writing, jotting down *seed ideas* (see Fletcher 1996a, 1996b) and *try-its* in their writing notebooks, and writing and publishing other pieces that they have decided to pursue (e.g., they may be writing additional pieces that a previous unit of study inspired, such as writing poetry or how-to books). They will publish a piece for the genre study, but given all the work that has preceded it (e.g., in the sifting, immersion, and try-its stages), the writing of this piece is a continuation of what they have been already doing, rather than a sudden demand to now write a memoir (or essay or poem, etc.). That is, just as writing is a recursive process, so is the writing of a published piece for a unit of study. Depending on the age of students, the focus of the unit of study, and the progress of inquiry, publication is likely to occur about once every three to four weeks.

- *Reflecting/Assessing*—at the end of the study, the students and teacher reflect upon and assess individual student's accomplishments during the unit of study, which includes both the product (the piece of writing) and the processes involved in writing it. Some teachers ask their students to write a letter to readers in which they identify where the elements being tried or developed can be found in the piece of writing. This type of reflective assessment can be done orally and/or in writing.

Depending on the focus of the unit of study, the inquiry can last for as little as one week (e.g., a ministudy on revision) or up to about three to four weeks (e.g., a unit of study on poetry or nonfiction writing). Sometimes, a class will return to a unit of study later in the year so that students have time to process what they have learned and apply that learning over time to their writing (e.g., see Goldfarb 1999).

Theoretical Underpinnings of a Unit of Study Approach

A unit of study approach to writing workshop/teaching writing is a particularly rich illustration of the sociocultural nature of learning to write, one in which children become increasingly more competent through collaboration with (or apprenticeship to) more knowledgeable others, whether peers, teachers, or published authors. In this respect, it integrates Vygotsky's Zone of Proximal Development (1978). In addition, because children's interests and expertise are at the core of this approach, and writing instruction builds on students' interests, needs and areas of expertise, it is possible for all children to succeed, not just those whose home experiences with print are congruent with school literacies.

Implications of the Research for Teachers of Writing

Research discussed in this chapter points to the compelling influence of the environment on ELLs' writing. Hence, when writing is approached as the conveying of genuine messages, this is reflected in children's writing. When writing is approached as an exercise, a mechanism to practice discrete parts of language and writing, that is also reflected in ELLs' writing. ELLs are capable of conveying important thoughts in writing, even when they are new to the language, and they benefit from being challenged and supported as writers. Key findings in the research discussed in this chapter about the impact of the environment include the following:

- The school environment exerts a powerful influence on ELLs, so the kinds of writing experiences they encounter in school will have a profound impact on how they view and approach writing, and their success as writers.

- ELLs need to write from their first days in an English-speaking environment. They need to write often and for authentic purposes in order for writing to become an automatic part of their lives.

- It isn't enough to give ELLs time to write. There also needs to be time for focused instruction that is grounded in the needs of learners. That is, teachers need to observe carefully, engage with each writer, and teach according to observed needs.

- ELLs need time to read, think, talk, and write in order to become effective writers.

- What ELLs read affects what they write. Therefore, if their reading diet is limited to the stilted and inauthentic writing often found in basal readers, exercises, and worksheets, then their writing is likely to reflect this kind of writing. Or, if they are introduced to and discuss beautifully written, substantive texts, then their writing is likely to more closely resemble this kind of writing.

- Teachers' beliefs about writing (and what they value) affect ELLs' writing. Hence, if teachers value powerful leads and interesting and accurate information, that is what ELLs will attempt to incorporate into their writing. On the other hand, if teachers value length and correct spelling, that is what ELLs will focus on.

- Writing experiences need to allow ELLs to immerse themselves in, incorporate, and build on their knowledge of and expertise about communication, life, and literacy, while also extending it.

- Writing in the native language can be an invaluable resource to ELLs, and should be fostered whenever possible.

Revisiting the Survey

It may be interesting for you to revisit the survey at the beginning of Chapter 2, and see if you would modify any of your responses. As the research presented in this book indicates, ELL children can write in English before they are fluent speakers or readers of English, and the natural integration of all language modalities is beneficial to their language and literacy development. Also, and very importantly, ELLs benefit from being offered authentic reasons and opportunities to write, just as native English speakers do.

Although an occasional writing exercise may be enjoyable and even useful to ELLs, research indicates that they learn to write from writing naturally, from exploring how others write, from having opportunities to discuss their writing processes, development and goals with others, and from being taught writing skills and strategies in context and as needed. Teachers who are careful observers of children and who provide writing instruction geared to the observed needs of learners are likely to have more success than if they follow writing programs that have predetermined writing activities and teaching points, as these programs are not geared to the needs of any class or any learner at any given moment.

A still controversial topic in the United States is the role of the native language in the schooling of ELLs. Despite much of the politicized public rhetoric, research shows us that children who are participants in well-designed maintenance bilingual education programs (i.e., long-term instruction in both English and the native language) typically have greater academic success than those who are submerged in English (see Samway and McKeon 1999). The native language is a key component in any child's language and literacy development. The more literate a person is in the native language, the greater the ease with which that child is likely to become literate in English.

While the native language is often reflected in ELLs' writing (e.g., word order and spelling patterns reflective of the native language), this is a natural, developmental phenomenon that reflects the process of *creative construction*, illustrating how children are resourceful acquirers and learners of oral and print language. Although some educators fear that providing writing instruction in the L1 will cause confusion for ELLs, the research indicates that developing literacy in the L1 is a very important resource to students when writing in English.

References

AMMON, P. 1985. "Helping Children Learn to Write in English as a Second Language: Some Observations and Some Hypotheses." In *The Acquisition of Written Language*, ed. S. W. Freedman, 65–84. Norwood, NJ: Ablex.

ANDERSON. C. 2000. *How's It Going?: A Practical Guide to Conferring with Student Writers*. Portsmouth, NH: Heinemann.

APPLEBEE, A. N. 1978. *The Child's Concept of Story*. Chicago: The University of Chicago Press.

ATWELL, N. 1985. "Writing and Reading from the Inside Out." In *Breaking Ground: Teachers Relate Reading and Writing in the Elementary Years*, eds. J. Hansen, T. Newkirk, & D. Graves, 147–65. Portsmouth, NH: Heinemann.

———. 1987. "Building a Dining Room Table: Dialogue Journals About Reading." In *The Journal Book*, ed. T. Fulwiler, 157–70. Portsmouth, NH: Boynton/Cook Heinemann.

———. 1998. *In the Middle: New Understandings About Writing, Reading, and Learning*. 2d ed. Portsmouth, NH: Heinemann.

AUERBACH, E. 1989. "Toward a Socio-Contextual Approach to Family Literacy." *Harvard Educational Review* 59 (2): 165–81.

AVERY, C. [1993] 2002. *And with a Light Touch: Learning About Reading, Writing, and Teaching with First Graders*. Portsmouth, NH: Heinemann.

BARBIERI, M. 1987. "Writing Beyond the Curriculum: Why Seventh Grade Boys Write." *Language Arts* 64 (5): 497–504.

BEREITER, C. 1980. "Development in Writing." In *Cognitive Processes in Writing*, ed. L. W. Gregg & E. R. Steinberg, 73–93. Hillsdale, NJ: Lawrence Erlbaum.

BEREITER, C. & M. SCARDAMALIA. 1984. "Learning About Writing from Reading." *Written Communication* 1 (2): 163–88.

BIRNBAUM, J. C. 1982. "The Reading and Composing Behavior of Selected Fourth- and Seventh-Grade Students." *Research in the Teaching of English* 16 (3): 241–60.

BISHOP, W. 1999. *Ethnographic Writing Research: Writing It Down, Writing It Up, and Reading It*. Portsmouth, NH: Boynton/Cook.

BISSEX, G. L. 1980. *GNYS AT WRK: A Child Learns to Write and Read*. Cambridge, MA: Harvard University Press.

BLACKBURN, E. 1985. "Stories Never End." In *Breaking Ground: Teachers Relate Reading and Writing in the Elementary School*, eds. J. Hansen, T. Newkirk, & D. Graves, 3–13. Portsmouth, NH: Heinemann.

BLAIR, H. A. 1998. "They Left Their Genderprints: The Voice of Girls in Text." *Language Arts* 75 (1): 11–18.

BLOOMFIELD, L. 1933. *Language*. New York: Holt.

BOUTWELL, M. A. 1982. "Reading and Writing Process: A Reciprocal Agreement." In *A Study of Children's Rewriting*, comp. Lucy McCormick Calkins. Urbana, IL: National Council of Teachers of English. 423–432. ERIC ED 229 750.

BRIDWELL, L. S. 1980. "Revising Strategies in Twelfth Grade Students' Transactional Writing." *Research in the Teaching of English* 14 (8): 197–222.

BRITTON, J., T. BURGESS, N. MARTIN, A. McLEOD & H. ROSEN. 1975. *The Development of Writing Abilities*. London: Macmillan.

CALKINS, L. M. 1982. *A Study of Children's Revising*. National Council of Teachers of English. ERIC ED 229 750.

———. 1983. *Lessons from a Child: On the Teaching and Learning of Writing*. Portsmouth, NH: Heinemann.

———. [1986] 1994. *The Art of Teaching Writing*. Portsmouth, NH: Heinemann.

CARSON, J. G. 1992. "Becoming Biliterate: First Language Influences." *Journal of Second Language Writing* 1 (1): 37–60.

CHEW, C. 1985. "Instruction Can Link Reading and Writing." In *Breaking Ground: Teachers Relate Reading and Writing in the Elementary School*, eds. J. Hansen, T. Newkirk & D. Graves, 169–73. Portsmouth, NH: Heinemann.

CHI, M., M-Y. 1988. "Invented Spelling/Writing in Chinese-Speaking Children: The Developmental Patterns." In *Dialogues in Literacy Research*, eds. J. Readance & R. Baldwin, Thirty-seventh Yearbook, National Reading Conference, 285–96. Chicago: National Reading Conference.

CRONNELL, B. 1985. "Language Influences in the English Writing of Third- and Sixth-Grade Mexican-American Students." *Journal of Educational Research* 78 (3): 168–73.

CROWHURST, M. 1991. "Interrelationships Between Reading and Writing Persuasive Discourse." *Research in the Teaching of English* 25 (3): 314–38.

DAIUTE, C. 1990. "The Role of Play in Writing Development." *Research in the Teaching of English* 24 (1): 4–47.

DANIELS, H. 1994. *Literature Circles: Voice and Choice in the Student-Centered Classroom*. York, ME: Stenhouse.

———. 2002a. "Expository Text in Literature Circles." *Voices from the Middle* 9 (4): 7–14.

———. 2002b. "The Literature Circle: Rethinking Role Sheets." *Voices from the Middle* 10 (2): 44–45.

———. 2002c. *Literature Circles: Voice and Choice in Book Clubs and Reading Groups*. York, ME: Stenhouse.

D'ARCY, P. 1987. "Writing to Learn." In *The Journal Book*, ed. T. Fulwiler, 41–46. Portsmouth, NH: Boynton/Cook.

DRESSEL, J. H. 1990. "The Effects of Listening to and Discussing Different Qualities of Children's Literature on the Narrative Writing of Fifth Graders." *Research in the Teaching of English* 24 (4): 397–414.

DUKE, N. K. 2000. "For the Rich It's Richer: Print Experiences and Environments Offered to Children in Very Low- and Very High-Socioeconomic Status First-Grade Classrooms." *American Educational Research Journal* 37 (2): 441–78.

DYSON, A. H. 1982. "Reading, Writing and Language: Young Children Solving the Written Language Puzzle." *Language Arts* 59 (8): 829–39.

———. 1983a. *The Emergence of Visible Language: Interrelationships Between Drawing and Early Writing.* Paper presented at the Annual Meeting of the American Educational Research Association (Montreal, Canada, April 11–14, 1983). ERIC Document Reproduction Service No. ED 230 280.

———. 1983b. "The Role of Oral Language in Early Writing Processes." *Research in the Teaching of English* 17 (1): 1–30.

———. 1989. *Multiple Worlds of Child Writers: Friends Learning to Write.* New York: Teachers College Press.

———. 1990. "Research Currents: Diversity, Social Responsibility, and the Story of Literacy Development." *Language Arts* 67 (2): 192–205.

———. 1991. "What Happen When a Duck Egg Crack? Or Unexamined Assumptions of Current Writing Pedagogy." *The Quarterly of the National Writing Project & the Center for the Study of Writing and Literacy* 13 (4): 27–30.

———. 1992. "*Whistle for Willie*, Lost Puppies, and Cartoon Dogs: The Sociocultural Dimensions of Young Children's Composing." *Journal of Reading Behavior* 24 (4): 433–62.

———. 1993. *Social Worlds of Children Learning to Write in an Urban Primary School.* New York: Teachers College Press.

———. 1994. "The Ninjas, the X-Men, and the Ladies: Playing with Power and Identity in an Urban Primary School." *Teachers College Record* 96 (2): 219–39.

———. 1995. "Writing Children: Reinventing the Development of Childhood Literacy." *Written Communication* 12 (1): 4–46.

———. 1997. *Writing Superheroes: Contemporary Childhood, Popular Culture, and Classroom Literacy.* New York: Teachers College Press.

ECKHOFF, B. 1983. "How Reading Affects Children's Writing." *Language Arts* 60 (5): 607–16.

EDELSKY, C. 1982a. *The Development of Writing in a Bilingual Program.* NIE Final Report. Tempe: Arizona State University, ERIC ED 221 057.

———. 1982b. "Writing in a Bilingual Program: The Relation of L1 and L2 Texts." *TESOL Quarterly* 16 (2): 211–28.

——— 1986. *Writing in a Bilingual Program: Había Una Vez.* Norwood, NJ: Ablex.

EDELSKY, C. & K. JILBERT. 1985. "Bilingual Children and Writing: Lessons for All of Us." *Volta Review* 87 (5): 57–72.

EEDS, M. & R. PETERSON. 1991. "Teacher as Curator: Learning to Talk About Literature." *The Reading Teacher* 45 (2): 118–26.

EEDS, M. & D. WELLS. 1989. "Grand Conversations: An Exploration of Meaning Construction in Literature Study Groups." *Research in the Teaching of English* 23 (1): 4–29.

EMIG, J. 1971. *The Composing Processes of Twelfth Graders*. Urbana, IL: National Council of Teachers of English.

ERDRICH, L. 1988. *Tracks*. NY: Henry Holt.

ERNST, G. & K. J. RICHARD. 1994/1995. "Reading and Writing Pathways to Conversation in the ESL Classroom." *The Reading Teacher* 48 (4): 320–26.

FERREIRO, E. 1980. "The Relationship Between Oral and Written Language: The Children's Viewpoints." In *Oral and Written Language Development Research: Impact on the Schools*, eds. M. Haussler, D. Strickland, & Y. Goodman, 47–56. Urbana, IL: International Reading Association.

FINNEGAN, E. M. 1997. "Even Though We Have Never Met, I Feel I Know You: Using a Parent Journal to Enhance Home-School Communication." *The Reading Teacher* 51 (3): 268–70.

FLETCHER, R. 1996a. *Breathing In, Breathing Out: Keeping a Writer's Notebook*. Portsmouth, NH: Heinemann.

———. 1996b. *A Writer's Notebook: Unlocking the Writer Within You*. New York: Avon.

FLOWER, L. & J. R. HAYES. 1977. "Problem-Solving Strategies and the Writing Process." *College English* 39 (4): 449–61.

———. 1981a. "A Cognitive Process Theory of Writing." *College Composition and Communication* 32: 365–87.

———. 1981b. "The Pregnant Pause: An Inquiry Into the Nature of Planning." *Research in the Teaching of English* 15 (3): 229–43.

FOSTER, D. 1997. "Reading(s) in the Writing Classroom." *College Composition and Communication* 48 (4): 518–39.

FRANKLIN, E. & J. THOMPSON. 1994. "Describing Students' Collected Works: Understanding American Indian Children." *TESOL Quarterly* 28 (3): 489–506.

FULWILER, T. 1987. *The Journal Book*. Portsmouth, NH: Boynton-Cook.

GARMON, M. A. 2001. "The Benefits of Dialogue Journals: What Prospective Teachers Say." *Teacher Education Quarterly* 8 (4): 37–50.

GARCÍA, C. 1992. *Dreaming in Cuban*. New York: Knopf.

———. 1997. *The Agüero Sisters*. New York: Knopf.

———. 1998. Speech at Mills College, Oakland, CA. March 13.

GIACOBBE, M. E. 1986. "A Writer Reads, a Reader Writes." In *Understanding Writing: Ways of Observing, Learning, and Teaching*, eds. T. Newkirk and N. Atwell, 114–25. Portsmouth, NH: Heinemann.

GOLDFARB, C. 1999. "Ninja Turtles, Space Aliens, and Regular Folks: A Fifth-Grade Genre Study of Fiction." *Primary Voices K–6* 8 (1): 22–28.

GONZÁLEZ, N. & L. MOLL. 2002. "Cruzando El Puente: Building Bridges to Funds of Knowledge." *Journal of Educational Policy* 16 (4): 623–41.

GONZÁLEZ, N., L. C. MOLL & C. AMANTI, eds. 2005. *Funds of Knowledge: Theorizing Practices in Households, Communities and Classrooms*. Mahwah, NJ: Lawrence Erlbaum.

GOODMAN, K. & Y. GOODMAN. 1983. "Reading and Writing Relationships: Pragmatic Functions." *Language Arts* 60 (5): 590–99.

GOODMAN, K. S., E. B. SMITH, R. MEREDITH & Y. GOODMAN. 1987. *Language and Thinking in Schools: A Whole-Language Curriculum*. New York: Richard C. Owen.

GOODY, J. 1977. *The Domestication of the Savage Mind.* Cambridge, England: Cambridge University Press.

GORDIMER, N. 1991. *Jump and Other Stories.* New York: Farrar, Strauss, Giroux.

GRAVES, D. H. 1975. "An Examination of the Writing Processes of Seven Year Old Children." *Research in the Teaching of English* 9 (3): 227–41.

———. 1978. *Balance the Basics: Let Them Write.* New York: Ford Foundation.

———. 1979. "What Children Show Us About Revision." *Language Arts* 56 (3): 312–19.

———. 1980. "A New Look at Writing Research." *Language Arts* 57 (8): 913–19.

———. 1982. *A Case Study Observing the Development of Primary Children's Composing, Spelling and Motor Behaviors During the Writing Process.* Final Report. Washington, DC: National Institute of Education, ERIC ED 218 653.

———. 1983. *Writing: Teachers and Children at Work.* Portsmouth, NH: Heinemann.

———. 1989. *Investigate Nonfiction.* Portsmouth, NH: Heinemann.

GRAVES, D. H. & M. E. GIACOBBE. 1982. "Questions for Teachers Who Wonder If Their Writers Change." *Language Arts* 59 (4): 473–79.

GUZZETTI, B. J., J. P. YOUNG, M. M. GRITSAVAGE, L. M. FYFE & M. HARDENBROOK. 2002. *Reading, Writing and Talking Gender in Literacy Learning.* Newark, DE: International Reading Association.

HALL, N. & A. ROBINSON, eds. 1994. *Keeping in Touch: Using Interactive Writing with Young Children.* London: Hodder & Stoughton.

HAN, J. W. & G. ERNST-SLAVIT. 1999. "Come Join the Literacy Club: One Chinese ESL Child's Literacy Experience in a 1st-Grade Classroom." *Journal of Research in Childhood Education* 13 (2): 144–54.

HARSTE, J., V. WOODWARD & C. BURKE. 1983. *The Young Child as Writer-Reader Informant.* Final report (NIE G–80–0121).

———. 1984. *Language Stories and Literacy Lessons.* Portsmouth, NH: Heinemann.

HARVEY, C. B., L. OLLILA, K. BAXTER & S. Z. GUO. 1997. "Gender-Related Topics and Grade-Related Differences in Writing Topics in Chinese and Canadian Children." *Journal of Research and Development in Education* 31 (1): 1–6.

HARVEY, S. 1998. *Nonfiction Matters: Reading, Writing, and Research in Grades 3–8.* Portland, ME: Stenhouse.

HAYES, J. 1988. "Research on Written Composition: A Response to Hillocks' Report." *Research in the Teaching of English* 22 (1): 99–104.

HAYES, J. R. 2000. "A New Framework for Understanding Cognition and Affect in Writing." In *Perspectives on Writing: Research, Theory, and Practice,* eds. R. Indrisano & J. R. Squire, 6–44. Newark, DE: International Reading Association.

HAYES, J. R. & L. S. FLOWER. 1980. "Identifying the Organization of Writing Processes." In *Cognitive Processes in Writing,* eds. L. W. Gregg & E. R. Steinberg, 3–30. Hillsdale, NJ: Lawrence Erlbaum.

HEALD-TAYLOR, G. 1986. *Whole Language Strategies for ESL Students.* Toronto, Canada: Ontario Institute for Studies in Education.

HEARD, G. 1989. *For the Good of the Earth and Sun: Teaching Poetry*. Portsmouth, NH: Heinemann.

HEATH, S. B. 1983. *Ways with Words*. London: Cambridge University Press.

HILGERS, T. L. 1984. "Toward a Taxonomy of Beginning Writers' Evaluative Statements on Written Compositions." *Written Communication* 1 (3): 365–84.

———. 1986. "How Children Change as Critical Evaluators of Writing: Four Three-Year Case Studies." *Research in the Teaching of English* 20 (1): 36–55.

HILL, A. 1998 (December 9). *Reality Feeds Imagination of Author Wolfe*. The Oakland Tribune, Cue 1–2.

HILLOCKS, G. 1986. *Research on Written Composition: New Direction for Teaching*. Urbana, IL: ERIC Clearinghouse on Reading and Communication Skills and National Conference on Research in English.

———. 1988. "A Response to the Commentators." *Research in the Teaching of English* 22 (1): 108–16.

HOYT, L. 1993. "How Do They Learn to Read and Write?: Literacy Instruction in a Refugee Camp." In *Common Threads of Practice: Teaching English to Children Around the World*, eds. K. D. Samway & D. McKeon, 67–77. Alexandria, VA: Teachers of English to Speakers of Other Languages.

HUBBARD, R. 1985. "Write and Tell." *Language Arts* 62 (6): 624–30.

HUCK, C. S. 1960. *Inventory of Children's Literary Background*. Chicago, IL: Scott, Foresman and Co.

HUDELSON, S. 1983. *Janice: Becoming a Writer of English*. Paper presented at the 17th Annual Meeting of the Teachers of English to Speakers of Other Languages. Toronto, Canada.

———. 1984. "Kan yu ret an rayt en Ingles: Children Become Literate in English as a Second Language." *TESOL Quarterly* 18 (2): 221–38.

———. 1986. "ESL Children's Writing: What We've Learned, What We're Learning." In *Children and ESL: Integrating Perspectives*, eds. P. Rigg & D. S. Enright, 25–54. Alexandria, VA: Teachers of English to Speakers of Other Languages.

———. 1989. "A Tale of Two Children." In *Richness in Writing*, eds. D. M. Johnson & D. H. Roen, 84–99. New York: Longman.

———. 2005. "Taking on English Writing in a Bilingual Program: Revisiting, Reexamining, Reconceptualizing the Data." In *Second Language Writing Research: Perspectives on the Process of Knowledge Construction*, eds. P. Matsuda & T. Silva, 207–220. Mahwah, NJ: Lawrence Erlbaum.

HUGHES, J. 2000. "Writing for Each Other." In *Integrating the ESL Standards Into Classroom Practice: Grades 3–5*, ed. K. D. Samway, 27–51. Alexandria, VA: Teachers of English to Speakers of Other Languages.

HUSS, R. L. 1993. "Story Writing and Young Second Language Learners: The Influence of Context and Control." In *Literacy: Text and Context*, ed. D. Wray, 106–12. Exeter, England: United Kingdom Reading Association.

———. 1995. "Young Children Becoming Literate in English as a Second Language." *TESOL Quarterly* 29 (4): 767–74.

HUSS-KEELER, R. L. 1997. "Teacher Perception of Ethnic and Linguistic Minority Parental Involvement and Its Relationships to Children's Language and Literacy Learning: A Case Study." *Teaching and Teacher Education* 13 (2): 171–82.

Jaggar, A. M., D. H. Carrara & S. E. Weiss. 1986. "Research Currents: The Influence of Reading on Children's Narrative Writing (and Vice Versa)." *Language Arts* 63 (3): 292–300.

Kamler, B. 1993. "Constructing Gender in the Process Writing Classroom." *Language Arts* 70 (2): 95–103.

Kingston, M. H. 2003. *The Fifth Book of Peace.* New York: Knopf.

Kooy, M. & J. Wells. 1996. *Reading Response Logs: Inviting Students To Explore Novels, Short Stories, Plays, Poetry and More.* Markham, Ontario, Canada: Pembroke.

Kreeft, J., R. W. Shuy, J. Staton, L. Reed & R. Morroy. 1984. *Dialogue Writing: Analysis of Student-Teacher Interactive Writing in the Learning of English as a Second Language.* (Final report, National Institute of Education Grant No. NIE–G–83–0030). Washington, DC: Center for Applied Linguistics. ERIC Document Reproduction Service No. ED 252 097.

Kuball, Y. E. & S. Peck. 1997. "The Effect of Whole Language Instruction on the Writing Development of Spanish-Speaking and English-Speaking Kindergartners." *The Bilingual Research Journal* 21 (2 & 3): 213–31.

Lancia, P. J. 1997. "Literary Borrowing: The Effects of Literature on Children's Writing." *The Reading Teacher* 50 (6): 470–75.

Langer, J. A. 1986. *Children Reading and Writing: Structures and Strategies.* Norwood, NJ: Ablex.

Lay, N. D. 1982. "Composing Processes of Adult ESL Learners: A Case Study." *TESOL Quarterly* 16 (3): 406.

Loban, W. 1976. *Language Development: Kindergarten Through Grade Twelve.* Urbana, IL: National Council of Teachers of English.

Lyman, R. L. 1929. *Summary of Investigations Relating to Grammar, Language and Composition.* Chicago, IL: The University of Chicago.

MacGillivray, L. & A. M. Martinez. 1998. "Princesses Who Commit Suicide: Primary Children Writing Within and Against Gender Stereotypes." *Journal of Literacy Research* 30 (1): 53–84.

Many, J. E., R. Fyfe, G. Lewis & E. Mitchell. 1996. "Traversing the Topical Landscape: Exploring Students' Self-Directed Reading-Writing-Research Processes." *Reading Research Quarterly* 31 (1): 12–35.

McCarthey, S. J. 1997. "Connecting Home and School Literacy Practices in Classrooms with Diverse Populations." *Journal of Literacy Research* 29 (2): 145–82.

McCarthey, S. J., G. E. García, A. M. López-Velásquez, S. Lin & Y-H Guo. 2004. "Understanding Writing Contexts for English Language Learners." *Research in the Teaching of English* 38 (4): 351–94.

McIntyre, E., A. Rosebery & N. Gonzalez, eds. 2001. *Classroom Diversity: Connecting Curriculum to Students' Lives.* Portsmouth, NH: Heinemann.

Merriam, S. B. 1988. *Case Study Research in Education: A Qualitative Approach.* San Francisco, CA: Jossey-Bass.

Moll, L. C., C. Amanti, D. Neff & N. González. 1992. "Funds of Knowledge for Teaching: A Qualitative Approach to Developing Strategic Connections Between Homes and Classrooms." *Theory Into Practice* 31 (2): 132–41.

Naipaul, V. S. 1967. *The Mimic Men.* Harmondsworth, England: Penguin Books.

NATIONAL CENTER FOR EDUCATION STATISTICS (NCES). 2005. Website at http://nces.gov.

NATIONAL COMMISSION ON WRITING IN AMERICA'S SCHOOLS AND COLLEGES, THE. 2003. *The Neglected "R": The Need for a Writing Revolution*. The College Board. www .writingcommission.org.

NATIONS, M. J. 1990. *Turn up the Volume and Sing Along with Pedro*. Unpublished manuscript.

NEUMANN, S. B. & D. CELANO. 2001. "Access to Print in Low-Income and Middle-Income Communities: An Ecological Study of Four Neighborhoods." *Reading Research Quarterly* 36 (1): 8–26.

NEWKIRK, T. 1985. "The Hedgehog or the Fox: The Dilemma of Writing Development." *Language Arts* 62 (6): 593–603.

———. 1987. "The Non-Narrative Writing of Young Children." *Research in the Teaching of English* 21 (2): 121–44.

NIA, I. T. 1999. "Units of Study in the Writing Workshop." *Primary Voices K–6* 8 (1): 3–11.

ORELLANA, M. F., J. REYNOLDS, L. DORNER & M. MEZA. 2003. "In Other Words: Translating or "Para-Phrasing" as a Family Literacy Practice in Immigrant Households." *Reading Research Quarterly* 38 (1): 12–34.

PARATORE, J. R., A. HOMZA, B. KROL-SINCLAIR, T. LEWIS-BARROW, G. MELZI, R. STERGIS & H. HAYNES. 1995. "Shifting Boundaries in Home and School Responsibilities: The Construction of Home-Based Literacy Portfolios by Immigrant Parents and Their Children." *Research in the Teaching of English* 29 (4): 367–89.

PARSONS, L. 1994. *Expanding Response Journals in All Subject Areas*. Portsmouth, NH: Heinemann.

PEASE-ALVAREZ, C. & O. VASQUEZ. 1994. "Language Socialization in Ethnic Minority Communities." In *Educating Second Language Children*, ed. F. Genesee, 82–102. New York: Cambridge University Press.

PERL, S. 1979a. "The Composing Processes of Unskilled College Writers." *Research in the Teaching of English* 13 (4): 317–36.

———. 1979b. "Unskilled Writers as Composers." *New York Education Quarterly* 10 (3): 17–22.

———. 1980a. "A Look at Basic Writers in the Process of Composing." In *Basic Writing: Essays For Teachers, Researchers, and Administrators*, eds. L. N. Kasden and D. R. Hoeber, 65–73. Urbana, IL: National Council of Teachers of English.

———. 1980b. "Understanding Composing." *College Composition and Communication* 31 (4): 363–69.

PERSKY, H. R., M. C. DAANE & Y. YIN. 2003. *The Nation's Report Card: Writing 2002*. Washington, DC: U.S. Department of Education. Institute of Education Sciences. National Center for Education Statistics. (2002 NAEP report).

PETERSON, S. 1998. "Evaluation and Teachers' Perceptions of Gender in Sixth-Grade Student Writing." *Research in the Teaching of English* 33 (2): 181–208.

PETERSON, R. & M. EEDS. 1990. *Grand Conversations: Literature Groups in Action*. Richmond Hill, Ontario, Canada & New York: Scholastic.

PEYTON, J. K. & L. REED. 1990. *Dialogue Journal Writing with Nonnative English Speakers: A Handbook for Teachers*. Alexandria, VA: Teachers of English to Speakers of Other Languages (TESOL).

PEYTON, J. K. & M. SEYOUM. 1989. "The Effect of Teacher Strategies on Students' Interactive Writing: The Case of Dialogue Journals." *Research in the Teaching of English* 23 (3): 310–34.

PIANKO, S. 1979. "A Description of the Composing Processes of College Freshmen Writers." *Research in the Teaching of English* 13 (1): 5–22.

PORTALUPI, J. & R. FLETCHER. 2001. *Nonfiction Craft Lessons: Teaching Information Writing K–8.* Portland, ME: Stenhouse.

PURCELL-GATES, V. & K. L. DAHL. 1991. "Low-SES Children's Success and Failure at Early Literacy Learning in Skills-Based Classrooms." *Journal of Reading Behavior* 23 (1): 1–34.

QUANDAHL, E. 1994. "The Anthropological Sleep of Composition." *Journal of Advanced Composition* 14 (2): 413–29.

RAIMES, A. 1985. "What Unskilled ESL Students Do as They Write: A Classroom Study of Composing." *TESOL Quarterly* 19 (2): 229–58.

RAY, K. W. 1999. *Wondrous Words: Writers and Writing in the Elementary Classroom.* Urbana, IL: National Council of Teachers of English.

———. 2001. *The Writing Workshop: Working Through the Hard Parts (and They're All Hard Parts).* Urbana, IL: National Council of Teachers of English.

REYES, M. DE LA LUZ. 1991. "A Process Approach to Literacy Using Dialogue Journals and Literature Logs with Second Language Learners." *Research in the Teaching of English* 25 (3): 291–313.

ROBINETT, R., P. ROJAS, & P. BELL. 1970. *The Miami Linguistics Readers.* Boston: D. C. Heath.

ROSENBLATT, L. M. 1988. *Writing and Reading: The Transactional Theory.* Center for the Study of Writing, University of California Berkeley, Carnegie Mellon University, Technical Report No. 13.

ROUS, E. W. 1993. "Teaching English in Estonia: Using Reading and Writing Process Methods to Teach English as a Foreign Language." In *Common Threads of Practice: Teaching English to Children Around the World,* eds. K. D. Samway and D. McKeon, 120–32. Alexandria, VA: Teachers of English to Speakers of Other Languages.

SAMWAY, K. DAVIES. 1987a. "Formal Evaluation of Children's Writing: An Incomplete Story." *Language Arts* 64 (3): 289–98.

———. 1987b. *The Writing Processes of Non-Native English Speaking Children in the Elementary Grades.* Unpublished doctoral dissertation, University of Rochester.

———. 1993. "'This Is Hard, Isn't It?': Children Evaluating Writing." *TESOL Quarterly* 27 (2): 233–58.

SAMWAY, K. DAVIES & D. MCKEON. 1999. *Myths and Realities: Best Practices for Language Minority Students.* Portsmouth, NH: Heinemann.

SAMWAY, K. DAVIES & D. TAYLOR. 1993a. "The Collected Letters of Two Collaborative Researchers." In *Delicate Balances: Collaborative Research in Language Education,* eds. S. J. Hudelson and J. Wells Lindfors. Urbana, IL: National Council of Teachers of English.

———. 1993b. "Inviting Children to Make Connections Between Reading and Writing." *TESOL Journal* 2 (3): 7–11.

SAMWAY, K. DAVIES & G. WHANG. 1996. *Literature Study Circles in a Multicultural Classroom.* York, ME: Stenhouse.

SAMWAY, K. DAVIES, G. WHANG, C. CADE, M. GAMIL, M. A. LUBANDINA & K. PHOMMACHANH. 1991. "Reading the Skeleton, the Heart and the Brain of a Book: Students' Perspectives on Literature Study Circles." *The Reading Teacher* 45 (3): 196–205.

SCARDAMELIA, M. & P. PARIS. 1985. "The Function of Explicit Discourse Knowledge in the Development of Text Representations and Composing Strategies." *Cognition and Instruction* 2 (1): 1–39.

SCHECTER, S. R. & R. BAYLEY. 2002. *Language as Cultural Practice: Mexicanos en el Norte.* Mahwah, NJ: Lawrence Erlbaum.

SCHICKEDANZ, J. A. 1990. *Adam's Righting Revolutions: One Child's Literacy Development from Infancy Through Grade One.* Portsmouth, NH: Heinemann.

SCHLICK, K. L. & N. J. JOHNSON. 1999. *Getting Started with Literature Circles.* Norwood, MA: Christopher-Gordon.

SERNA, I. A. & S. HUDELSON. 1993. "Emergent Spanish Literacy in a Whole Language Bilingual Classroom." In *At-Risk Students: Portraits, Policies, Programs and Practices*, eds. R. Donmoyer and R. Kos, 291–321. Albany: State University of New York Press.

SHANNON, S. 1995. "The Hegemony of English: A Case Study of a Bilingual Classroom." *Linguistics and Education* 7 (3): 175–200.

SHAUGHNESSY, M. 1977. *Errors and Expectations: A Guide for the Teacher of Basic Writing.* New York: Oxford University Press.

SKILTON-SYLVESTER, E. 2002. "Literate at Home But Not at School: A Cambodian Girl's Journey from Playwright to Struggling Writer." In *School's Out: Bridging Out-of-School Literacies with Classroom Practice*, ed. G. Hull and K. Schultz, 61–90. New York: Teachers College Press.

SMITH, F. 1982. *Writing and the Writer.* New York: Holt, Rinehart and Winston.

SMITH, K., C. ESPINOSA, E. ARAGON, R. OSORIO & N. ULLOA. 2004. Reconceptualizing Writing Workshop in a Dual Language Program. Unpublished manuscript.

SOMMERS, N. 1980. "Revision Strategies of Student Writers and Experienced Adult Writers." *College Composition and Communication* 31 (4): 378–88.

SOWERS, S. 1979. "A Six-Year-Old's Writing Process: The First Half of First Grade." *Language Arts* 56 (7): 829–35.

STATON, J. 1980. "Writing and Counseling: Using a Dialogue Journal." *Language Arts* 57 (5): 514–18.

———. 1985. "Using Dialogue Journals for Developing Thinking, Reading, and Writing with Hearing-Impaired Students." *Volta Review* 87 (5): 127–54.

———. 1987. "The Power of Responding in Dialogue Journals." In *The Journal Book*, ed. T. Fulwiler, 47–63. Portsmouth, NH: Boynton/Cook.

STEIN, P. 1993. "For a Brighter Future: SPEAK Project in Soweto." In *Common Threads of Practice: Teaching English to Children Around the World*, eds. K. D. Samway and D. McKeon, 7–19. Alexandria, VA: Teachers of English to Speakers of Other Languages.

TAN, A. 1989. *The Joy Luck Club.* New York: G. P. Putnam.

TAYLOR, D. 1983. *Family Literacy: Young Children Learning to Read and Write.* Portsmouth, NH: Heinemann Educational.

TAYLOR, D. M. 1990. "Writing and Reading Literature in a Second Language." In *Workshop 2: Beyond the Basal*, ed. N. Atwell, 105–17. Portsmouth, NH: Heinemann.

———. 2000. "Facing Hardships: Jamestown and Colonial Life." In *Integrating the ESL Standards Into Classroom Practice: Grades 3–5*, ed. K. D. Samway, 53–81. Alexandria, VA: Teachers of English to Speakers of Other Languages.

TEALE, W. H. 1982. "Toward a Theory of How Children Learn to Read and Write Naturally." *Language Arts* 59: 555–70.

THOMAS, D. [1954] 1959. *A Child's Christmas in Wales*. New York: New Directions.

TOWNSEND, J. S. & D. FU. 1998. "A Chinese Boy's Joyful Initiation into American Literacy." *Language Arts* 75 (3): 193–201.

TSE, L. 2001. *"Why Don't They Learn English?": Separating Fact from Fallacy in the U.S. Language Debate*. New York: Teachers College Press.

TSUKIYAMA, G. 1991. *Women of the Silk*. New York: St. Martin's Press.

———. 2003. Speech at Mills College, Oakland, CA.

URZÚA, C. 1986. "A Children's Story." In *Children and ESL: Integrating Perspectives*, eds. P. Rigg and D. S. Enright, 93–112. Washington, DC: Teachers of English to Speakers of Other Languages.

———. 1987. "'You Stopped Too Soon': Second Language Children Composing and Revising." *TESOL Quarterly* 21 (2): 279–304.

VASQUEZ, O. A., L. PEASE-ALVAREZ & S. M. SHANNON. 1994. *Pushing Boundaries: Language and Culture in a Mexicano Community*. New York: Cambridge University Press.

VYGOTSKY, L. S. 1962. *Thought and Language*. Cambridge, MA: MIT Press.

———. 1978. *Mind in Society: The Development of Higher Psychological Processes*. Cambridge, MA: Harvard University Press.

WOLLMAN-BONILLA, J. E. 1989. "Reading Journals: Invitations to Participate in Literature." *The Reading Teacher* 43 (1): 112–20.

———. 1991. *Response Journals: Inviting Students to Think and Write About Literature*. New York: Scholastic.

———. 2000. "Teaching Science Writing to First Graders: Genre Learning and Recontextualization." *Research in the Teaching of English* 35 (1): 35–65.

ZAMEL, V. 1982. "Writing: The Process of Discovering Meaning." *TESOL Quarterly* 16 (2): 195–209.

———. 1983. "The Composing Processes of Advanced ESL Students: Six Case Studies." *TESOL Quarterly* 17 (2): 165–87.

Children's and Young Adult Literature

ADOFF, A. 1986. *Sports Pages*. New York: HarperCollins.

BABBITT, N. [1977] 1989. *The Eyes of the Amaryllis*. New York: Sunburst Books.

———. [1977] 1985. *Tuck Everlasting*. New York: Sunburst Books.

CARROLL, L. [1865] 1981. *Alice's Adventures in Wonderland*. New York: Bantam.

CISNEROS, S. 1989. *The House on Mango Street*. New York: Random House.

CLEARY, B. 1983. *Dear Mr. Henshaw*. New York: Morrow.

CUSHMAN, K. 1994. *Catherine, Called Birdy*. New York: HarperCollins.

HINTON, S. E. 1967. *The Outsiders*. New York: Viking.

JAMESON, C. (Adap.). 1973. *The Clay Pot Boy*. New York: Coward, McCann & Geoghegan.

LANGSTAFF, J. M. 1974. *Oh, A-Hunting We Will Go*. New York: Atheneum.

MARTIN, B., JR. 1970. *The Haunted House*. New York: Holt, Rinehart & Winston.

MAYER, M., & M. MAYER. 1971. *A Boy, a Dog, a Frog, and a Friend*. New York: Dial.

MEYERS, W. D. 1981. *Hoops*. New York: Delacourt.

NEWTH, M. 1989. *The Abduction*. New York: Farrar, Strauss & Giroux.

PAULSEN, G. 1987. *Hatchet*. New York: Bradbury.

RAWLS, W. 1974. *Where the Red Fern Grows*. New York: Bantam.

RYLANT, C. 1982. *When I Was Young in the Mountains*. New York: Dutton.

———. 1987. *Henry and Mudge: The First Book of Their Adventures*. New York: Simon & Schuster.

TAYLOR, M. 1976. *Roll of Thunder, Hear My Cry*. New York: Dial.

———. 1990. *Mississippi Bridge*. New York: Dial.

WARD, M., J. BURR, & J. AHLER. 1989. *The Mouse Raid*. Medora, ND: Theodore Roosevelt Nature and History Association.

Index

accents, differences in use of in children's
　　nonnative and native writing, 51
Ammon, Paul, 158
Applebee, Arthur N., 2
Aragon, Ernestina, 172
audience, role of, 160–162
audiences, gendered, 84

Barbieri, Maureen, 83
basal textbooks, impact of basal style on
　　writing, 117–118
Baxter, Kristin, 82
Bayley, Robert, 48
beliefs, impact of teachers', 165–167
Bereiter, Carl, 111
bilingual writing, 163–167. *See also* native
　　languages
　　children mediating learning experiences,
　　　　164–165
　　holistic approaches, impact of, 164
　　needs, benefits of teachers adjusting
　　　　instruction to student, 167
　　sketches of bilingual writers, 61–78
　　teachers' beliefs and actions, impact of,
　　　　165–167
Birnbaum, June Cannell, 108–109
Bishop, Wendy, 4
Blackburn, Ellen, 113–114
Blair, Heather, 79, 84–85
book reviews, reflective writing and, 128
books
　　mentor texts, 176
　　socioeconomic status and access to, 94–95
　　touchstone texts, 176
Boutwell, Marilyn, 15
Britton, James, 2, 152

Burgess, Tony, 2, 152
Burke, Carolyn, 22–25, 95

Calkins, Lucy, 67, 73, 151
Carrara, Donna H., 112–113
Carson, Joan G., 55
Celano, Donna, 94
Center for Research on Education, Diversity
　　and Excellence (CREDE), 18
Center for Research on the Education of
　　Students Placed At Risk (CRESPAR), 18
Center for the Improvement of Early Reading
　　Achievement (CIERA), 18
Center for the Study of Writing, 18, 19
Chew, Charles, 106
Chi, Marilyn, 50
classrooms. *See also* environment
　　children's understandings about writing and
　　　　school, interplay between, 152
　　influence of, 54
　　learner-centered approach with ESOL
　　　　students, impact of, 151–152
　　peer support and the role of audience,
　　　　160–162
　　similarities and differences in classrooms
　　　　that foster writing, 158
　　teachers' beliefs and actions, impact of,
　　　　73–74, 165–167
code switching, by ELLs, 49–50
cognitive-developmental model of writing,
　　early research on, 5
cognitive processes
　　early research on, 3–4
　　in Hayes-Flower Cognitive Model, 10, 12
　　of skilled versus less-skilled writers, research
　　　　on, 8

use of symbols to express complex thoughts by ELLs, 35–38
cognitive process theory, 4
cognitive theory, misunderstanding about, 13
collaborative learning styles, 57
communicative approach to teaching writing to ELLs, 170–172
community, influence of, on children's writing, 152–154
content
    explicit, in ELL writing instruction, 175
    reading content influences on writing, 118–119
contextual influences
    on writing development, 45
crafting
    element, partial understanding of a craft, 53–54
    issues, attention to, 53
creative construction principle, 26, 179
Cronnell, Bruce, 46–47
Crowhurst, Marion, 110
culture
    awareness of features of native written languages, young children's, 23–25
    drawbacks of ignoring, 96–97
    literacy being viewed aculturally, dangers of, 92–93
    ways of learning, culturally grounded, 86–89
    writing as expression of, 89–92
curriculum
    influence of school curricula on children's writing, 152
    social class influences on, 95–96

Dahl, Karen L., 152–153
Daiute, Colette, 83
developmental stages in early writing, 2, 38–44
dialogue journals, 127, 130–134
    student-to-student, 132–134
    teacher-student, 130–132
    variations in ELL children's responses to, 141–143
Dorner, Lisa, 138–139
Dressel, Janice, 111–112
Dyson, Ann Haas, 15, 19, 79
    culturally grounded differences, research on, 92–93

on early writing not growing out of speech, 3
on educators viewing literacy in an acultural way, 96
on giving students space for reading and writing that is important to them, 99
superhero characters, research on children transforming dominant images, 81–82

Eckhoff, Barbara, 117–118
Edelsky, Carole, 3, 48–50, 51
    children's writing stagnating without guidance, research on, 165–166
    patterns of writing development, research on, 38
    writing development as process of reorganizing systems, research on, 45
Emig, Janet A., 6
English for Speakers of Other Languages (ESOL)
    children evaluating writing, study of, 52–54
    contextual influences on writing development of, research on, 45
    dialogue journals with, research on, 139–141
    lack of authentic writing, research on 158–160
    learner-centered, workshop approach, impact on, research on, 150–152
    mainstream and ESOL classes, dissonances with home culture, 85–86
    oral fluency not necessary for writing growth, 28–30
    peer support and role of audience with, 160–162
    role of talk with, 27–28
    sociocultural contexts, influences of, 61, 66–76
    writing influenced by textbook reading, 118–122
English Language Learners (ELLs)
    actions, impact of teachers', 73–74, 165–167
    authentic writing, lack of, 158–160
    best writing program for. *See* writing programs for ELLs
    developmental stages in early writing, 38–44
    educators getting to know families, importance of, 100

English Language Learners (ELLs), *continued*
gender. *See* gender
as having rich literacy experiences at home,
97–98
literacy development, ELLs reflecting on
their, 143–148
personality, learning styles and writing
development, intersection of, 76–77
research about writing of. *See* English
Language Learners (ELLs), research
about writing of
risk taking, 71–72
sketches of writing development of
bilingual, 61–78
successful writers, what ELLs need to
become, 167–169
writing programs for. *See* writing programs
for ELLs
English Language Learners (ELLs), research
about writing of, 21–60
code switching, 49–50
contextual influences, 45
conveying important messages in writing,
28, 29
errors as evidence of language
resourcefulness, 48–49
errors as hypothesis testing, 48
evaluating writing, ELL children. *See*
evaluating writing, ELL children
expressing complex thoughts and emotions
in less than fluent English, 30, 34
functions of print, young children's
awareness of, 22–26
how writing works, young children's
understanding of, 25–26
literacy development, role of talk in, 27–28
native languages. *See* native languages
nonlinear writing development, 44, 61–62,
77
oral fluency not necessary for writing
growth, 28–30
oral language/writing connections, 26–28
prior literacy experiences, influence of. *See*
literacy experiences, influence of
role of talk in young children's writing,
26–27
similarities and differences in children's
writing, 50–52

symbols to express complex thoughts, use
of, 35–38
understanding more than they can write,
34–35
write in more than one language, ability of
children to, 49
environment
beliefs and actions, impact of teachers',
73–74, 165–167
bilingual writing, influence of environment
on. *See* bilingual writing
children mediating learning experiences,
164–165
children's understandings about writing and
school, interplay between, 152
classroom, influence of, 54
influence of, on children's writing, 150–179
learner-centered approach, impact of,
151–152
peer support and role of audience, 160–162
school and community, influence of,
152–154
school experiences, influences of. *See* school
experiences, influences of
similarities and differences in classrooms
that foster writing, 158
teacher, influence of the, 154
Ernst, Gisela, 27
Ernst-Slavit, Gisela, 56
errors
as evidence of language resourcefulness,
48–49
as hypothesis testing, 48
Espinosa, Cecilia, 172, 175
ethnicity
culture, writing as expression of, 89–92
home-based and school-based literacy
practices, dissonances between, 85–86
influence of, on writing, 84–93
literacy being viewed aculturally, dangers of,
92–93
ways of learning, culturally grounded, 86–89
evaluating writing, ELL children, 52–60
classroom environment, influence of, 54
craft element, partial understanding of a,
53–54
crafting issues, attention to, 53
reflexive powers, displaying, 52–53

Ferreiro, Emilia, 25–26
Flower, Linda, 7, 9
Foster, David, 122
Franklin, Elizabeth, 89–92
Fu, Danling, 157–158
Fulwiler, Toby, 138
Funds of Knowledge, 97
Fyfe, Laurie M., 81

García, George E., 158–160
gender, 79–84
    access to literacy, 80
    audiences, gendered, 83
    character portrayals in writing, gendered, 82
    genre and topic selection by, 80
    how teachers treat children's writing,
        influence of gender on, 84
    images of power and gender, transforming,
        81–82
    meanings in children's writing, gendered,
        82–83
    and role play in writing, 83
    and writing topics, 83
genre
    awareness of genre differences when
        writing, 107
    selection by gender, 80
Giacobbe, Mary Ellen, 154
Goodman, Kenneth S., 105–106
Goodman, Yetta, 105–106
Graves, Donald, 4, 73, 83, 151, 156
Gritsavage, Margaret M., 81
Guo, Song Zheng, 82
Guo, Yi-Huey, 158–160
Guzzetti, Barbara J., 81

Han, Jofen W., 56
handwriting, differences in children's
    nonnative and native, 51
Hardenbrook, Marie, 81
Harste, Jerome C., 22–25, 95
Harvey, C. Brian, 82
Hayes, John R., 7, 9
Hayes-Flower Cognitive Model, 9–13
Heald-Taylor, Gail, 38, 43–44
Hilgers, Thomas L., 52
home-based writing versus school-based
    writing, 85–86

Hoyt, Lauren, 28, 30, 155–156
Hubbard, Ruth, 26–27
Hudelson, Sarah, 45, 61–65, 66, 74–77
    on learning through writing original
        messages, 119
    political issues embedded in sociocultural
        factors, 17–18
    role of environment in writing
        development, research on, 28, 163–167
Hughes, Jim, 17
Huss, Rebecca, 157
Huss-Keeler, Rebecca, 98–99

inquiry, in ELL writing instruction, 175
interlanguage, 46–47
invented spelling, 46, 51

Jaggar, Angela M., 112–113
Jilbert, Kristina, 3, 45, 48–50, 165–166
journals
    with bilingual ELL primary students, 63
    dialogue, 127, 130–134, 139–140, 141–143
    double-entry, reflective writing with, 128
    reading logs, variations in ELL children's
        responses to interactive, 141–142
    reading response journals in EFL setting,
        139
    reflective writing through, 126, 127, 128,
        130
    role of teacher in dialogue journals with
        ELLs, 130–132, 139–140
    student-to-student dialogue journals,
        132–134
    variations in ELL children's responses to
        dialogue, 141–142

Kamler, Barbara, 82–83
Kuball, Yazmin E., 164

Lancia, Peter, 113
Langer, Judith A., 7, 16–17, 106–108
learner-centered approach with ESOL
    students, impact of, 151–152
learning, process approach to, 119–120
learning experiences, social class bias on,
    95–96
learning styles in ELL writing development,
    role of, 77–78

Lin, Shuman, 158–160
listing, leads to more complex writing, 28, 30–32
literacy
    development, ELLs reflect on their, 143–148
    ELLs have rich literacy experiences at home, 97–98
    experiences at home and school, determining which has more influence, 162–163
    reflective writing in literacy development, 138
    silencing of literacy stories, 99
    viewed aculturally, dangers of, 92–93
literacy experiences, influence of, 54–60
    collaborative learning styles, 57
    dissonance, potential for, 57–58
    experiences at home and school, determining which has more influence, 162–163
    holistic language instruction, 164
    literacy for social cohesion versus for individual expression, 55
    part-to-whole versus whole-to-part approaches, 55–56
    resiliency and, 56–57
literary techniques, influence of, 121
Loban, Walter, 3
López-Velásquez, Angela M., 158–160
Lyman, Rollo L., 1

MacGillivray, Laurie, 82
Martin, Nancy, 2, 152
Martinez, Ana Maritza, 82
McCarthey, Sarah J., 95–97, 158–160
McLeod, Alex, 2
mentor texts, 176
Meredith, Robert, 105–106
Meza, María, 138–139
Moll, Luis, 97

National Assessment of Educational Progress (NAEP), 19
National Center for Education Statistics (NCES), 80
National Commission on Writing in America's Schools and Colleges (2003), 19–20
National Institute of Education (NIE), 50

National Research and Development Center on English Learning and Achievement (CELA), 18
Nations, Mary Jane, 57, 87, 89
native languages
    children's awareness of features of their written native language, 23–25
    being taught in, as asset, 47–48, 163
    ELLs write in native and nonnative languages without confusion, 48–50
    influence of, on spelling of ELLs, 46–47
    influence of, on writing of ELLs, 46–47
    similarities and differences in children's writing, 50–52
    sketches of bilingual writers, 61–78
    write in more than one language, ability of children to, 49
Neumann, Susan B., 94
Newkirk, Thomas, 2, 3
Nia, Isoke Titilayo, 176

Ollila, K. Lloyd, 82
oral language
    early research on oral language and writing, 3
    ELL literacy development, role of talk in, 27–28
    fluency not necessary for writing growth, 28–30
    role of talk in young children's writing, 26–27
oral reading, impact of books read aloud on children's writing, 111–112
Orellana, Marjorie Faulstich, 138–139
Osorio, Rebecca, 172, 175

parents
    importance of teachers getting to know, 100
    limited communication between teachers and, impact of, 98–99
    supportive, defined, 98
part-to-whole approach to writing, 55–56
Peck, Sabrina, 164
peer support and the role of audience, 160–162
personality in ELL writing development, role of, 76–77
personal style, differences in children's nonnative and native writing, 51
Peterson, Shelley, 84

Peyton, Joy Kreeft, 139, 140
prewriting and prereading, 104
print
    research about young children's awareness
        of, 22–26
    socioeconomic status and access to, 94
process approach to learning, 119–120
process approach to writing, 160–162
psychological dimension to writing, 13–14
Purcell-Gates, Victoria, 152–153

race
    home-based and school-based literacy
        practices, dissonances between, 85–86
    influence of, on writing, 84–93
    literacy being viewed aculturally, dangers of,
        92–93
    ways of learning, culturally grounded, 86–89
reading
    children's writing, impact of books read
        aloud on, 111–112
    content influences on writing, 118–119
    differences between writing and, 105–106,
        107–108
    focusing on writing needn't ruin reading
        experience, 102–103
    like a writer, 101–103
    part-to-whole versus whole-to-part
        approach, 55–56
    persuasive texts, relationships between
        reading and writing, 110
    reading/writing connections. *See* reading/
        writing connections
    writing, influence of reading on, 109–122
reading/writing connections, 101–124
    awareness of genre differences, 107
    borrowing text features, 112–113
    children's writing, impact of books read
        aloud on, 111–112
    connections between reading and writing,
        103–109
    differences between reading and writing,
        105–106, 107–108
    different emphases in children's thinking,
        generation of, 107–108
    established authors, borrowing from,
        112–113
    focusing on writing needn't ruin reading
        experience, 102–103

grounded in language, both reading and
    writing are, 106–107
impact of reading/writing discussions on
    writing, 113–114
impact of self-selected reading on writing,
    114
influence of reading on writing, 109–122
literary techniques, influence of, 121
meaning-making processes, both are, 105
persuasive texts, relationships between
    reading and writing, 110
processes of more and less proficient readers
    and writers, 108–109
reading content influences on writing,
    118–119
similar processes, reading and writing are,
    104–105
as social acts, 108–109
textbooks on writing, impact of, 117–118
recursive nature of writing, research on, 6–7
reflective writing, 125–149
    book reviews, 128
    complaint books, 126, 131
    field notes, 128
    idea bookmarks, 128, 135, 136
    incorporating into classroom, 126–138
    interviews, 128, 134–135
    journals. *See* journals
    letters, 129, 135, 137–138
    literacy development, ELLs reflecting on
        their, 143–148
    questionnaires, 128, 134–135
    reflective powers, displaying, 52–53
    role of, in language and literacy
        development, 138
    supporting ELLs, 139–148
    teacher's interactive style on reflective
        writing, effect of, 140
    types of, 126–130
resiliency, in ELL literacy learners, 56–57
Reyes, María de la Luz, 141–142
Reynolds, Jennifer, 138–139
Richard, Kerri J., 27–28
risk taking, 71–72
Rosen, Harold, 2, 152
Rosenblatt, Louise, 105
Rous, Emma, 139, 156–157

Samway, Katharine Davies, 15–16, 66, 79
  ability of ELLs to reflect on their growing
    literacy, research on, 143–148
  Alexis, a struggling second grade writer,
    research on, 66–74
  children's resilience as writers, 57–58
  ELL children evaluating writing, research
    on, 52–54
  idea bookmarks, reflective writing and,
    135
  influence of the environment on children's
    writing, research on, 150–152
  patterns of writing development of ELL
    children, research on, 38
Scardamalia, Marlene, 111
Schecter, Sandra, 48
school
  access to print, and socioeconomic status,
    94–95
  influence of, on children's writing, 152–154
  literacy experiences at home and school,
    determining which has more influence,
    162–163
school-based writing versus home-based
  writing, 85–86
school experiences, influences of, 155–163
  authentic writing in US, lack of, 158–160
  England, case study of student writing in,
    157
  Estonia, case study of student writing in,
    156–157
  international perspective, 155–157
  literacy experiences at home and school,
    determining which has more influence,
    162–163
  Philippines, case study of student writing in,
    155–156
  similarities and differences in classrooms
    that foster writing, 158
  South Africa, case study of student writing
    in, 155
  in United States, 157–163
scribble writing, 38–39
segmentation, 51
Serna, Irene, 17, 61–65, 66, 167
Seyoum, Mulugetta, 139, 140
skills-based approach to teaching writing to
  ELLs, 170–172
Skilton-Sylvester, Ellen, 85–86

Smith, E. Brooks, 105–106
Smith, Frank, 4, 7–8
Smith, Karen, 172, 175
social acts, reading and writing as, 108–109
social-behavioral model of writing, research
  on, 5, 14–15, 16
social class
  in literacy curricula and learning
    experiences, 95–96
  middle-class literacy values, 95
  teacher expectations and, 80
  and writing, 94–97
social cohesion, literacy for, 55
sociocognitive model of writing, research on,
  15–17
sociocultural influences on writing, 17–18,
  81–82
socioeconomic status (SES)
  access to school-related print experiences,
    94–95
  teacher expectations and, 80
  and writing, 94–97
Spanish
  being taught in native language an asset,
    47–48
  dialogue journals, 140–141
  holistic language approach, impact of, 164
  influences of native language on writing of
    ELLs, 46–47
  part-to-whole versus whole-to-part
    approach, 55–56
  similarities and differences in children's
    writing, 50–52
  sketches of writing development of
    bilingual students, 61–78
  writing instruction with, 158
spelling
  developmental, 46
  influence of native languages on spelling of
    ELLs, 46–47
  invented, 46, 51
  Spanish, 62–63
stages in early writing development. *See*
  developmental stages in early writing, 2,
  38–44
Stein, Pippa, 17, 155
students
  needs, benefits of teachers adjusting
    instruction to student, 167

peer support and the role of audience, 160–162

validating students' lives, 173

symbols, ELLs use of, 35–38

syntax, differences in children's nonnative and native writing, 51

talk. *See* oral language

Taylor, Denny M., 35

Taylor, Dorothy, 28, 34, 119–120, 143–144

teachers

    actions, impact of teachers' actions on students' writing, 73–74, 154, 165–167

    awareness of cultural differences by, 97

    beliefs, impact of teachers', 165–167

    changes in what teachers taught, 173–175

    effect of, interactive style of response on reflective writing, 140

    influence of gender on how teachers regard children's writing, 84

    limited communication between parents and, impact of, 98–99

teacher-student dialogue journals, 130–132

terminology, impact of, on children's writing, 73

textbooks, impact of, on children's writing, 117–118

Thompson, Jackie, 89–92

tildes, differences in children's nonnative and native writing, 51

topics

    gender and children's writing, 83

    selection by gender, 80

touchstone texts, 176

Townsend, Jane S., 157–158

Ulloa, Nora, 172, 175

unit of study approach, features of, 172–177

Urzúa, Carole, 28, 141, 160–161, 162–163

Vygotsky, Lev, 177

Weiss, Sara E., 112–113

Whang, Gail, 79, 132, 135

whole-to-part approach to writing, 55–56, 61

Woodward, Virginia A., 22–25, 95

writers

    borrowing text features, 112–113

    established authors, borrowing from, 112–113

    processes of more and less proficient, 108–109

    reading like a writer, 101–103

    similarities and differences in classrooms that foster, 158

    successful writers, what ELLs need to be, 167–169

writing

    authentic writing, lack of, 158–160

    awareness of genre differences when, 107

    bilingual. *See* bilingual writing

    children's understandings about writing and school writing, interplay between, 152

    children's writing, impact of books read aloud on, 111–112

    defined, 22

    development, personality and learning styles in, 76–77

    developmental stages in writing, 2, 38–44

    differences between reading and, 105–106, 107–108

    early focus on cognitive processes involved when, 3–4

    environment. *See* environment

    focusing on writing needn't ruin the reading experience, 102–103

    gender, influence of. *See* gender

    how writing works, young children's understanding of, 25–26

    impact of reading/writing discussions on, 113–114

    impact of self-selected reading on, 114

    influence of native languages on writing of ELLs, 46–47

    influence of reading on, 109–122

    literary techniques, influence of, 121

    mechanics in books, influence of, 121–122

    nonlinear writing development by ELLs, 44, 61–62, 77

    oral fluency not necessary for ELL writing growth, 28–30

    part-to-whole versus whole-to-part approach, 55–56

    reading content influences on, 118–119

    reading/writing connections. *See* reading/ writing connections

writing, *continued*
  reflective. *See* reflective writing
  research. *See* writing research
  similarities and differences in children's
      writing, 50–52
  as socially-constructed, meaning-making
      process, 17
  social-behavioral view of, research on,
      14–15, 16
  textbooks on writing, impact of, 117–118
  unit of study approach to teaching,
      176–177
writing process
  lack of emphasis on in early research, 1, 2
  similar across languages, 50–52
writing programs for ELLs, 169–177
  best type of, 169–177
  skills-based and communicative approaches,
      170–172
  unit of study approach to teaching writing,
      172–177
writing research
  about writing of ELLs. *See* English Language
      Learners (ELLs), research about
      writing of
  cognitive model of writing, 5
  current, 18–20
  focus on product, 1, 2

functions of print, awareness of, 22–26
Hayes-Flower Cognitive Model of the
      writing process. *See* Hayes-Flower
      Cognitive Model
historical overview, 1–18
implications of, 20, 77–78
intersection of writing, sociocultural factors,
      and politics, 17–18
lack of early emphasis on writing processes,
      2
oral language, writing as subordinate to, 3
psychological dimension, 13–14
recursive nature of writing, 6–7
skilled versus less-skilled writers, research
      on, 8
social-behavioral view of writing, 14–15, 16
sociocognitive model of writing, 15–17
writer/writing processes, focus on, 4–14
writing as a meaning-making, thinking
      process, 5–8
writing as not transcribing thoughts, early
      research on, 7–8
writing workshop, 172

Young, Josephine Peyton, 81

Zamel, Vivian, 6–7